Human nature has the tendency to avoid philosophy. This is not because of any high-brow thinking, but because the problems in philosophy are inherently psychological. Philosophy requires the study of knowing, and no one wants to change their personal immortality formulas that give them false comfort against the scarecrows of reality.

Samuel Dael

The Platonic Idiom is the first in a series of books by Samuel Louis Dael that deals with a classical epistemology towards philosophy science, psychology, economics, religion and politics.

Soon to be published: *The Einstein Illusion*

The Platonic Idiom

Samuel Louis Dael

Vision Impact Publishing
P.O. Box 1338, St. George, Utah 84771
editor@visionimpactpublishing.com
Samuel Dael htpp://www.platonic-idiom.com

This book is dedicated to Socrates, and to the world which suffers from modern education's lack of Socratic discourse. It is not written to those who look to modern authority, but to those who look far back in time to the authority of antiquity that had the mind to understand, ears to hear, and eyes to see.

The Platonic Idiom
Copyright © 2007 Vision Impact Publications.
All rights reserved.
Printed in the United States of America

ISBN 978-0-615-24674-1

The Platonic Idiom

We all have a tendency to alter the meaning of words in order to justify our world view. One might feel guilty or jealous because of a human situation, but rather than accept the guilt, we change the meaning of words to curb our regret.

Samuel Dael

Contents

Contents vi
Preface viii
Introduction xii
1. Understanding the Masters 1
2. Philosophical Motive 17
      Conclusion 34
3. The Socratic Method 35
4. The Platonic Position 49
5. Objective Reality 61
      Figure 5-1 Energy's Continuous Exchange 62
      The Field Concept 63
      Figure 5-2 Analog of an Electron 65
      Figure 5-3 Particle Relationship 67
      Figure 5-4 Emission of Light 70
      Magnetic Space 78
      Control Monopole 80
6. Subjective Reality and Intelligence 87
7. Subjective Reality and Reason 113
      Considering Kant's View 133
8. The Nature of the Predicate 141
      Figure 8-1 The Nature of Equality 156
      Figure 8-2 The Predicate Process 158
      The Law of Invariance 161
9. The Epistemology of Meaning 169
      Figure 9-1 Basic Epistemology Tree 179
      Figure 9-2 Equality 183
      Figure 9-3 The Subjective 187
      Figure 9-4 The Predicative 192
      Figure 9-5 The Objective 193
      Figure 9-6 The Objective 197
      Figure 9-7 Complete Epistemology Tree 203

10. Pushing Reality Around 205
    Metaphysics 207
    Epistemology 208
    Ethics 213
    Aesthetics 214
    Logic 217
    Monism 218
    Materialism 218
    Idealism 219
    Dualism 219
    Pluralism 220
    Rationalism 221
    Empiricism 222
    Absolutism 224
    Relativism 224
    Existentialism 225
    Egoism 228
    Predicativism 228
11. The Way of Socrates 231
12. The Platonic State 247
    Aristotelean Considerations 266
13. A Vanishing Republic 271
    Changing Our Republic 279
    A Change for the Worst 289
    Bureaucratic Nightmares 295
14. A Manifest Constitution 303
    Representation 314
    Taxation 325
    Capitalism And Freedom 335
References 343
Index 347

Preface

The *Platonic Idiom* by Samuel Louis Dael is a book about the meaning of words. More particularly, it is an epistemology of meaning, which makes it the first of its kind.

When the *Platonic Idiom* came to my attention from a friend who demanded that I "read it," the first thing that caught my eye was not the title of the book, but rather the audacity in the subtitle that read, "The infirmity of western civilization." Ever since my early days in college, it has been assumed, even without any serious discussion that I can recall, that western civilization has grown more imminent from the time of the first Greek philosophers. According to Samuel Dael, western civilization has descended from its true Greek forum and embraces a great infirmity postulated by the mind of Plato. The infirmity is having the spirit of Socrates converse the words of an idiom contrary to the way of the master himself. Perhaps this is the folly of civilization—to change the mind of heaven.

This very claim pulled me into a book that has caused me to rethink everything I know with a discipline I have never had. Surprisingly, this is part of the western tradition that has yet to be reborn. The other part is a complete philosophy of responsibility rather than another positional thesis. This makes it timely and certain to impact the statesmen and the student. All things from the desert seem to have this potential, which makes the *Platonic Idiom* that much more impressive in that it has no ties to the academic world. It was written not for advancement but for impact.

The impact begins with the creation of a predicate epistemology and crescendos as it challenges the most influential minds and ideas in history with a series of five books to follow. The next to be published is the *The Einstein Illusion* and the last is a book Mr. Dael has asked that I keep to myself for now. *The Platonic Idiom* is the first and the foundation for all.

So how does one writer effectively challenge so many dominant thinkers and beliefs? It is done with an epistemology unique in the history of philosophy and known only by the masters themselves. Mr. Dael argues that philosophy has been so busy perfecting subjectivity on the one hand and objectivity on the other that the original intent of apparent action has been neglected. When Socrates labored to find meaning in words, he was searching for meaning in "right action" and was not toying with a wasteful debate between what is real and not so real. In this respect, *The Platonic Idiom* shows the failure of Platonism and instead delivers a philosophy of action and responsibility rather than another polemic position.

The problem with our so-called western civilization is found in splintered dichotomies that exist because we neglect to find equilibrium with reality. We have indeterminism vs. determinism, subjectivism vs. objectivism, the ideal vs. the real, liberalism vs. conservatism and even faith vs. reason. In today's hotbed of polarization, the problem arises with each person thinking that taking a position is the key. Just as you cannot position faith as the pendulum opposite of reason, you cannot position reality in opposites. What is thought to be opposite must more likely be complimentary. This is why we need a third reality that gives agreement, proportion, and equilibrium rather than something that negates the other side. The *Platonic Idiom* reveals this third reality appropriately called the reality of predicativism.

When we negate the other side of a position, we are left with ideologists that talk of freedom yet avoid the responsibility required by the gift of agency. While the patriot positions himself on the side of freedom from the state, the ideologist positions her philosophy within the force of the state. Neither side accepts responsibility and, instead, western civilization followed the Platonic dichotomy rather than the predicate act of responsibility.

You will find that *The Platonic Idiom* communicates an inclusive philosophy unsurpassed in its ability to define words free from contradiction. Mr. Dael challenges the Platonic and Aristotelian duality that has plagued western thinking, and he does this by applying the psychology of fear, the conservation of meaning, the law of invariance, the predicate axis of action, and through his epistemology tree I believe he will give birth to a western tradition that pangs to be delivered.

Mica Ron Thomas
Editor Vision Impact Publishing.

Quoting accepted authority in order to propagate a personal view causes one to question the intent. Many will seek for a myriad number of authoritative facts in order to avoid responsibility toward understanding.

Samuel Dael

Introduction

Readers familiar with antiquity will find *The Platonic Idiom* a version of philosophy different in content and different from traditional views. The attempt is: To make philosophy less highbrow and give meaning more responsibility. This required a process that is for the most part neglected in philosophy yet considered paramount by Socrates and perhaps the prophets of antiquity. Plato is here considered the first to depart from not only Socrates, but also from sound thinking. Western Civilization continues to make the same mistakes as Plato.

In finding the academic forms of philosophy very strange, I have fallen back on the Socratic method and the meaning of words. This is not the form found in scholastic circles, but will make perfectly good sense once understood. This thesis is not a traditional scholarly work that simply references prior authorities. Rather, the maturation of this approach comes from the study of classical physics, the origins of classical religion, and also through a process of solving the paradoxes of modern relativity. Much of these views will be found in *The Einstein Illusion* and other books to follow, but they are referred to in this book because of their philosophical nature. This process was not without the development of an epistemological philosophy that requires that terms used in logic and reason must hold their meaning with more self-evident precision. The intellectual can argue rhetorically from any view he wishes, but making good sense takes a more classical, Socratic approach.

All meaning must be axiomatic or self evident and perceivable. Despite theories to the contrary, these concepts support the foundation of philosophy. Classical philosophy has always depended on a proper approach of defining the terms axiomatically including the recognition of self-evident truth based on prior axioms. For this reason I would like to suggest that this book is an essay in epistemological philosophy. I do not mean philosophy as usually practiced today, but in the classical sense, a science investigating the principles of reality. This epistemological approach not only encompasses physical reality, but also places faith in axiomatic meaning at the predicate center of reality and does not dwell in the subjective or objective positions only. Axiomatic means to have an axis at the center of reality and does not position one side of reality over another in order that one might justify questioning the self-evident.

The Platonic Idiom not only provides a philosophy that solves the division found in modern systems but also injects a long overdue predicate reality to compliment the traditional subjective and objective positions. This altogether new method places the definitions of words such as conservation, freedom, and almost every important word into invariant relationships rather than accepting a relative concept based on traditional usage and precedent. Precedent is not always the best solution to a decision. Unless the classical invariant meaning of terms is sought after, an opinion will hold errors and perfect meaning will be avoided. The popular path is of tradition and conventional knowledge that changes only when authority allows it. We fail to seek after absolute principles. As you shall see, fundamental words are compared numerically and through other classical means and concepts. The entire method fixes words into such perfect form that the meanings are preserved rather than twisted for intellectual altering. Ultimately, sophistic decay can hopefully be averted.

The customary procedure of thinking follows a process of deduction from traditional meaning. In this book, however, truth is postulated first using induction or a process of inducing sound meaning before deduction begins. This type of thinking usually does not survive in the academic world because the thought processes are conceptually slower and do not weather the quick acquiescence of fact. In the academic world, terms are assumed from conventional or authoritative knowledge and are not questioned. For this reason, the thoughts in this book come from the desert with literally no direct contact with the academic world. The approach, however, is not new. It is classical and begins with Socrates who probably learned the approach from a residue of Hebrew origins.

The attempt will be to formulate a proper explanation of philosophy without reverting to modern forms of positioning reality into a particular form as initiated by Plato. As historically recorded, Plato was the first to depart from the truly classical form. He separated the whole of reality and insisted that the subjective was the only true reality. Since Plato, the dichotomy of subjective and objective has pulled reality and philosophy apart. This was simply caused by sophisticated knowledge overshadowing sound meaning. We lost the classical means to define our terms. *The Platonic Idiom* will produce a sufficiently striking view for the religious, but a trial will certainly surface with the teacher of philosophy, if he or she has already found security in his or her own position.

Those who contemplate the use of this book should be warned that they will have to abandon the common prejudice that observed fact remains the soundest test of physical understanding. The basis of this conclusion comes from recognizing that *reason, observation,* and *objective fact* represent different parts of reality much the same way that the *subjective, predicative,* and *objective* represent different parts of speech. If we write in a precise way, should we not also think in the same manner? All ideas start with the thinking processes and therefore should be written in the same manner. The problem comes from the human mind rarely thinking in the predicate. Socrates tried to overcome this neglect and every time he pushed his opponent to define a word, the opponent simply changed the subject or brushed Socrates aside. This is how modern authority pushes the predicate reality under the rug. The predicate reality makes us question our traditions and it requires that we accept responsibility for meaning.

Many will certainly ask, "How can the philosophy of Socrates be separated from Plato when we only know Socrates through the writings of Plato?" It is not much different than when a modern preacher talks of a view he claims as Christ's and yet many know it not to be true. Reading Paul, for example, will give a slightly different color than Christ himself. A Cleric of Muhammad will certainly distort the original. I am sure that many a Rabbi will have taken the Law of Moses and turned it into idolatry—the worshiping of existing authority rather than something to study and live by. When you see a master defining the meaning of things and how it promotes responsibility, you can easily see the distortion when a student of the master introduces the need for a system to control the people. With skill, you can see it in every philosophy and you can see it in science. Even in modern times you can study the words of the American Prophet Joseph Smith and with the same skill note that Brigham Young, his prodigy, distorted the meaning of two key concepts and thus changed the future of this new American church. You can also see it in modern physics and you can see it in philosophy, education, and politics. If you have the skill to see the meaning change from the master to the student, you will have the skill to see the difference between Plato and Socrates. The key difference between how Socrates would define justice and how Plato attempted his form is clearly manifest between the *Republic* and other books of Plato's earlier writings. How one obtains the skill to decipher change in meaning is hopefully illustrated in this book.

It is understandable that the student may take the master's words differently when the master usually does not speak specifically. The master rather asks questions or speaks in similes or parables. Thus, the student never has the eye to see as clearly as the master and writes something different. This is the beginning of conventional knowledge—something the master never intended.

In depending upon meaning, I strongly encourage the creation of a third reality in which to place the act of observation and most of the words philosophy and religion have distorted since all the masters laid down the truth. Observation must retain power to show agreement between reason and fact and not try to become fact itself. It should have been concluded long ago that something must be wrong when observation creates paradoxical solutions or when fact and reason differ.

I take the position that the unspecialized thinker has access to basic questions which transcend technical proficiency, and that these basic questions can be approachable insofar as one resists getting sidetracked by philosophical muddle. We must maintain an awareness of a complimenting whole. *The Platonic Idiom* maintains this whole by explaining how the parts of reality fit together. Modern philosophy has been so busy perfecting reason on the one hand and objectivity on the other that the original intent of *right action* has been neglected. For when Socrates labored to find meaning in words such as justice, love or one's responsibility, he was searching for meaning in *right action* and was not toying with a wasteful debate between what is real and not so real. So, too, did Christ appropriately attempt to introduce proper action into the lives of His listeners. In this respect, *The Platonic Idiom* is a philosophy to better understand the workings of predicativism or right action and help one see the infantile thinking of isolated reality constructs.

Once Plato's terms become scanty, it can be illustrated epistemologically that the meaning of the subjective idiom he created affected unjustifiably all of philosophy. I will emphasize Plato's *Republic* and illustrate how it has affected all of political thought since. With a final view of our own vanishing republic, I will note that the thing most neglected in every republic and constitution is the method of taxation. This is because proper taxation yields to responsibility and the neglect of a good form of taxation leads to political control.

The most destructive philosophy preventing man from attaining the highest values is the egoism of Ayn Rand. Our country thrives on the need of greed, but it is sequentially killing every opportunity for a new and better way. Plato started things in the opposite direction with subjectivity, and Ayn Rand is a pendulum in the other direction called objectivist epistemology. We have come full circle in order to worship objectivity and a false sense of freedom and yet we completely avoid responsibility in the process. The tendency to think that big brother should be the responsible source on the one hand or rely upon natural greed on the other destroys all responsibility within man. The result is a loss of freedom, legal lawlessness, hypocrisy, and corruption.

Since the debate between subjectivism and objectivism has lasted so long, many *isms* have come upon the scene of philosophy, but all walk a tight rope eventually falling to one side or the other trying desperately to find a compromise with such philosophies as Empiricism and Existentialism. Both of these philosophies may recognize reason and to some extent objective existence, but they seem to gloss over the need of a third reality with existentialism having the greatest avoidance. I will cover most every ism on record and compare it with predicativism. This does not mean that predicativism stands alone. It means that the verb of reality is a connector of all reality.

In searching back and trying to find the place where philosophy jumped track, I came to a psychologically based conclusion. There appeared to be certain benefits to shift the meaning of words and thereby position a word to one side of reality or the other in order to deny the predicate reality of responsibility. The benefit seemed to cloak the traditional image of both God and reality and thus avoid accountability. If one finds a wailing and gnashing of teeth, I mean no harm. The problem of philosophical positioning is born out of irresponsibility and has little to do with intelligent insight.

A positioned reality is not a reality unto itself any more than one can stress position using a prepositional phrase without referencing the verb. It is the verb that delivers the ultimate solution. Subjective and objective positioning is destructive to the verb and misses the essential reality of philosophy. As did

Plato, those who negate one position for another, do so in order to bolster their own position. They play politics with meaning and truth. Platonic rhetoric will always emphasize authoritative control by taking responsibility away from the people and giving it to the state. On the other side is sophistic talk of more freedom from responsibility by keeping the state out of our lives. Neither side will talk of accepting more responsibility. It is like the liberal who negates the conservative in order to bolster his view rather than say to the conservative, "where is the right action that both of us are missing?" If we never reach agreement, we must be missing the predicate, the responsible thing, the ultimate solution, and the ultimate truth. As far as the state is concerned, the missing truth will be laid out in the last chapters where the intent will be to find equality and equilibrium between taxation and representation. This is what the founding fathers wanted, but our modern democracy has steered from it because of our need for Platonic positioning. It is imperative to understand the predicate because it will become the only salvation for our communities, states, nations, and the world.

Human beings take philosophical positions to satiate a personal acceptance formula rather than for the sake of humanity.

Samuel Dael

The Platonic Idiom

1. Understanding the Masters

Teachers of literature often fail in their dissemination of literary ideas by assuming that the masters can be interpreted by reading their works. When one writes to be understood, this is usually clarified with various examples and expressions of meaning that the masters used. We should remember, however, that the masters were not always writers to be understood but were writers to be heard. This was the case with Shakespeare. His venue was not the written work but the stage and the spoken word. To understand Shakespeare, one must listen to allow the inflections and interaction of all the actors to yield up the intent of Shakespeare.

Other masters never wrote a word but spoke as one man speaks to another. We have their words only through the eyes and ears of followers. Out of antiquity and through the oral traditions come the thoughts of the masters and of the prophets. It is only through the writing of their followers that we know them. There was once a man named Socrates, the "acknowledged master of all the eminent thinkers who have since lived," said John Stuart Mill.[1] We must be reminded, however, that everything we know about Socrates along with every piece of wisdom that he had given us comes to us second hand from his disciples and hearers of the word rather than by our hearing or reading the direct words of Socrates himself. Socrates did not write a book nor can we even find a jotting that has survived. All his ideas came to us in oral form. The only written form comes to us through Plato and other disciples.

Jesus was another master who had a following, but he did not put to pen his words of wisdom. If only we could have been there to listen and to watch the mood and inflections of a master in order to truly come to a better understanding. The hearing of the word was often not as important as understanding the word. For this reason, Jesus referred to this by asserting that those with eyes may not see nor those with ears may not have a guarantee of hearing. How much less would one who only reads the words second hand come to the proper understanding? And if another wrote an interpretation, how much more would true understanding fall to darkness?

When we try to understand the masters, the various disciples have injected some subtleties, of which we are unaware, into the dialogue. The further distant from the spoken event, when the words were eventually transcribed, the more we become suspicious of what was actually said. When Plato wrote his *Apology of Socrates*, the book came so soon after the actual event that distortion in substance would have caught the attention and aroused the criticism of the many readers of the *Apology* who were present. This was not the case with Jesus of Nazareth. It was many years afterwards that the disciples began to transcribe the words of the master. It is believed by many authorities that this posed a difficult problem especially when each disciple may have had a slightly different view.

Some words of the masters were written with the intent to be read and not heard. Such was the case of the Old Testament prophets. Their words were written in allegory and could not be understood easily. Consider the case with Isaiah.

> The Spirit of the Lord GOD is upon me; because the LORD hath anointed me to preach good tidings unto the meek; he hath sent me to bind up the brokenhearted, to proclaim liberty to the captives, and the opening of the prison to them that are bound;
> To proclaim the acceptable year of the LORD…
>
> Isaiah 61:1-2

3 | *The Platonic Idiom*

It was generally believed that only those who had the same gift as the prophets could reveal the meaning intended. Jesus made this very attempt according to Luke. Jesus was able to read the above from a scroll in the synagogue. He quoted the same as follows:

> The Spirit of the Lord is upon me, because he hath anointed me to preach the gospel to the poor; he hath sent me to heal the brokenhearted, to preach deliverance to the captives, and recovering of sight to the blind, to set at liberty them that are bruised,
> To preach the acceptable year of the Lord.
>
> Luke 4:18-20

Translations are apt to render things differently than written or even intended. Luke's use of the word 'poor' rather than 'meek' and adding 'recovering the sight to the blind' leads one to believe that Luke was injecting a point of view that was more Christian. Most authorities question the authenticity of the gospels because they were written so long after the oral word.

Slight variations should be expected when going from one language to another. Jesus did not read from the King James Version nor was the King James Version translated from the exact scrolls Jesus had read. In this respect, Luke could have been correct and the Old Testament we have today may not have come through the same language transformation as did the gospels. The two originals may have been the same and only what we have today is two completely different versions, including the Old Testament.

What was most unique about this reference from Isaiah came from the spoken words of Jesus when he said, "This day is this scripture fulfilled in your ears." Accidental change can be understood, but this announcement was consistent with other claims that Jesus had made in identifying his mission as something predicted by the prophets. It was as if Jesus was testifying of Isaiah and Isaiah was testifying of Jesus. This connection commands a certain degree of respect.

This transcending of time should teach us to consider more respectfully. Let me give another example from Matthew:

> Jesus saith unto them, Did ye never read in the scriptures, The stone which the builders rejected, the same is become the head of the corner: This is the Lord's doing, and it is marvelous in our eyes?
>
> Matthew 21:42

This is from Psalms 118:22 as beginning with: "The stone which the builders refused is become the head stone of the corner." The verses were essentially identical. These words would not offend some as feeding the poor and healing the blind did in the earlier reference, but Jesus again indicated in his own allegory that it would be fulfilled when he said:

> Therefore say I unto you, the kingdom of God shall be taken from you, and given to a nation bringing forth the fruits thereof.
>
> Matthew 21:43

Was Matthew making up something to justify taking the gospel to the Gentiles because the Jews had rejected His word? If not, then here were certainly words that transcended not only the past, but also into the future when Paul would be instructed to preach the Kingdom of Heaven to the Gentiles.

Here is another point: Even as recently as the 20th century writers were telling us that the Great Pyramid had a chief cornerstone that was rejected in its construction. The significance of this was had among the Masons who inscribe it onto U.S currency beneath the *All Seeing Eye*. This suggests that the Pyramid is a prophecy many centuries further back in time than the prophets. For something to transcend the beginning to modern times is very enlightening indeed, especially when the Master himself was the focal point of this prophecy and one who claimed to be the God of Abraham by saying, "Before Abraham was I Am."

Following a concept through history helps us to understand the original intent. By not making the links, one will follow some form of conventional knowledge initiated by

5 | The Platonic Idiom

later interpreters. The allegory simply sounds poetic and could be almost anything tradition will put upon it. Linking through time makes for the most powerful words. Masters that have so little linkage from the past to modern knowledge were either misunderstood or were never truly masters. Words cannot be just traditional; they must not diminish the past. Rather they must be meaningful and eternal.

Muhammad the prophet must here be mentioned. Unlike many masters who were submissive to the enemy as were Socrates and Jesus, Muhammad had a history of being unmerciful. He was painted by many as a poor sage in the desert who died with only the clothes on his back. It was even said that his education was limited and that he could not write. Yet traditions say that he wrote the words of the Koran as given to him by the angel Gabriel. It is not unlike the Christian attributing the words of Paul to Christ simply because Christ talked to Paul from heaven. We therefore attribute every word from Paul as the word of Christ.

Like Jesus, we interpret the words of Muhammad more through the writings of tradition than directly from Muhammad. We rarely realize that words change through each generation—especially through transcription and translation. If a cleric wants control, it is natural to overlay wisdom with rigid doctrine. It is almost sinister to make the master the author of new traditions, but it happens in every generation. We often shudder to think that Christ was the author of the crusades, but the originators of such seemed to indicate that they were following their master.

Muhammad's claim to knowledge comes from the Koran. The following reference mentions Gabriel as perhaps giving Muhammad some kind of authority:

> Say: Whoever is an enemy to Gabriel—for he brings down the (revelation) to thy heart by Allah's will, a confirmation of what went before, and guidance and glad tidings for those who believe,
>
> Koran 2:97

A more descriptive account follows in detail—seemingly at a far later time. This suggests an embellishment:

> Endued with Wisdom: for he appeared (in stately form);
>
> While he was in the highest part of the horizon:
>
> Then he approached and came closer,
>
> And was at a distance of but two bow-lengths or (even) nearer;
>
> So did (Allah) convey the inspiration to His Servant—what He (meant) to convey.
>
> The (Prophet's) (mind and) heart in no way falsified that which he saw.
>
> Will ye then dispute with him concerning what he saw?
>
> For indeed he saw him at a second descent,
>
> Near the Lote-tree beyond which none may pass:
>
> Near it is the Garden of Abode.
>
> Behold, the Lote-tree was shrouded (in mystery unspeakable!)
>
> (His) sight never swerved, nor did it go wrong!
>
> For truly did he see, of the Signs of his Lord, the Greatest!
>
> Koran 52:6-18

Despite the above, Muhammad taught that authority was a vice and to this day Islam does not have clergy or authority. All look to Allah as the only authority. Here is another verse of interest:

> Say ye: "We believe in Allah, and the revelation given to us, and to Abraham, Ishmael, Isaac, Jacob, and the Tribes, and that given to Moses and Jesus, and that given to (all) prophets from their Lord: We make no difference between one and another of them: And we bow to Allah (in Islam)."
>
> So if they believe as ye believe, they are indeed on the right path; but if they turn back, it is they who are in schism; but Allah will suffice thee as against them, and He is the All-Hearing, the All-Knowing.
>
> (Our religion is) the Baptism of Allah. And who can baptize better than Allah. And it is He Whom we worship.
>
> Koran 2:136-138

All were prophets from Abraham, and from Moses to Jesus. If any of them go amiss it is they who turn back and not Allah. Who is going to determine which prophet turns back? Allah, of course, but who tells us what Allah says? Evidently Muhammad claimed some sort of perfect authority when he evidently dismissed authority in others. Muhammad often condemned the prophets of old for turning back and advised those reading the Koran not to look back to the "ancients" as he called them. This kind of process destroys the link of truth out of the past from reaching the present and prevents truth from arising in the future. Truth is not a byproduct of only one prophet. Rather it weaves in and out of history without someone negating the past simply to get control. To condemn all of the past in order to justify your personal view and yet claim to be the only true authority is as much darkness as medieval Christianity distorting the words of their master. The atheist does the same by negating all that has passed before.

Muhammad was concerned about idolatry and the worshiping of authority, but nonetheless put himself up as the ultimate authority. "We should worship Allah (God only) and no other," says Islam, but I know no other nation that pays tribute to the authority of the tribal clerics than the Muslims. Rather than following the Koran, idolatry in worshiping clerics and even militant leaders overshadows the mind and breaks the very thing Muhammad was trying to establish. When no one speaks as one having authority, it is like taking any form of scripture you can find in order to justify any action that will fit your view with lust, power, and control. If we consider the Koran as the words of Muhammad, how are we to decipher them from the words of Allah? It really takes more than one prophet to decipher the truth. It is essential that we read between the lines of a disciple in order to extract truth from the manipulation manifest.

Muhammad was a merchant who traveled extensively. He most certainly understood Christianity, and his view is expressed as follows:

> The Jews call 'Uzair a son of Allah, and the Christians call Christ the son of Allah. That is a saying from their mouth; (in this) they but imitate what the unbelievers of old used to say. Allah's curse be on them: how they are deluded away from the Truth!
>
> They take their priests and their anchorites to be their lords in derogation of Allah, and (they take as their Lord) Christ the son of Mary; yet they were commanded to worship but One Allah. There is no god but He. Praise and glory to Him: (Far is He) from having the partners they associate (with Him).
>
> Koran 9:32-33

To worship but one God was not only the salutation of Muhammad but also of Christ. This God we owe allegiance to has the makings of the most nebulous concept in philosophy because we know this God or Allah only through the writings of prophets. It is like we are damned if we follow prophets because they might lead us astray and we are damned if we do not follow them because there may be some truth in them. The problem that needles Moslem, Jew, Christian or atheist is the prophetic authority that is implied in an opponent's choice of prophet. When a prophet comes along, sees a vision, and writes all his words that are original and different from all previous masters, this says something about the twisting of meaning and of the truth. But when a master fulfills the words of a previous master and also predicts the words of one yet to come, that is prophetic authority that cannot be dismissed. Prophesy has a thread in it that seems eternal to every generation, and when a prophet comes along and says that all the old should be done away with, he or she is either wrong or something prior has been lost through darkness. Christ wanted to do away with the old wine but sought for things lost before the law. You have to pull something out of antiquity in order to measure truth against the backdrop of change. The Law of Moses was a change from the past and perhaps was needed to manage ignorance, but you do not dismiss things altogether as did Muhammad.

The Platonic Idiom

I do not intend to doubt Muhammad's visit of Gabriel or of Moses speaking face to face with God, or even Joseph Smith's testimony of receiving visitors from heaven. I do not care to doubt the experiences of heaven that Emanuel Swedenborg had. I only doubt the words of the Prophets who do not clarify reason and nullify tradition. And when they demean the masters that preceded them or attempt to change the original, I am there to challenge them with every form of rationality possible. This is the problem with tradition. It changes the meaning of things. Just as Muhammad said that he had no authority, so also did Paul the apostle say, "I speak of myself and not by commandment"[2] and again "I speak not by commandment, but by occasion of the forwardness of others..." Even Christ made it a point to stress the important difference between speaking of one's self or by commandment from God.

> For I have not spoken of myself; but the Father which sent me, he gave me a commandment, what I should say, and what I should speak.
>
> John 12:49

Muhammad made it a point on several occasions to acknowledge the authority of Jesus Christ:

> And remember, Jesus, the son of Mary, said: "O Children of Israel! I am the apostle of Allah (sent) to you, confirming the Law (which came) before me, and giving Glad Tidings of an Messenger to come after me, whose name shall be Ahmad." But when he came to them with Clear Signs, they said, "this is evident sorcery!"
>
> Koran 61:6

This was used by Muhammad to give additional authority to himself rather than what was intended. "Ahmad" in the above refers to the second comforter that Jesus mentioned. Islam generally believes this to be Muhammad. Islamic people are Christians in this sense, only they do not believe Christ was crucified nor was He the Son of God, yet the Koran has 73 references to the day of Resurrection and that Christ will come and Judge the people. Many Islam writers criticize Christianity with the same energy as the Protestants criticize the Catholics. They claim that Christianity has gone astray, yet they deny the words of the ancients altogether.

When tradition is mixed with truth, it becomes a horrific controller of the people. Jesus understood this problem when the Pharisees and certain of the scribes came from Jerusalem:

> And when they saw some of his disciples eat bread with defiled, that is to say, with unwashen, hands, they found fault.
>
> For the Pharisees, and all the Jews, except they wash their hands oft, eat not, holding the tradition of the elders.
>
> And when they come from the market, except they wash, they eat not. And many other things there be, which they have received to hold, as the washing of cups, and pots, brasen vessels, and of tables.
>
> Then the Pharisees and scribes asked him, Why walk not thy disciples according to the tradition of the elders, but eat bread with unwashen hands?
>
> He answered and said unto them, Well hath Esaias prophesied of you hypocrites, as it is written, This people honoureth me with their lips, but their heart is far from me.
>
> Howbeit in vain do they worship me, teaching [for] doctrines the commandments of men.
>
> Mark 7:2-7

When a disciple, cleric, or traditional authority talks of petty things such as the many traditions of Jewish law or the insurmountable superstitions of any religion (including Islam) that make God a God of meticulous habits such as one must pray a certain number of times or must repeat a particular prayer that tradition demands, all this simply indicates the need of control by the one in authority and the need of acceptance by the follower. Religious leaders following such traditions are in the gall of bitterness and teach for doctrines the commandments established by tradition. Even Christianity adds a multitude of traditions to satiate the need of acceptance. Essentially this breeds self-righteousness. God does not command in every detail. It is the hallmark of tradition and the way of dictators, despots, and controlling clergy and clerics. The people follow because they cannot suffer rejection and they must feel accepted so a little meticulousness is a sign of doing the acceptable thing.

Rather than disavow the ancient masters, we should disavow traditions that follow disciples who add in a new twist of terms. The Mormon religion made the same attempt as Muhammad during the eleventh hour of the 20th century. Mormon authority spoke often of not paying attention to the words of dead prophets, but to follow living prophets. This was an attempt to control the many wandering away from the church in order to practice polygamy. The dead prophet subtly referred to was Brigham Young, who taught the doctrine of polygamy. The Mormon Church, to this date, still has difficulty deciphering the difference between tradition added by Brigham Young and truth as intended by the master Joseph Smith. This problem will continue until they announce a better understanding rather than hold Brigham Young as a perfect prophet and in the same breath expect that we put away dead prophets, as did Muhammad.

It is important to root out tradition rather than condemn any great master, but traditional leadership and authority will not do this. Either they will disavow old authority or keep it and never separate ideas as one would separate the wheat from the tares. Prophets and all masters in science and philosophy are not perfect. The truth must be gleaned from their words and reestablished with long standing values while the errors of their ways are described simply as conventional knowledge of the time.

Einstein has been placed as a master of physics and one who comprehends the ultimate truth. Few will question the paradoxes of the Special Theory of Relativity. Instead, they say that only the best minds can understand it. This is no different than the special status given to religious clerics. Such denial is a manifestation of control by the disciples of relativity. Modern physics accepted every word of Einstein as truth and twisted the terms of reality into new terms that actually prevent us from perusing the ultimate in truth. This was due, in part, to

Einstein himself, but largely his contemporaries fostered a new contemporary knowledge or change in meaning about space, time, and mass. Modern science has not the skill to remove this new tradition and has thus allowed modern relativity to lead the people into the same kind of darkness that many disciples have done with various religions. Einstein tried on two occasions to correct the problem, but it was too late. The modern mind preferred magic to accountability. There is so much insight from Einstein that we tend to accept everything he stated and cannot separate conjecture from truth. We treat him as an absolute authority as did the disciples of Muhammad.

Even though toleration and diversity have eventually crept into our modern culture to justify different views, we are still very authoritative. The so-called diversity of liberal attitudes in education really does not create freedom from darkness because approval from the cleric is supplanted by approval from the professor. Nothing under any culture is learned about obeying sound principles of the masters and eliminating tradition or false ideas. Over time, the words of the masters will always be turned upside down. It is human nature and the goal of most every disciple.

An interesting analogy has surfaced as we change the meaning of terms. Consider the liberal as the liberating culture and the conservative as the traditional culture. We have none other than two divergent positions where both avoid responsibility and both muster a semblance of freedom. The liberal lacks personal responsibility and pontificates about the right for all to obtain a share. The conservative is guilty of a lack of social responsibility and pontificates the freedom to do as he wishes. The liberal sees social injustice and social inequality where the conservative denies that there should be any social concern and says that liberty is survival of the fittest. In Plato's *Republic* one can get the liberal position of government control. And by reading Aristotle's *Politics* we see a similar imbalance in conservative thinking. The conservative and the liberal both abuse freedom by defining it incorrectly. One is a selfish right to take and the other is a selfish freedom to keep. The liberal seeks to gain power through government and the conservative seeks to gain leverage through capitalism. Neither maintains personal or social responsibility as taught by the masters. If one does not individually help the poor and if one does not encourage a local social structure to aid the same, then being a liberal or being a conservative is pride, greed, and simply a tradition, whether old or new, that continues to grind the faces of the poor. The nature of responsibility and how it is avoided defines the nature of many cultures. The correct meaning of freedom as well as faith, justice, and judgment inspires responsibility. Distorted meanings are buried in fastidious traditions. Ignorance becomes our bliss in order to avoid accountability and tradition inspires ignorance whether old or new. It is just our nature to twist the terms of the masters.

Every old or modern culture preserves its own type of darkness in order to say that we must follow the true and living way without having to do anything for the week and the afflicted. The ultimate truth is avoided for this very reason. Truth requires responsibility and hard work. It is easier to perform a ritual to be accepted than consider another as one would think of himself. Those who do see the suffering see it in the world and not around them. For this reason they establish governments, organizations, and bureaucracies to fix things they are unwilling to personally attend to. They will go to the utmost length to raise funds to feed a social machine rather than give a personal touch to those in need.

Modern education in its most advanced form has also created a subculture establishing diversity of ideas as a form of freedom from ignorance. Our educational system simply develops its own hierarchy of authority that replaces cultural authority. Nothing is really accomplished because education does not teach one to define correctly. Higher education simply supplants religious control with the control by the degree holder. Its doctrines are relativity, the mechanism of evolution, the darkness of a programmed psychology, and the greed of capitalistic concepts. The professionals do not select a profession in order to serve, but to get gain. One never becomes a teacher save he or she avoids defining reality and accepts the twisted terms given under some formal educational process. New cultures create new masters over time who will position reality into blind corners simply to avoid the responsibility of meaning that Socrates, Christ, and other masters taught through self-awareness of the whole of reality rather than a one-sided form of it. Nothing learned is ever absolutely new. Correct meaning was so important to the masters that they would die for it. Without this testament, any new authority is apt to foster traditions that work on the fear of the people rather than understanding.

Whenever the commandments of men ask us to consider the poor or forgive our enemy, we note that none will follow a prophet stating such requirements. If the prophet tells us to bow ourselves to God seven times a day, this we will do. If we are asked to take up the sword to kill the enemy, this we will do also. If we are told to hate someone who does not love God, this we will do. But to love our neighbor and care for the fatherless, this we will not do. We leave it to the few and to the government. We all have hearts of guile, for obedience proves our acceptance of those over us, but giving to the poor means only those less than we appreciate our good will. Men will do evil and even sacrificial things to be appreciated by those above or by the masses, but no one wants to be appreciated by the least in the kingdom. The scriptures we accept and reject are only to satisfy our acceptance formula and maintain our prejudice. We lie to ourselves because we do not understand the intent of the masters.

Like Plato, the wisdom of men concocts special reality theories to position us into a corner far away from accountable action and the predicate reality of responsibility. Every culture provides its own idiom to establish tradition, acceptance formulas, and the denial of true meaning. It is this meaning of things that the masters wanted us to consider while it is the traditions of the disciples that keep us in darkness by injecting false meaning. The attempt by Plato to twist the meaning intended by Socrates has caused such devastating results that few can wade through the proverbial traditions and see what Socrates intended. Plato was guilty of the same crime as Muhammad, Christians and Jews who talk of the masters but change meaning to fit their own views. These differing views cause divisions and war between cultures. Because of term twisting, the proponents of freedom offer no more of a solution to peace than the despot. We are in darkness because no one will sit down and define things clearly in order to remove the hold tradition has upon us.

    We continually say how evil idolatry is, but we practice it daily within a culture we have come to relish as true. Our social acceptance and our denial of death become the driving force for our belief and anyone who suggests we discuss the meaning of things becomes the enemy of our tradition. The problem is a psychological one and has little to do with a philosophical debate. A predicate philosophy of meaning can remove our scarecrows, but too many condemn philosophy because they prefer psychological darkness rather than the light of meaning and understanding that transcend from time immemorial and on into the future.

The motive of authority is to maintain ignorance among the people in order to limit questioning minds. We know this problem exists with religion but we fail to recognize that it is also found within philosophy, science, and politics.
Samuel Dael

2. Philosophical Motive

It is not in the nature of man to understand the masters. Humanity prefers to accept only that which will support a particular philosophy based upon a psychological motive such as popular acceptance formulas that satisfy common worldviews. Consider that history gives us a common worldview that describes the sacrifices of many religious origins in which early saints went through great difficulties in order to worship according to their own dictates. Generations after will never attempt some of the trials that their ancestors suffered. This particular worldview of our ancestors is quite different than our worldview for our own generations. We seem to apply different worldviews for the early Christians than we do to ourselves. What we do not understand is that these trials were byproducts of rejection and prejudice. The Jews in Germany were a perfect example. Also the Tibetan Monks and Mormon pioneers suffered similar forms of persecution. There seems to be a tendency for those once persecuted to be eulogized for their sacrifices. I am not talking of sacrifices one does for another, for a principle, or for the poor; I am talking about the persecuted that are forced to find freedom from persecution because of their beliefs. They do not choose to sacrifice but are forced into it because of their rituals and beliefs.

Ever since Moses led the children of Israel out of Egypt, religious trials were never one's choosing, but were thrust upon the people. When we look back, we do not do as they did because it is now a choice and not a necessity or something forced upon us. In a sense, they were no different than we are today, for how can you judge the early saints as more righteous if it was forced upon them?

If we too were forced, perhaps we would become as the saints of old. We cannot assume that there is a difference between a former generation and a modern one. If we do not volunteer to sacrifice, perhaps we may eventually be forced to suffer. The worldview of sacrifice has been misapplied to all people who are forced to adjust their lives. Sacrifice should really mean that we do unto others as we would like to be treated. Thus, we have two types of sacrifice. The one is a responsible action and the other is forced suffering. We must ask, "Why do people accept trials by force, but do not place a burden upon them voluntarily? Humanity hangs onto tits beliefs at all costs, even to give up one's very life, but they will not sacrifice for the poor or the fatherless. Even the homeless and the widow are neglected. Sometimes, under catastrophic duress, you will find many pitching in to help, but as soon as the storm is over the volunteers go home and still neglect their neighbors.

Regardless of the culture, every man and his family are pretty much economic islands unto themselves. What they do have in common is a belief system. They fall in line to some authority and to various systematic rituals. You find that they have a strong need of acceptance, but rarely will one love his neighbor as himself. This need of acceptance will actually cause class divisions over time. It will cause prejudice and self-righteousness. It will eventually generate poor and rich. When we volunteer to help some distant crisis, but fail to help our own neighbor in need, are we not doing it for the acceptance and the notoriety of the world? For some reason we feel more immortal helping in a catastrophic situation than we do simply giving to a poor neighbor. It is this feeling of exhilaration and immortality that we seek and we do not look to the least in our communities.

The Jews eventually found their own state, but do they care for one another any more than one American does for another? They wanted a state to practice their beliefs. Those who fight for freedom of religion can be honored, but those who fight for their own religion usually care less for the rest of humankind. They are imprisoned by their belief. I suggest this in part for the Jews but with great disgust for the Muslim extremist. Even the Mormon has similar tendencies to the Jew. Individually they do not "cleave one to another"[1] except there is a reward of honor in it. Even families in the world do not care for each other past the generation of the parents. What appears as caring is superficial at most.

Where are the principles aside from social ritual and family tradition, and where are the human values for the community? Each community still has rich and poor, gossiper and prejudicial icon, social dictators, and obedient followers. Their principles are in their rituals, but not in their behavior toward one another. Why do we believe so strongly in a doctrine, but cannot live the way Christ taught and lived? Even our politics is muddied with prejudice as we stand strong to a belief system but care little for those on the other side. We are downright fixed on a tradition and not on principles for all.

I am sure at some time in history the Jews may have expressed the same spirit of prejudice as the Muslims. Certainly the Christians felt their belief was paramount during the Crusades. It is all done in the name of a belief system. But once the system is finally in place, there is little concern for the weak, the poor, or the downtrodden. It is not for principle that these people sacrifice their lives; it is for acceptance by those who get power over them, or for freedom that they obtain to control those under them. This cultural process requires that the poor politically work to the top of the prejudice ladder rather than be a beneficiary of compassion. It is often not for humanity or for principle that people espouse a religion and make a sacrifice. It is for personal acceptance. Many say they do it for God, but they lie. It is a problem of psychological motive to them and they do not know it. You do not give up your life to your God. He doesn't need it. If you think he does, your view of God is that of a fundamentalist or extremist, having little social value. You give up your life for others. Thus the expression: When you do it unto the least in the kingdom you do it unto God.

Families are cohesive to a lesser or greater degree, but when it comes to one family and another it is the survival of the fittest. If it were not for government and laws, families would destroy each other economically through prejudice and pride. The community is the pulse of goodness because it is voluntary, but when the government or church does well for its people, it is not voluntary. If you find rich and poor, drug addict and dealer, socially accepted and socially rejected in a community, you have a people who do things only for themselves, their church, and their social group, but nothing for the least in the community. Many will come forth with good ideas, but they want funds and power to fix a sick community. The bureaucracy they build only increases the problem. The problem in any government small or large is the search for power where many will come forth saying, "Give me the funds and the power and I will show you what great works I can do." What does happen when the people give power over to others is that they eventually suffer more corruption, a greater division of rich and poor, more restrictive laws and a higher cost of government.

Regardless of the religious convictions and the sacrifices made in the name of religion, every cultural community will eventually fail when it does not care for the least. Because of this we have big government and the principles espoused by the religion are a hiss and a byword. This whole problem is a psychological dilemma and not a moral or ethical problem. Human beings are basically ethical, but their psychological baggage and the false meanings are killing the community. Consider that it is a psychological problem that causes one to gossip, shoplift, exalt himself, become destructive, seek for power, intimidate others, establish his own image, or push others out. This problem is a problem in every community and even though all worship the same God and believe the same things, we are sick with motive. It is this sickness that is the subject of this chapter. This sickness does not go away with reasoning or education. It is there because individuals have not been taught proper meaning, such as in the case of sacrifice. They have instead been fed false meanings in everything from faith to grace and also about the truth in helping the least in the kingdom. The whole lot of Christianity has shifted in meaning from its origin toward hypocrisy and guile.

Now the cause of this is primarily psychological. Man needs a feeling of immortality without responsibility. He will die for the feeling, but will not consider the poor. Whether one is religious or not, the need is the same. A daredevil performer gets a sense of immortality when he comes close to death in a challenging act and is exhilarated to a level of immortality when he comes out alive. Young people flock to a scary movie for the very same reason. The feeling of leaving alive is exhilarating. Competitive sports, hunting, gambling and other so-called recreational pastimes achieve the same effect. Each person chooses different means to accomplish the same psychological uplift. We do not have to be religious. In fact the atheist has a special psychological method. If he can attack prayer and God in any way, he accomplishes an unusual thing psychologically. It is not unlike the hunter out for the kill. If you can kill God, then you are above God. You are alive. Killing reminds those who are sick with the fear of death that they are still alive.

Escaping death is not as much a survival instinct as it is a psychological problem. The same is true of rejection. A teenage boy who feels neglected by his father may destroy property just to get the attention he is seeking. It is a denial of rejection. A twisted religion is the denial of death as are so many things in our lives. To justify our need to deny death and rejection we foster new worldviews that allow us to practice our psychological religion. The old religion has been given a new meaning just to allow us the freedom we want. If our religion asks us to sacrifice our lives for a cause, we will do it if the doctrine has been changed sufficiently to make us a hero. Perhaps the denial of death is more of a problem in some cultures than in others. In any case, we are warmongers because, like the daredevil, we can see how close we can come to death and live and if we die we become immortal as we are honored as heroes. The need to be a hero is more important to us psychologically than helping someone in need.

The denial of death and rejection is what is driving us. The will to do something for others is a rarity. We are sick with a curse. The philosopher is not exempt. If a philosopher can change the traditional mind, it would indicate that he has been awarded a spot in immortality. The scientist may very well do the same. The need for honor is so important and stimulated by the need to publish that it is imperative to come up with something different to get attention. What really works best is if an idea can be somewhat rational and allow the hearer of the idea to benefit psychologically as well. It does not matter if the idea is true or not. It sells. If one comes up with an idea that would require more responsibility, it will be rejected. Einstein, for example, came up with relativity, but he did not get a Nobel Prize for it. Even though it has become popular because of its magic, the Special Theory of Relativity is still unproven. What Einstein did get a Nobel Prize for was his photoelectric effect. This demonstrated that light could be treated as bundles of particles, but we still consider light pure energy because it is more magical to see how energy can change into mass and back again. We follow the new traditions of relativity rather than a responsible view that light is bits of matter. We love changing the meaning of things to give us the mysticism we need to deny death and rejection. That is the philosophical motive each of us suffers from.

You cannot blame a lack of meaning in the lives of people because that is not the root cause. Sound meaning is only a long-term cure for what on the inside that sickens us. We all have some sort of moral or religious values, but we have found a problem in dealing with death. Something is wrong, but we cannot put our finger on it. We sense the hypocrisy in others, but fail to see the hypocrisy in ourselves. It seems that we are all somewhat sick and need something to believe in. This is the vacuum from which false ideas and false religious doctrines are created modified and continue. It is the cause of false meaning and the inevitable destruction of a cohesive community. It seems that we need a cure or are looking for one. When we find it, most likely it furthers our destruction because we become sick when we see the responsibility needed. A rational scientist or philosopher when approached with a religious or intuitive concept will want proof or some logical explanation. I would say to them that they are in denial and cannot handle the truth. I heard a similar line delivered in a recent Ghost Whisper TV series in response to one wanting logic. The basis of the expression really originated from the movie *A Few Good Men*. It is mentioned here that the tables can be turned. Usually one would say that the believer couldn't handle the truth. This chapter and the need to deny death and rejection can just as well apply to the logician who wants proof. The truth may be that the logician cannot face the responsibility required if he had to follow his intuitive truth. The problem with logic and philosophy is that the meaning changes as much as it does in religion. This is all in an attempt to deny death and rejection in hopes of becoming immortal and rise to the hero status. What we cannot see is that philosophers are just as sick as we are. We cannot see through their mesmerizing rhetoric and the creating of so many philosophical positions for the truth. This alone should tell us that they are sick with motive.

The psychological sickness that all of us have is the anxiety about life and apprehension over our eventual death. Any doctrines that can sooth over this problem become the eventual doctrine of tradition and not true meaning. These false doctrines can come from religion, politics, education, and especially Hollywood. The terror of life and death will eventually cause extremism at both ends of the spectrum. That is what fear does. It divides the meaning of life into two corners. The more one pushes to the left, the greater the push to the right and, in return, a greater push to the left. Whether we are in a community of the accepted and non-accepted or in a nation of rich and poor, polarization is inevitable because of false meaning. The problem is that each individual will deal with his problem differently either overtly or with silence. He either quietly works into power or becomes more overt about it. Power seems to be the natural propensity to deal with the anxiety of life and death. If we do not have power, we lust after those who do. How we do it is determined by whether we hold to the invert subjectivist method or the overt objectivist mode. We thus create two poles of false meaning to deal with our sickness of fear.

Now the basis of this psychology comes from Otto Rank—a contemporary of Freud. Also, the Pulitzer Prize winner Ernest Becker made note of this psychology in his book *The Denial of Death*. Neither talked of false doctrines or polarization, but they did discus the need to deny the reality of death and rejection because, at our core, we are afraid. As Becker and Rank so eloquently established, all manner of sin is a byproduct of fear. For this reason they explained the need of sound religious principles. Otto Rank was the editor of Freud's writings and those of other psychologists. He had a broad view and a religious conviction and applied his fear-based psychology to legends, myths, and art and to all things created by man's lust to deny death. He did not study the neurotic in hospitals but rather the neurotic in life who are said to be normal. His own writings gave the correct answers that his contemporaries failed to see because they could not apply their theories to the sick community. Freud and others were overly focused upon the individual and personal trauma and not of the innate fear that is already present and only further traumatized by poor parenting and poor communities. There is no attempt here to demean the treatment of the individual, but unless we can treat the community with sound meaning rather than false meaning the treating of the individual will be an endless and expensive process.

Essentially, false meaning originates from the subconscious need to deny death and to deny rejection. This comes in religious forms that promise salvation in the next life and in youthful forms that require one to prove that he is not afraid. There are countless psychological methods in between.

The Platonic Idiom

The idea is that one is to write a great philosophy that, if accepted, makes one immortal. This may apply to art, music or anything creative. We do things more for the acceptance and denial than for the good of humanity. We have unconscious motive that drives our achievements and our behavior. The problem is not what we accomplish, but what we do with our worldviews and the meaning we attribute to our behavior. If others eulogize us, then they too are caught up in the false meaning and philosophical motive.

Sin satiates this same motive of denial, but the religious mind cannot sin so they attempt to introduce doctrines that solve their dilemma. It becomes important that they convince others in order to justify their beliefs and eventually their strange acts. This same psychology can be demonstrated among youth who satiate their fear of life and death by seeking out a horror movie. If the fear of death and of life begins to rise out of their subconscious, they seek the terror simply to consciously say they are not afraid. When they come out of the movie alive, they say, "I came close to death and lived." For this same reason, images of the sacrifice of Jesus upon the cross became more interesting to worshippers than the resurrection. We can walk in a church, look at death and then walk out alive. This is all a psychological need to deny death and rejection.

The real solution to the denial of death and life is to apply faith in meaningful principles. The spirit of motive will often confuse us, but we must stand firm with sound meaning—meaning that requires responsibility. Confusion comes from a misinterpreting of many principles. Take the meaning of Christ's statement:

> Jesus said unto her, I am the resurrection, and the life: he that believeth in me, though he were dead, yet shall he live:
> John 11:25

John was telling the story of the raising of Lazarus. Jesus seemed to know and understand how the fear of death among the people governed their lives. He also wanted to teach them that there should be no fear of death because he would bring the resurrection and they should have no fear of life if the people would but believe and really live what he taught them. Christ's whole mission was designed to teach us how to overcome. Christ's story provided the grandest scheme to overcome fear. Sin was not the problem, but a symptom. It was the fear of life and death that needed to be overcome. Sin was only a sign of the problem. Jesus cared little about one's sins for he associated with sinners teaching them how to overcome fear in order to sin no more. Man places too much emphasis upon the sinful act and not enough on its psychological basis. The Lord's anger arises more for meticulous doctrines than sin, for the endless doctrines become chains of denial that prevent one from overcoming the fears of life and death.

Religion over time has turned meaning around by pushing the act of believing into a subjective process rather than truly living the gospel of Christ. Part may be due to translation and part may be in the way Christ expressed the message. When people want to believe in the easy way they will, and if they want to take the responsible direction they will act accordingly. If we have ears to hear, we will hear correctly; but, if we cannot see the true meaning, we will take the easy meaning to cover our fear. We will even create new ideas as leaders to feed the needs of the psychologically sick. Leaders often give "gall to drink"[2] instead of milk because followers want malignity and bitterness to deny their fear of death. We are all sadists in degree. We watch the typical violent television series just to see blood, guts, and death. It makes us feel alive. For the same reason, we watch the nightly news.

As no one desires death, loneliness or oblivion, few want to admit they are afraid of such realities. The pride in us intimidates by saying, "The strong survive. If we are afraid, we are not strong." Human nature is forever attempting to bully away fear and never learning to overcome it. We do not overcome fear by denying it. We learn to understand it. We would rather avoid responsible action by talking more of fastidious cultural rules and of blind obedience. This is done specifically to give us a false sense of immortality. All of us seek for special worldviews in order to feel liberated from reality. All of human nature to one degree or another does not consider what's really bugging them. No one is exempt from this dilemma save they reach the wisdom of Socrates and Christ. For, when we can accept death and life through concern for others, we have reached the pinnacle of faith. Faith is the enemy of this fear and of denial.

Intellectualism can be just as dark as dogmatic religious views and just as dark as a sportsman facing death in order to see if he can come out alive.

> For life is at the start chaos in which one is lost. The individual suspects this, but he is frightened at finding himself face to face with this terrible reality, and tries to cover it over with a curtain of fantasy, where everything is clear. It does not worry him that his "ideas" are not true; he uses them as trenches for the defense of his existence, as scarecrows to frighten away reality.
>
> Jose Ortega y Gasset[3]

Few will consider that the eternal nature of individual intelligence, through its evolutionary process from some preexisting condition, may be the precursor of such terror. If such is the case, Christ may have known this condition as he attempted to sooth the spirit as mentioned above in John 11:25. Within psychology as well as in biological evolution theory, preexistence is not considered. Therefore all things must be hereditary or environmental. This conclusion is so limiting that it explains why the denial of death and rejection is not taught as it should be. It just may be the same reason philosophy has never developed a predicate reality. These views may sound too religious, but consider that if preexistence dominates our behavior in any way, religious insight out of the mouths of the masters may have something more to say than we give it credit. It is not sufficient to be good, but one must overcome. Sin is only a means of denial of fear and not a product of a temptation to do evil. Temptation is the lust to do something to help us to scare away reality.

The different modes of religious or even political ideologies are nothing but positions of denial. Each thinks his method is that of God or some true form. Followers think a traditional leader knows all and the average mind cannot decide for itself. If individuals could learn to define more clearly, they could choose better leaders and make better decisions. Without clear meaning, we fall prey to an entire library of methods to push fear into the background.

Few want the responsibility of life, or to accept the laws of conservation in a physical existence. Too many bask in the magic of religion and various forms of psychological denial that defy some law of conservation. This is found in philosophy, economics, physics, religion and evolution. They do this in an attempt to prove to themselves that they are not afraid. Economics is the most fluent manifestation of denial and the avoidance of responsibility. We all understand equity, but most think that what we have becomes ours by some eternal right. Many seek for governments, kings, and dictators to care for their needs and, in so doing; they break the law of economic conservation. No one wants the responsibility to love his neighbor as himself, so we choose instead to believe in the power of religious magic and the strict, orthodox worship of a God of one fundamental theology or another in order to justify our neglect. Anytime a choice is made to soften or excuse personal responsibility, a serious error has occurred. The result leads to further denial, the justification of neglect and even mental illness. Almost all choose some form of idolatry by placing one human magically above another. We do not trust our own spirit and we do not trust in a God who must obey the same laws of the universe that we must obey. Everyone wants a God of magic, or they deny God altogether. Like philosophical bullies, we cloak our fear by saying, "There is no God."

Jesus wanted to teach something to Peter, James and John, but after three attempts he evidently considered that the time had passed. This was when he asked them to come and watch him pray. They fell asleep upon three attempts. Jesus was 'exceeding sorrowful unto death' and in his prayer he knew of the Father's power and therefore admitted his fear of pain unto death: 'Abba, Father, all things are possible unto thee; take away this cup from me: nevertheless not what I will, but what thou wilt.' Though Christ did not abandon virtue, he did confess his fear. One need not think that facing death without fear epitomizes strength. In fact, one cannot face death without fear. If you think you can, you are in denial of the inevitable. Courage, then, cannot foster denial of one's fear wherein one brushes danger in defiance. An act of courage approaches death in light of fear. It overcomes by faith in a better outcome for all.

Like Peter, James, and John, man has fallen asleep to this understanding. We do not see the message. We will not awake and see that it is important to confess our fear and recognize it. Man instead cloaks it in denial. Pagan Christianity dresses death in mysticism and excuses a lack of virtue. All fail in understanding the core meaning of Christ's psychology. Few understand that all behavior more easily fosters some level of denial.

Many use tradition, popular assumptions, and a false sense of reason to defend their worldview. This is understandable, but claiming reason as part of their process is usually presumptuous. Reason too often is used as a dialectic process rather than a sound method of removing contradiction in false meaning. We often, in a subtle way, change the meaning of terms in order to curve-fit our own desires into the argument. Our meaning is often not the meaning of others, but if the many also like our change of connotation, we foster what is properly called conventional knowledge. It is knowledge based upon accepted tradition and not sound meaning. The intellectual is often so darkened by the twisting of terms that he or she can even distort reason itself.

If it were really possible to reason, we would do it better. Because of its problems, some religious believers think reason is not of God. Yet God himself said, "Come let us reason together."[4] I have countered professors of traditional theory with a different view and since I was nobody important, they simply dismissed my inquiry. Socrates had the same problem. People carry psychological problems about being wrong. It needles their immortality formulas and prevents them from really reasoning. Opponents tend to intimidate rather than rationalize. You can see it in political rhetoric more than anywhere else. The masses respond more to intimidation or the suggestion of a false assumption than they do to reason. Authority keeps their executive distance that they may never face the fact that they are ignorant about clear meaning. No one wants his or her worldview to be challenged because it represents all that they stand upon. Most teachers would rather captivate the ignorant student than face a challenging question.

Debates go on all the time, but few care to clarify their terms during the debate. Clarifying takes time, and the listener already has a false sense of the terms. If you attempt to clarify your opponent's positions, you anger most of the audience. A debate can argue endlessly on differing ideologies because they have differing definitions. In fact, you can generally come to a conclusion as to what a person's worldview is by finding out their meaning of God. In the extreme sense, atheists are more likely to be liberal and those who believe in a God of magic are apt to be superstitious. The conclusions are almost endless. It all depends upon what reality of God they prefer. For this reason there is no way to reason without first defining the basic words used. That is often an endless and fruitless task because we are not taught through open discussion. Rather we are taught to read authority and give them what they want. We may be diverse in color and nationality, but we are not diverse as to open expression inside the classroom. It takes too much time away from establishing accepted knowledge.

Some think mathematical logic can solve problems and give us a peek into reality. This is only if the terms in the equation are agreed upon. Mathematical logic provides terms that are often easily accepted, but may be incorrect. Take the equation $E=mc^2$. Modern physics says that the equation defines the conversion of mass into energy, but that is not what the terms say. *Energy*, in all classical terminology, is proportional to the motion of a certain mass in which the greater the motion or mass the greater the energy. *Mass* has meant the resistance of motion, or in the subatomic sense, a compilation of bits collectively resisting motion or a push. *C* defines the velocity of light. With these terms you cannot convert pure mass substance into pure motion. Without mass there is no motion to measure the energy. Think of mass as angular subatomic particles orbiting at the speed of light. Once their bonds are released, some of these particles of light[5] are released into linear motion. The remaining ones recoil with the remaining mass, like a rifle that fires a series of bullets tells us that the rifle weighs less after firing. Is this a conversion of mass to energy? This is no different than an atom firing a photon particle. Just as the rifle and its bullets are composed of mass, so too is the electron and the light it fires composed of subatomic mass. Light and Mass are composed of the same thing. Twisting the term of light to mean energy or pure motion caused a seemingly irreversible problem in modern physics. This problem was nothing more than the twisting of terms and the twisting of meaning. Challenge a modern physics student with this and note his reaction. You had better have a clear understanding, because he will change the subject to relativity theory.

Aristotle developed rules for chains of reasoning that would, if followed, never lead from true premises to false conclusions. In reasoning, the basic links are pairs of propositions that, taken together, give a new conclusion. For example, "All humans are mortal" and "All Greeks are humans" yields the valid conclusion "All Greeks are mortal." The problem with this traditional sample, used so often to illustrate logic, is that it has two assumptions. Of course everyone accepts the assumptions, but what if one had a different meaning of the word human or of mortal? Would it be so easy? Scientific results come from constructing more complex systems of reasoning, but new ideas are always there to push old ideas asunder by changing the meaning of the terms. In his logic, Aristotle distinguished between dialectic and analytic. Dialectic, he held, only tests opinions for their logical consistency; analytic works should be deducted from principles resting on experience and precise observation. This is clearly an intended criticism of Plato who preferred the dialectic as the only proper method for science and philosophy. Often it becomes rhetorical rather than analytical. But often, the analytical follows a rhetorical path. This is paramount in politics. Whatever the process or the method or even the name you give it, meaning has to be at the foundation. A good speech of sounding brass that tingles our ears is not analytical in the sense of defining the terms clearly without contradiction. Few want to see clearly. They prefer the conventional knowledge they have been taught.

It would be nice to think the dialectic method would work for philosophy, but it does not. Consistent processes do not guarantee the truth any more than coincidence. Without a full understanding of every term, any consistency found will still be based upon one assumption or another. The analytic process assumes that experience will shed light on the truth. Experience is used too often to justify rather than confirm. What we experience is sifted into our preferred worldview and is not totally new knowledge because we assume certain terms to have certain meanings, which may not be true. Experience is nothing but conformance to conventional knowledge.

If truth could be reasoned, we would not be so politically divided from election to election. Every argument on both sides has presuppositions that are assumed to be true without first dealing with the assumption before starting any analytic process or debate. We need first to open discussion on the meaning of terms before we attempt to draw conclusions. People are afraid to do this because they are afraid of losing the audience, which prefers distorted terms.

An atheist may conclude that there is no God and I foolishly might ask, "What is your definition of God?"

Of course the reply would be something like, "There is no God, so why ask me the meaning of God."

I would then stubbornly ask, "How do you know?"

He would reply after many back and forth arguments, "If there were a God, why does he allow so much starvation in the world?"

I would reply, "You have just given me your definition of God."

"How," he might ask.

I would reply, "Your definition of God is one who would not allow starvation to exist."

I would continue, "Your definition is that God is a God of magic. Because there is no magic in the world, you then assume that there cannot be a God. Your assumed definition of God is your problem."

If God were a very intelligent human with extensive powers but totally unable to break the law of conservation and totally unable to make something out of nothing, we have a meaning of God that can be reasoned more easily. The atheist's problem comes from the traditional meaning of God by superstitious cultures. The atheist has accepted conventional knowledge without asking the right questions. When he felt the knowledge wrong, he dismissed God rather than correct the meaning of God.

This indicates the simple process of demonstrating that an atheist may have a propensity about starvation that drives his conclusions. Every person may differ as to his or her own propensity. If forced to define their terms, the psychological truth will eventually surface. It's not much different than a psychoanalyst continuing questions in hopes that the patient will realize for himself what ails him. Most individuals will sense something and will cleverly avoid the questions thinking they are talking to a stupid questioner. Their problem is denial and its many facets of fear manifesting death or rejection. The atheistic example reveals a probable fear of starvation and its symbol of death. Denying God masks the fear. Forcing others to deny their God proves their worth.

Conclusion

Up to this point I have simply introduced psychological motive and suggested that faith in clear meaning is the way out of the human dilemma. I titled the chapter *Philosophical Motive* to illustrate that our worldviews are psychologically based. Motive does mean psychological and perhaps I should have titled this chapter *Philosophical Psychology*. From what has been said thus far we can come to four conclusions:

> **1. We do not understand the masters.**
> **2. There is no perfect authority we can trust.**
> **3. Our personal world views are psychologically motivated.**
> **4. We generally fail to define our terms.**

The first three are simply the result of the failure of the fourth. For this reason I will focus next on the Socratic Method and how it is neglected. Later, I will show how Plato curve fits meaning to his liking and uses Socrates' voice to lend authority. There is a lot that Plato wrote that did not question meaning. He instead brought us assumptions. We shall see that Plato most likely had a philosophical motive based on the desire for eminence.

3. The Socratic Method

Socrates is only a name but the principle of discussion for which Socrates has been given credit deserves a place in epistemology. Christopher Phillips called it socratizing.[1] Philosophy, logic, and reason are founded upon the epistemological act of socratizing. Socratizing or the act of open discussion, gives terms more precise meaning. In formal education, many terms are avoided such as justice, liberty, and responsibility. Traditional meanings are implied in generalizations that avoid the intended meaning or proper origin of the terms. Currently, discussion is too structured in education, religion, and politics. In antiquity socratizing was informal and done only in oral conversation. Even numbers were used to fix the meaning of terms as Pythagorean theory tried to emulate. This subject will be dealt with in a later chapter. It is here that one needs to understand meaning from only two parameters. One is the meaning of a term from rational grounds and the other is a meaning from intuitive foundations. This represents both a masculine and feminine approach. Open discussion needs both of these views in order to justify sound meaning. You cannot rationalize meaning, but rather every one must contribute his own intuitive expressions that all may be edified with various possibilities. As the discussion proceeds, the meaning will come closer and closer to classical terminology.

Socratic thinking looks for deeper meaning and is both masculine and feminine in its process. It asks questions and is never satisfied with conventional knowledge or traditionally accepted parameters. "Just as philosophy is the foundation of science, epistemology [*of meaning*] is the foundation of philosophy."[2] Ayn Rand was right in a grand way. When one relates to the epistemology of the meaning of things it can also be said that intelligence could manifest the foundation of epistemology. Meaning thus requires intelligence and the ability to relate and seek deeper for original meaning, but we should keep in mind that anyone desirous should participate no matter in how a way small. When argumentation surfaces between two participators, it is a sign of alter egos rather than a search for meaning. The use of deeper or original meaning means only that terms change in use over the years. This would not be too much of a problem if valuable concepts were not left without words to reference them. You can see this in the developing youth who coin terms that can be understood among certain generations. Sometimes those terms transcend to older generations. Such is the case with the word *cool*. It is used in many contexts—all of which are implied to render superiority to the one addressed as being *cool*. In some cases it might describe a concept of helping someone, but this is very unlikely amidst the generalizations of the word. When a word becomes too generalized, it allows each person to fabricate his own personal meaning. When a word can describe the denial of rejection as in the clothes one wears to get accepted and also describe the act of coming to the aid of someone, you develop a real problem. Over time there is no word to describe certain acts of responsibility and many words are used to describe various forms of the opposite. Society eventually loses the concepts of real value. This is done by creating new words or changing the old ones. You ask a teenager what love or justice is and you will get distorted meanings or you might even get programmed or traditional connotations. Rarely will you get the meaning intended through classical epistemology.

Once the meaning of any word is changed there is no word left for the concept illustrated classically. The popular mind then grows up without the concept needed to generate responsibility. In other words, we do not know what it means to be responsible because all words that imply it have been changed to mean something less responsible. There is a tendency to distort terms in order to differentiate our behavior from prior cultures. Essentially, we liberalize meaning. If we focused more on meaning, we would find that we can correct the hypocritical change prior generations have instigated. We then become more responsible. Meaning is not learning the acceptable, but understanding that which is lost.

Once the meaning is dissected and related through socratizing, each participant can learn, from another, certain ways to sharpen their definitions. Whether art as in intuition or a science as in reason, meaning really requires both to create a good harmonic meaning.

> Socrates says that a combination of sobriety and madness impels the soul to philosophize, and I'm wondering if the same is true with art.[3]

On one side of the equation, challenging the status quo appears as social madness. On the other side, this madness is what makes one see clearly. After time, it appears that the status quo was madness and the challenge became the clarity of thought. The clarity of thought is what develops understanding, and dogmatism fades as the security of conventional knowledge disappears. Over many generations the once clear thought begins over time to be distorted into a conventional form, again losing a sure footing. Knowledge then must wait many more generations for what many will think as madness when an individual arises to protest the vice of darkness in order to expound the virtue of meaning. This new madness inspires those with a new spirit of understanding and the madness dies away only to once again lead the people astray into darkness by creating the status quo of some form of conventional wisdom. The only way out of this historical revolving door is open dialog in which every one can participate at every stage of life.

> When Socrates was tried and convicted of heresy for impiety and for corrupting the youth of Athens, his prosecutors hinted that if he'd agree to keep his mouth shut they wouldn't put him to death. But Socrates said he'd rather die than quit asking question.[4]

So madness can be defined as when one tries to add value to life or take life away. It all depends upon your point of view. Such was the case with Jesus of Nazareth. The social status quo wanted conventional knowledge left alone. The reason a constant test of meaning is required is that each generation must question in order to learn. Since there are always some who have the gold and when the same wish to control, irresponsibility eventually develops in the meaning of terms. Irresponsibility manifests in the need to avoid ideas that upset one's power. Many are intimidated to comply because of their desire for acceptance of those in power. Those, like Socrates and Jesus, preferred death to a life of darkness and the madness of dogmatism. Who is really mad? Is it Socrates and Jesus or the ones killing the Socratic method of asking and answering questions?

Formal education once inspired minds to discuss, ask questions, and search for truth. That is no longer the case. The demise of socratizing has been to the detriment of our society. We now learn what to think and when to think it, and we have lost our way in how to think. The cause of this demise is the irresponsibility of those in power. They avoid discussion because everyone expresses the desire to escape the faith needed to apply axiomatic meaning to life. Too many prefer darkness rather than light. They look to the beyonds of others and the vanity of authority to determine what we learn rather than the sovereign responsibility everyone must learn—how to think.

Insanity is the child of neglect and also of intimidation. If the truth in us wants to come out, the world around should clap with joy rather than look upon us as simply mad. Because of intimidation we all seem to prefer the dogmatism of darkness rather than the beauty of meaning. We suppress our intelligence rather than glorify it. The desire for beauty mirrors the same appreciation and concern that we have for the afflicted who need expression. Darkness is a denial of faith in meaning and also of the afflicted. True madness is darkness. Socrates was considered mad, but it was those who considered him foolish that were really the mad ones. It was the vigilante keepers of the status quo who have always been mad in their own conventional knowledge. Putting one to death on false pretences is real madness. The epistemology of meaning and the responsibility it engenders produce more value than the status quo and even life itself.

The Socratic method of questioning with the intent to find meaning helps us gain a better understanding of ourselves. There are, however, many who question everything and sustain nothing as to meaning. This method is designed to be intimidating and is not honest with the intent to define. We never come to the point of making better choices because we do not follow a good process in discussion. If there were more open discussion, there would be far less stupidity and the need to learn from radio personalities, broadcast television, Internet blogs, viral emails, and print media to tell us what is up and what to think. If we become emotionally disturbed, we might end up in group therapy trying to discuss the meaning of ourselves. This represents the neglected honest discussion we should have received. Those who think that Socratic discussion is not needed probably harbor self-reliant methodologies that are selfishly independent, dishonest and corrupting. There is a great need of Socratic discussion. It will make greater leaders and it will sharpen the mind. Laying out the meaning of words can be used like a game board of philosophy. No one really loses and everyone wins. The epistemology of words becomes an exercise program in removing true madness from our lives and puts traditional status quo hypocrisy and guile behind us.

There is no definitive proof that Socrates ever existed. Socrates never wrote a word as far as we know. The same was true with Jesus. Plato's dialogues provide us with the only hard evidence. Despite this, Plato revealed Socrates without correctly understanding him. Plato was more of a dramatist and poet and therefore took liberties with what Socrates truly meant. Many a scholar has said the disciples of Jesus did the same. Instead of trying to depict the wording of Socrates, we need to establish his emphasis on meaning, for the meaning intended can filter through all the over dramatization ever written. It is this ideal persona or ideal meaning that makes Socrates immortal to our minds and which should be of the greatest concern of the epistemologist. Plato did get the importance of ideal meaning, but dismissed the real and thus the harmony of meaning. Plato injected false meaning to muster his controlling view about the ideal state.

Science leads us to believe that things immeasurable cannot be studied. The Socratic Method does not demand this criterion. The method of measurement in philosophy is a broad-based perception of the meaning of words. When intuition is incorporated with reason, one can study things such as justice, love, sacrifice, and other words neglected by traditional education. This includes a far more feminine aspect and suggests that intelligence can lay hold of concepts without a so-called step-by-step logic. As this intuitive process continues to define more clearly in order to remove contradiction, a rigid epistemology can approach the realm of axiomatic self-evident meaning just by gradually removing contradictions. Intuition reaches high and reason brings things closer. The harmony between the two is truly an art more than a science, with a continual retouching until we grow in perfect understanding.

The Socratic Method can be humbling, and exhilarating, as well as perplexing at times. It seems that you can never stop putting those finishing touches upon the process of meaning. The more we begin to see our own contradictions, the more it becomes possible to face the scarecrows of reality. In time, group discussion on the meaning of things will eventually exalt us and cure us of the black hood of insanity. Like Socrates, we must delve into the depth of our souls. Everyone goes away richer save he who prefers tradition more than meaning.

To philosophize is to exercise the mind and prevent the social diseases of fundamentalism, economic conspiracy, and foolhardiness. We must be quickened to our own sense of value rather than expect others to accept us. He who accepts death and rejection through applied purpose can live with a true knowledge of understanding. We must learn to force open ourselves rather than be intimidated into the force of others. Socratizing forces us to confront our own worldview that we have used to flee from responsibility. Sometimes we have to embrace our own demise in order to escape the darkness of dogmatism. We must always question and never assume our meaning of things is as secure as we think. The more questions and the sharper our definitions, the more sure we become. This sureness is not rigidity, but rather peace.

The Socratic Method requires us to search out the meaning of things and not to accept the traditions of authority. We must know for ourselves. This process must be repeated with each generation, for when each grows up with the honest ability to ask questions, it may appear threatening to the social schemes, but youthful honesty clarifies and prevents conventional knowledge from becoming the status quo. We must consider that we are feeding the young mind with personal wisdom and understanding that can be added to the next generation. It is essentially remixing the feminine and masculine attributes of intuition and reason in order to procreate enlightened wisdom for the next generation rather than to instill the conventional wisdom of those in power.

> Philosophy is one of the greatest liberators of man. It saves him from folly, prejudice, and confusion; it guides him into a richer and more stable world. Without philosophy, man's life and thought are in bondage to dark forces from which, with it, he can become free.[5]
>
> Edwin A. Butt

Each generation must come to its own, for what joy there is when we read the words of an honest philosopher and notice that our own ideas have maturated to the same conclusion? Those who do not agree will treat philosophers as fanciful and picayune. To demean the value of philosophy is to escape the reality of responsibility. Each generation should not be of the same mold as the prior generations. Each must create a better mold with the tenacity to understand and agree rather than simply conform or diverge. When everyone repeats the same conventional mold with the same verbalization in order to give a false sense of security, everyone becomes truly dishonest to himself and to others. This form of rubber-stamping builds robots for society without the ethics required to add quality to our lives. This is what is meant to really be alive.

Asking good questions facilitates and impels the Socratic Method. Poor questions come from two methods. First, the loaded question expects or intimidates an acceptable answer, and second, most questions require several previous meanings to be settled first. When one calls attention to these two errors, we can better understand that someone is covering up. As we shall see, this covering up is neglecting a reality that the history of philosophy fails to include. In other words, terms misaligned usually belong in the predicate and are moved either to the subjective or the objective. The classical example has come down to us through religion as each authoritative generation has taken the word *faith* (an active word) and moved it into the subjective as thought by magic you can do anything just by thinking hard about it. Modern positive thinking is a byproduct of this error. Science, on the other hand, has taken relativistic concepts such as time and pushed them into the objective, as they also take a subjective concept referred to as space and push it into the objective. Moving any word, especially out of the predicate action intended is a sign of atheistic meandering that covers one's fear of insignificance.

When we explore the predicate more deeply, we will find that our ethics, values, and morals become more dynamic rather than the usual static form that occurs under conventional authority. The predicate is also where religious concepts are better defined. The predicate reality is neglected for the sake of expediency because the terms are difficult to define for academia. For this reason, predicate terms are pushed into the subjective as relative concepts lacking any form of firm meaning. Religious institutions neglect the true predicate by mystifying meaning as metaphysical.

We should keep in mind that meaning can be placed in three realities. They are intelligent reason or logic, quality action or value, and finely objective terms. Has anyone ever said, "That definition places the word in the incorrect reality?" This has never occurred because philosophy has argued that all meaning is subjective or all meaning is objective and never considered that some meaning is subjective, some objective, and some predicative. The two sides have been fighting for centuries like politicians, never considering that reality comes in three parts. If we communicate with three parts of speech we must also think in the same way. When one is trying to establish his own worldview he most likely wants to elevate one reality at the expense of another. He does this because all meaning in one reality makes it possible to dismiss the other.

Most philosophies jump track from the subjective to the objective or back again, skipping the greatest wealth in the predicate. Hashing out reason and then jumping to scientific objectivity misses the most important ideals found in the world of right action. Ideals are sapped to the subjective and never allowed to mature.

True axioms begin in the predicate and religion more aptly originates there also, but religious institutions seem to avoid the true predicate as much as atheistic science. Defining the more difficult words requires a predicate connotation such as faith, justice, mercy, love and patience. Some words in science have predicate connotations such as time, velocity, and energy. Seeking the correct meaning and asking the right questions require a holistic, across-the-board reality. When the action is defined clearly without being antagonistic to reason or objective fact, clear meaning becomes an axiomatic, self-evident or *a priori* concept. It is not statements that are axiomatic, but the meaning of words. Once they are properly fixed, reason can be used suitably in combining words in a statement.

Socratic questioning and meaning work very well with young children for it is most natural for them to attempt to define. They should not only be taught to question, but to answer with their own hearts rather than what seems expected of them. We have philosophy classes that teach young students to learn historical facts, dates, periods and ideologies rather than to learn meaning and values. No wonder the youth are a rebellious generation. There is rarely a class available to teach meaning through questioning. The curriculum follows a preset list of conventional facts rather than teach the exercise in insight. You cannot teach insight and understanding like you can teach math or history. You must learn understanding from a methodology of questioning in groups, allowing all to have an equal opportunity to speak. This is not a dialectic process controlled by one that intimidates others. It is also not a debate. It is a discussion of meaning.

Religious groups should allow the Socratic Method as a necessary part of instruction. The values learned would be far more implemented in the individual's life than the conditioning and intimidation that normally come from religious leaders. Likewise, political debates could foster more insightful discussion and the concept of positioning should be put aside. In the case of politics, instead of asking a candidate what he will do, ask him what it means to lead, what it means to conserve, what it means to protect, what it means to be free, what it means to be responsible, what it means to be equitable, what it means to be rich and what it means to be poor. By the time he gets to the poor, you will have a pretty good idea how he looks at things. There is no end to questions of meaning and, if asked, our leaders would truly be exposed to our understanding. We avoid questions like this because few think in active predicate values. We prefer objective questions that position our thinking from an opponent and do not seek for self-evident truth.

How one thinks is only a product of how one defines reality. To be political about meaning means one is avoiding the epistemology of meaning and the responsibility that it engenders. Public schools are the biggest culprits of avoiding the Socratic Method. High Schools and colleges teach us what to think so we can have an ignorant labor force that will not complain. Higher institutions teach us when to think so the market is overflowing with professionals. No one learns how to think. For this reason, professions carry conventional terms to wash away the real ones that may develop insight. The so-called liberal education has gone astray for lack of Socratizing. The high schools have so many extra curricular classes and activities and these periods are so short that there is no chance for even the wisest of teachers to create a discussion of questions and answerers about the meaning of things. The university wants to cram so much data into young minds so that they know what to do when they are sent into the world. This added knowledge only makes them more deceitful, money hungry, and puts them on the road to power with a desire for honor. These minds spread throughout the world and mingle with all men, but they do not cleave one to another or even care for one another because they have no meaning in life other than what a professor conditioned them to think. Yes, we have lost a liberal education and in its place we have built a liberal mind without meaning. The modern mind finds difficulty in the real world for it only has ideals planted there void of honest discussion. Graduates find their way comfortably into government, education, communications, and religion. They cannot survive in the real world unless they become dishonest, political, and lust for power. The young liberal is frustrated and sees the imbalance, but does not understand the solution. He would rather start a revolution that will only replace the old with a new dogmatism and never come to the knowledge of the truth that man needs to define, conserve, and measure, and then define again. The Socratic Method can only do this by asking honest questions and allowing all to answer again and again and again.

Philosophy comes from the basis of defining. Philosophy also means to draw a distinction.

> A philosopher is a strange man. He draws distinctions where nobody else sees any need of them and is puzzled by problems that are problems to none of his fellows.[6]

Within this drawing of a distinction there is implied an honest need to ask honest questions and speak honest answers. Free speech has spawned a much-distorted version of honest speaking. Instead of the expression of meaning, it has become a cesspool of degradation, dogmatism, and extremist idealism. This sort of reconfiguration comes from modern cultures without values. This includes religious factions as much as any part of the culture. Religions may share the greatest blame along with parents of children who tell youth what they should think and never encourage self-expression or conversation. You can follow the life of any despot, any warmonger, any extremist, and any dishonest politician or business man and you will see the level of intimidation coming from parent, culture, religion, and even the job market that conditions the mind to follow a certain path, to never question and to join the mood of politicizing rather than socratizing. We have come to believe that this is the true American way and have forgotten that true socratizing was the way of the founders of liberty in all free countries. We, as parents, want the most for our children in this new world, so stepping over others to get to the top is acceptable. We intimidate our children to conform to social values yet expect them to be deceptive as adults. It is like an unwritten rule. Those minds who see that something is wrong will become idealists wanting big brother to solve all the world's problems. Those who succumb to this new tradition aspire for power, honor, and prestige. The young of this modern generation learn methods of politicizing for gain rather than socratizing for meaning.

Some young minds had parents who often discussed things. If the parents did not try to control the lives of their children, they would turn out to be truly honest people. The religious factions think that modern life lacks religion. In general, dogmatic morals may be a good schoolmaster for many youth but if they are very intelligent and do not get more meaning, they will become terrors or be terrified themselves and end up in institutions. So many good minds are wasted for a lack of

Socratic meaning. It has been religion's responsibility to provide this natural process, but it does not. We have only a few wise parents and it is those who are saving the world, if it can be saved.

Like the Sophists of Socrates' time, the modern traditional authority thinks that philosophy may corrupt the young mind and turn him away from cultural traditions and make him disobedient to law. It is more a lack of understanding coupled with dogmatic trends that create disobedience and corrupt the youth. Cultural traditions can be minimized in the mind when we come to understand better value and it is that value that causes us to be more law abiding, honest, fair and giving. The modern Sophist is more afraid of seeing the truth than allowing a new mind to see and understand. We protect our scarecrows. We dress them up and keep them in good condition just so what we fear will be driven away. This is the beginning of prejudice and dogmatism and it is not from any words of the masters.

What does it matter that a new young mind gets a slightly distinct picture of reality than a previous generation? The net epistemology of meaning and human values will grow and grow in clarity with each subsequent generation. They will increase in faith and values while authority and dogmatism will become less and less a controlling factor. What does society have to lose? Let us put philosophy back into the schools and into our churches and into our families. Let business participate and the political method change from positioning to understanding. In time you will find that every religion, every institution, and every culture will eventually want to be called by this new process. If you are afraid of losing your view, you probably will, but it will be gradual and without force. It will come by way of better and better understanding. You will eventually put away childish scarecrows and make peace with your enemy. Try it in your family and in your Sunday school. Try it in your classroom and in your social club. You will see for yourself and certainly recognize that the Socratic Method has been missing in modern life.

It is a simple process. Begin by seeking words with implied action and try to find meaning that yields that action. Avoid magic, intellectualism, and set aside tradition. It does not matter if some put forth strange meanings; there will be plenty of voices to pull things together. If there is no freedom of expression, there will be no improvement. Like Mill said, "the silencing of discussion is an assumption of infallibility." Eventually ideologies will fuse themselves into axiomatic words through discussion. If anything, the method should be practiced in the teaching of philosophy. Instead, philosophy has been moving away from its inherited birth right of epistemology and the processing of distinctions. Philosophy has lost the intent and traded her inheritance for a pot of opinions amongst a dichotomy of two realities. Philosophy has faired no better than a religious tradition or political ideology. Philosophy needs to return to method rather than trying to state some sort of position. Philosophy should stick to defining and building a strong foundation of epistemology.

An epistemology tree will be introduced in a later chapter as a guide to discovering meaning. If what I have to illustrate is too complex, I can highly recommend Christopher Phillips *"Socrates Café"* that tells you how and why the questioning style of Socrates works with children and adults.

4. The Platonic Position

When one thinks of philosophy, it conjures up a complex view that is relatively difficult to position for the average mind. One can read Plato or Aristotle and understand the intent and the beginning of classical concepts, but contemporary philosophers and their injection of complex issues do not approach philosophy with the same process as classical philosophy. Every authority goes through an extensive dialectic process trying to express the evolution of philosophy with concern only for those who have the vocabulary for such dissertation. When the philosopher uses the words subjectivity, objectivity, and even the word philosophy itself, the average reader often feels alienated. But when I introduce the word predicativism to a philosopher he will look at me suspiciously as a common person would look at a philosopher. The reason for this comes from the use of a word in a particular way not found in a professional philosopher's vocabulary. Likewise, when common folk hear words not in their vocabulary, they will react strangely. It appears as if each philosopher desires the process of thinking up sophisticated words that those in the field will understand. To get attention, each philosopher coming on the scene will position himself at some point in the full spectrum of philosophy much the same way that a politician positions himself or herself in a position that will satisfy his constituents. The politician has an ulterior motive, and perhaps the philosopher's motive is also manifest. Somewhat psychologically driven, a philosopher establishes himself at a slightly different position from the norm to maintain his importance.

Writing about a field of science has a catalog of various words designed to depict discovered criteria, but philosophy does not develop words out of discovery. Philosophy does not discover—it defines. The added words are only depictions of a philosopher's corner and where he stands much in the same way as a politician. What I find interesting is the positioning and not so much the philosophical views of philosophy. Just as in politics, you can generally label a philosopher as a subjectivist or an objectivist with many finding a different middle ground. This positioning tells us more about an individual's world view than what they say. When modern philosophers use words such as 'subjective activity' or 'sense perception' I would rather use the realm of the predicate to position these expressions. They define an active process rather than ideas or objects. Also the expression 'objective reason' does not lend to a better understanding of objectivity, for reason fits better in a subjective context. Historically, philosophy has used the two realms of subjectivism and objectivism to determine the nature of knowing or of being. I have added a third I call predicativism. It is not a compromise, but an actual third reality. The origin of this concept came by obvious selection.

There are such an extensive number of theories in determining knowledge that one wonders why it should be so difficult and why each philosopher has positioned himself or herself to a particular idiom. The use of three realms rather than two makes it possible to define terms more precisely and thus avoid extensive dialogue to position one's idiom above another. Clarity of definition and the placing of terms in the proper reality can improve communication and simplify discussion. This process will be introduced in a later chapter, but first one will need to understand the dichotomy that philosophy has upheld for two thousand years and more. Within this dichotomy philosophers position their thinking like a pendulum to one side or another with sundry variations in an attempt to claim the middle ground. The true process of knowing is really predicative activity of agreement between subjective reason and objective existence in order to determine truth.

The Platonic Idiom

Writers who think they understand the dichotomy given them by the history of philosophy tend to see some sort of progress taking place. They tend to give credence to more experience, existential thought, and ever-increasing dialectic dialogue. They fine-tune their position totally neglecting responsibility that pivots on a predicate axis. The continued debate between knowledge as a form of prediction of objective events or the flux of so-called subjectivity continues. What is needed so desperately is a predicate reality that shows agreement between the subjective and the objective rather than the selection of only one or the other.

Another way of looking at the traditional dichotomy is to understand that philosophy generally gives nature a deterministic path and the mind a perceptible form of indeterminism. Determinism gravitates to an objective position with three basic requirements. The first is the ability to obtain complete prediction of all events in nature; the second is the ability to reduce causal control to objective laws, and the third is that these laws can be validated by objective reason. The problem arises with the third. Reason is not objective. Indeterminism, on the other hand, says that objective thought cannot explain change and therefore follows a more liberal and sometimes vague, uncertain methodology. Indeterminism gravitates to the subjective. Philosophy is like a tightrope of reality trying desperately to gain experience sufficient to walk the rope of true knowledge. Most humans do not attempt the difficulty and prefer a pragmatic approach to things. Pragmatism sounds like some middle realm, but negates one of the most important predicate aspects of faith and responsibility. Whatever the pragmatic approach, it will never have sufficient experience to reach a perfect conclusion as to the knowledge of things. Occasionally one must act and choose based upon intuition. Intuition may never become the sole source of knowledge, but gut feelings often evolve into great truths. Intuition, unlike pragmatic experience, follows a base principle of responsibility. With intuition one often asks, "Is this right?" The pragmatic approach only asks, "Does it work."

The Platonic Position

Whether one positions toward indeterminism, determinism or even pragmatism, responsibility is always avoided. This is a psychological process that the philosopher avoids in order to claim an intricate examination of useless levels of knowledge. Psychology motivates this philosophical pendulum in an attempt to legitimize ideas. Ideas are only products of a world view driven by a desire for eminence. It is not the idea that makes a man great; it is the things he does for humanity that change the course of events. We quote many a president for wonderful ideas, but often note that they have failed in implementation. Ideas, implementation, and measured results require a holistic approach and thus greatness requires the same. Such should be the road map of philosophy and not just some beautiful idea that someone may quote some day because it sounds good. Great sounding ideas do not always work. This is because we intuitively do not ask if it is right.

Plato's position in the whole spectrum of philosophy was with ideas. To him ideas were more real than sense perception of objective things outside. Plato introduced his analog by telling a story of a cave dweller who saw shadows on the wall from his cave fire within. Plato compared these shadows to objective reality. When the cave dweller went outside and saw so much more in full color detail under the light of the sun he was amazed at the greater accuracy of things. This Plato compared with a subjective definition of things as being more real than the thing itself. The analog reminds me of the same type of thinking that is supposed to explain curved space. In both cases, the storyteller uses a two-dimensional analog to represent common experience and a three dimensional analog to represent what the writer is trying to promote. Neither analog really works because each plays havoc with intuition. Intuition is what Plato despised and intuition is what the relativist dismisses. Without intuition, true meaning will not surface. Instead we are allowed to change the terms to suit a personal worldview where intuition wants to make better sense. Without intuition new concepts change the meaning of things and leave an intuitive concept without a word to describe it. Over time science and philosophy evolve with new ideas that intuition cannot fathom. If Plato had just said that the definition of an object can be more accurate than the object itself, this could be understandable, but to deny objectivity altogether was inexcusable. Plato's original concept of the ideal eventually became a philosophy of subjectivism. The Sophists of Plato's time believed in real things and thus laid the foundation of objectivism. Philosophy has been doing this tug of war between the ideal and the real for thousands of years. Science naturally followed objectivity, but philosophy continued to play games with reason, logic, and other ways of knowing things that in many respects were contrary to intuition. Science treated reason as objective and the subjectivists often questioned reason altogether. Though philosophy gave birth to science and the predictability of determinism, there remained a psychological need to uphold many indeterminate philosophies. Even modern physics, although born of objectivity, has moved into uncertainty and indeterminism by some writers. Some have called upon the indeterminate philosophy of Eastern mysticism to explain the paradoxes of relativity. It does not matter what you read, there is a full spectrum of positions with each writer generally falling to one end or another. One can find this not only in philosophy, physics, economics and politics, but also in religion.

Dichotomies of left and right are prevalent. They neglect finding equilibrium with reality. As mentioned, we have indeterminism vs. determinism, subjectivism vs. objectivism, the ideal vs. the real, liberalism vs. conservatism, and even faith vs. reason. The problem arises with each dichotomy by thinking that a position to one side or another is the key. Just as you cannot position faith as the pendulum opposite of reason, you cannot position reality in opposites. What is thought to be opposite may more likely be complimentary. This is why we need a third reality that gives agreement, proportion, and equilibrium rather than something that negates the other side.

Plato was looking for the eternal nature and the absolute. This he deemed as the love of truth. He attributed the forgetful person not having a good memory as destructive to the attainment of true understanding.

> And there is an absolute beauty and an absolute good, and of other things to which the term "many" is applied there is an absolute; for they may be brought under a single idea, which is called the essence of each.[1]

This essence of which Plato was referring to was what he called intelligible rather than visible. He condemned the Sophist for relying upon the sense experience of observation. Plato had no use for images. He preferred ideas:

> There are two subdivisions, in the lower of which the soul uses the figures given by the former division as images; the inquiry can only be hypothetical, and instead of going upward to a principle descends to the other end; in the higher of the two, the soul passes out of hypotheses, and goes up to a principle which is above hypotheses, making no use of images as in the former case, but proceeding only in and through the ideas themselves.[2]

Putting words into the mouth of Socrates, Plato distinguishes the cognitive processes where ideas are apprehended. He illustrated that geometricians are not required to reason the objects they study and never do they question whether the circle they study actually exists or not. They rely on visible images of circles that are physically drawn for their investigation. In contrast, dialecticians who study the ideas of a circle depend on no such physical images to test their hypotheses. Dialecticians do not take for granted the existence of the ideas they investigate. Geometrical objects differ substantively from the idea of each geometrical object, which are apprehended by the faculty of reason. In essence, Plato was saying that the idea is the meaning of the thing and not the thing itself. When Plato had Socrates hold up three fingers—a little finger, a second finger, and a middle finger, a point was made in that some objects invite distinction. Each finger appears as a finger regardless whether seen as a small, medium or large finger. Regardless of the distinction such as thick or thin, soft or hard, a finger is a finger all the same. Once the objects reveal a distinction between one and another, it invites the idea of a finger as a more universal term for various types of fingers. Objects that are uninviting do not form a distinction according to Plato. Under normal conversation a man is not compelled to ask the question, "What is a finger?" The eyes see small and large, thick and thin but the intuitive intellect comprehends the meaning of finger.

Out of all that Plato had written, the concept of an ideal object rather than a real object was a great contribution to philosophy, but he did not need to negate the objective. This ideal was the beginning of subjectivism although Plato did not call it such. A more appropriate word from Plato's vocabulary would be intellectualism or the ability to decipher. Essentially this came from the mind and the traditional sense perception referred to the objects or as objectivism. Objects were relative in dimensions and size, but the definition of a particular type of object was absolute, as a definition would be absolute. Therefore, idealism became the foothold into philosophy that never let go. Science took mathematics, geometry, and astronomy in one direction, and philosophy took idealism in another. Even before this split, Plato suggested the difference when he said through the character of Socrates:

> Yet anybody who has the least acquaintance with geometry will not deny that such a conception of the science is in flat contradiction to the ordinary language of geometricians.
>
> They have in view practice only, and are always speaking, in a narrow and ridiculous manner, of squaring and extending, and applying and the like—they confuse the necessities of geometry with those of daily life; whereas knowledge is the real object of the whole science.[3]

Modern technology suffers the same dichotomy when the engineer draws up astounding things to satisfy daily pleasure without as much as a single consideration of the meaning of things. The meaning of things "will draw the soul to truth, and create the spirit of philosophy, and raise up that which is now unhappily allowed to fall down"[4] to technologically meaningless levels. Thus science has failed to keep the vision that philosophy once had and philosophy has failed to continue the meaning of things as ideas became anything one could subjectively imagine rather than simply distinguish. Today philosophy is a highbrow club of intellectuals that are stuffily academic. Better philosophy has come from non-philosophers of other disciplines than philosophy could ever produce from its own kind.

Plato was a student of ideas more than meaning, although his base argument that he learned from Socrates was to define. When it came to particular views on how we should live in a state, he missed the mark by neglecting the definition process. This is primarily what all of philosophy does. It says what should be, but does not define the terms used in the argument. In reading the *Republic*, one should note the avoidance of the meaning of *justice* in the beginning only to subtlety thwart its classical meaning into Plato's new worldview of state control. I do believe that it was Socrates and not Plato who gave the grander first principles of finding meaning. Plato elaborated in his own subjective world trying desperately to become greater than Socrates.

Plato used Socrates as his main character in the *Republic*. This was done either out of respect or out of assuring acceptance. Plato needed Socrates. The motive of Plato is perhaps a psychological one, for his ideas fostered control over man. This demonstrated feelings of inadequacy and a lack of faith in man's being able to govern himself through solid first principles of clear meaning. This is why Plato avoided the Socratic Method in defining justice. Plato just assumed a meaning to be what each man must do in his ideal state. Plato twisted the term to justify control. If Plato had used the word *control* rather than the word *justice*, he would have been rejected. For the same reason, had Plato used himself rather than Socrates, he would have been rejected. This is the main reason that Plato has to be distinguished from Socrates and why Plato really did not fully understand the Socratic Method. This may be debatable among some authorities. I only wish to establish two things. Plato had a psychological motive in creating the ideal State and he avoided the Socratic Method by assuming the meaning of justice. Actually, Plato distorted the term to put across his ideal state. Plato negated the way of absolute meaning, which Socrates taught, and which all of philosophy since should have done. Every liberal subjectivist will start with some ideal to demonstrate how things should be, but straightway shut up intuitive meaning in exchange for deterministic state control. This process is in the nature of man and the ideas are manufactured to deal with one's lack of control.

Ideas should not originate without first establishing the meaning of words or the concepts they establish. Ideas do not define things simply because they are stated as ideal. Ideas must be based upon self-evident principles, right action and conservation before they can suggest implementation through individual responsibility. Each word must be defined with the goal to remove every contradiction in meaning with the prime intent to avoid personal reality formulas that satiate some underlying psychological need. Equilibrium and agreement between words are needed more and thus meaning of words must be laid down first. If not, then ideas must be intuitively *a priori* rather than pontificating jargon.

There is nothing wrong in seeking for something absolute about the meaning of something, but that does not deny the objective aspects independent in the world in which they exist. Things vary from observation to observation, but the ideal meaning is fixed and can be considered absolute. Keep in mind that it is the object that receives the action of the predicate "is" as being equal to the ideal meaning or definition. From this point, the epistemology of meaning should and can be established to prove the objective, but this is not a subjective process as Plato and others have tried to demonstrate. Meaning is predicated upon the verb of equality. A definition incorporates the verb "is" as its central axis. Both a chosen subject and a chosen object are related by this predicate or harmonic axis. Predicativism and the meaning, or definition, of words is holistic and not subjective only, as Plato implied, or objective only as the Sophist might have stated.

Epistemology is the true foundation of philosophy and not the dialectics of Platonic rhetoric. Intelligent subjectivity, as one might call it, really does not work from the subjective only. True meaning is a relationship. It is the meaning of something objective that helps us come to know. Meaning is paramount, and increases knowledge. Better put, knowledge and wisdom are harmonics of reason and intuition. Reason seeks for meaning and intuition already has a sense of it. Reason is guided by the intuition in us to make sense and not to alter meaning to gain psychological control. A writer or any philosopher can carry an argument step by step in the most careful dialectic fashion, but will often reveal his motive when the terms are not clarified. Terms are often assumed without explanation. In most cases, the nearly all-important issues are missed. For example, in Plato's *Republic* there is no mention of how the people will be taxed. It was a travesty for Plato to think that the ideal State had no method of taxation. Plato talked of all living in common, but this sort of idealism does not work without a specific economic plan of taxation for funding. A method of legislated force generated by ideals does not work. It only generates political bureaucracies. When people share, there has to be a form of taxation based upon one's existing wealth and not by a nebulous byproduct of labor. As will be shown later, this takes the bureaucratic force out of the system and places the responsibility in the hands of those who take more out of the system than others. Plato brushed over his taxation within his communistic concept in one paragraph and spent pages and pages on marriage, sex, and having children in common. In a certain way, Plato wrote what sells. The reader would say, "The state will save us and we will have no personal responsibility." One having the propensity to control the people will never mention the responsibility of budgeting such an endeavor. This is the propensity not only of the liberal of antiquity but of modern times—there is no personal responsibility to conservation. They mistakenly think that the state brings about equity and justice and not the individual or community.

The Platonic Idiom

The need to mask one's responsibility with idealism camouflages personal fear. The best way for the intelligent to bring an end to death, poverty, and desolations is to find a way to control the objective world that causes their anxiety. Such was the intent of Plato and his *Republic*. It has been the same intent of dictators, religious dogmatists, and political parties. This idiom of claiming the world of the subjective and controlling the events of the objective seems to contradict reality when the subjective becomes absolute and the objective is now relative. The two worlds do not agree and therefore the ideal is wrong.

As one traces the history of philosophy, the turning of things up side down is strange indeed. One is only left to see an underlying psychological motive rather than a desire for seeking truth. It is like turning away from the objective world because it is painful to look at while trying to control it from the subjective without any responsibility.

The human mind is a complex entity and perhaps needs more study in this regard. On the one hand, the subjectivist or indeterminist cannot look at death so he turns from it and wants the government to make it right through determinism that he does not espouse. The objectivist or determinist, on the other hand, is willing to face death in the face and say that injustice is overcome by survival and natural greed. We are free to take advantage, as we will. Both the subjectivist and the objectivist abhor responsibility. To say it in a simpler form, both the idealist and the realist do not foster responsibility. In modern times the conservative is guilty of lacking social responsibility and the liberal is guilty of lacking personal responsibility. The liberal wants the government to make things right as did Plato, and the conservative demeans any community responsibility—we are on our own. The liberal wants to tax the rich to pay for the poor and the conservative wants a flat income tax so the laborer pays for everything. No one ever accepts the responsibly for paying equally according to their wealth and according to what they possess. One's total possessions represent that what he pulls out of the economic system is greater than what he needs. A proper taxation structure encourages both personal and social responsibility. The reason Plato did not resolve a method of taxation was that no one wanted to hear the subject. Still to this day, every one talks of freedom and rights but no one wants to take upon them economic accountability.

A compromise between Plato's Subjectivist Ideal and perhaps the modern Ayn Rand's Objectivist Epistemology does not solve the problem of personal and social responsibility. Various philosophies since Plato have made many attempts to clarify the subjective, to defend the objective, and perhaps to find some middle ground reality. This is none other than positioning one's view to a particular setting in the same way that the politician positions his or her speech. We need a holistic reality that includes the subjective, the predicative, and the objective. We should place reason and perhaps the dialectic process in the subjective as did Plato. We can discover consistent meaning only when it lies at the predicate axis of reality where agreement becomes the way of understanding. We can then determine if the objective receives what the predicate defines and agrees with the subjective. That is the whole statement of reality.

The verb used in the sciences is the axiom of equality as in the case of mathematics, geometry, and physics. As we shall see, there are other axioms such as distinction and proportion. The sciences have used proportion as a way to understand the elements and it behooves us to apply it to philosophy. Proportional thinking seeks more than the so-called pragmatic process. Proportional thinking is more intuitive. It sees the distinction in things rather than simply asking, "Does it work?" It asks for understanding about how things work. There are many poor philosophies in science, psychology and especially politics and religion. They all push reality around without any effort to define the terms and consider motive. They assume meanings and neglect the predicate process of agreement. The next chapter will cover a view of objectivity. The attempt will be to come to some considerations which science have not yet resolved. Again, I think this is a psychological problem similar to the problem that the atheist harbors.

5. Objective Reality

Reason and logic are not aspects of this chapter but will be reserved for the next. The attempt in this chapter will be to define an all-inclusive objective reality that satisfies a unified field theory. Also, objective reality has to begin with a foundation concept as if all things are composed of some basic substance. This would include metaphysics, if things beyond physics were composed of substance that we cannot see or measure. This does not include any mystical ideals or the concept of right action other than found in physical conservation. Since matter is so nebulously compared to energy, a more appropriate base is needed. I will first attempt to find that basis here.

In antiquity, the philosopher attempted to explain three components of objective reality such as earth, fire, and water. This may have served well in the beginning, but as time progressed, with science paving the way, this depiction was not all-inclusive. One can always ask, "Is there anything outside of earth, fire, and water that depict something different and distinct and that can also demonstrate in an obvious manner something that exists either dynamically or statically along side earth, fire, and water without intermixing or exchanging roles? Also, can earth, fire, or water be divided into smaller components? These questions I am sure were asked many times by many philosophers, but we must rethink the process in order to determine if anything was missed and consider the possibility of something broader and more inclusive than the typical physical properties of the earth's proximity or what the physicist can measure.

Objective Reality | 62

The philosopher might attempt to include another type of liquid than water with a different viscosity. To include such introduces the meaning of liquid, solid, and gas. This trilogy depicts exchangeability and therefore denies distinct roles. It also discloses that earth and water might be exchangeable. Nuclear physics of course shows this to be so. We also know that fire can be both a mixture of light and perhaps gas. The gas portion depicts exchangeability with earth, and light under modern physics is exchangeable with matter and thus earth also.

We need to draw a distinction in our investigation of objective reality by discussing the difference between the concept of light and energy. Physics often mistakenly equates them, but as to reality they differ as a verb differs from an object. Energy is a mathematical center of mass point that moves from one point to another at a constant velocity. If we take the impact of one billiard upon another we actually measure the energy passing from the first billiard to the next. Keep in mind that substance does not pass; it is the concept of action that passes. **Figure 5-1** illustrates this concept.

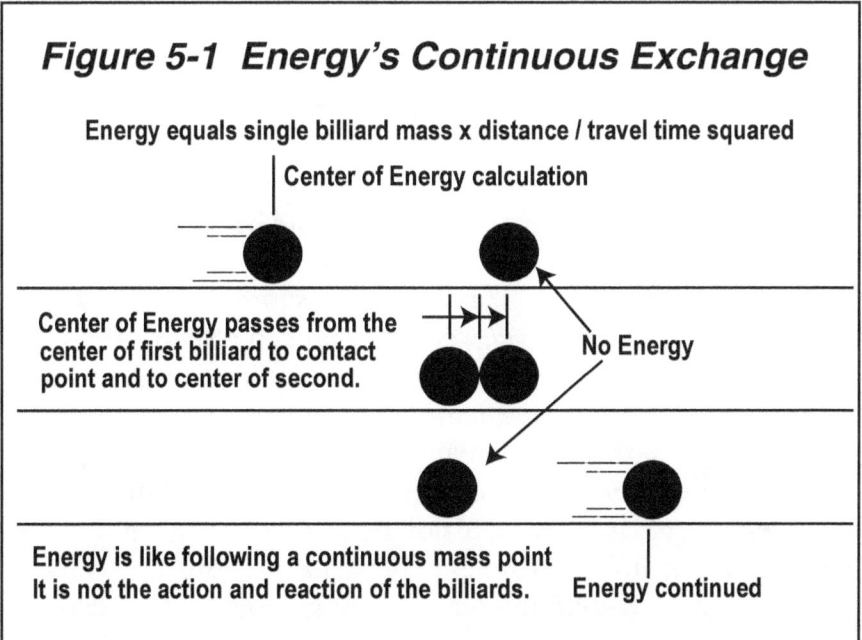

The first billiard carries the action or total kinetic energy. Upon impact the first billiard stops and the next billiard instantaneously takes up the action. It is as if the center of action (or mass that is used to calculate the total energy) moves from the center of the first billiard to the contacting edge and then to the center of the receiving billiard in a continuous non-accelerating motion. Each billiard decelerates or accelerates but not the action or energy. Energy has a constant motion excluding friction, but the particular mass does not. Because energy describes a certain type of mathematical action that is constant and the billiard describes a quantity of mass that is also constant in existence and quantity, but not motion, we need to separate the two as different realities or as an action verb (energy) differs from the objective noun (mass). Energy and mass are separate realities, but modern physics meshes them into one objective exchangeable reality. It is true that energy cannot exist without substance because energy is the action of substance in the same way that an object receives the action of a verb. The verb disappears in mind when there is no object to receive the action. Despite the association of mass and energy, their realities differ.

The Field Concept

Once energy is separated as it should be, then light can be better understood as a field concept that carries energy *linearly* and can be measured in terms of kinetics; while mass is a field concept that contains *angular* energy that can only be measured gravitationally. The conversion is from angular energy to linear energy and not from one reality to another. This conversion occurs in the same way linear momentum is converted from angular momentum. The conversion is from one type of field arrangement to another and not from one reality to another. Just as light is an electro-magnetic field relationship so too is matter. Light and solid matter differ in geometrical concepts as linear differs from angular concepts. Modern physics talks of mass turning into light and light turning back into mass. This makes sense as long as light is a net angular electric field in mass and linear upon leaving the confines of an atom, but when the same physics talks of mass turning into energy and back again, it becomes a problem in understanding and thus indicates a lack of proper definition and the nailing of physical terms in physics.

Epistemologically, light and energy define different reality concepts. Light is the substance and energy is the action of substance. Energy is a mathematical *verb* convention only and the epistemology of the conversion has not been established. To talk of a conversion requires the changing of the meaning of terms and this is precisely what the relativist has done. One cannot say that water turns into vapor without explaining the mechanics. One cannot say matter turns into light without revealing the necessary workings. Labeling light as energy and not as pieces of mass demonstrates the physicist's inability to explain the workings. I will make some generalizations that give the workings based upon traditional experiments and also keep the realities separate when they should be.

Just as earth, fire, and water are exchangeable, light and matter are exchangeable. In this sense we have one single objective reality with energy the predicate action of both. It is, however, premature, for what we have done is simply depict that part of objectivity that can be measured by the five senses. I do not intend to suggest that just because something cannot be measured by the five senses that it cannot be real or be exchanged or even fulfill some role in physical reality. With what we know as objective reality, some frequencies of light cannot be seen or felt but we know that they are exchangeable as any form of light that we can see. Logical processes, using conservation, will often predict things that cannot be seen—something that we can define and demonstrate logically even to the point that it may in some way be used in equations to show conservation, harmony, equilibrium etc. That something must be considered just as real as what we see.

Creation of electric matter can be understood as the interrelationship of the electric and magnetic fields. **Figure 5-2** lends an explanation as an analog agreeable with reality, experiment, and mathematics. This is an epistemological look at an electron that may differ from other worldviews, but the model will fit the equations without a mythically unexplained change of roles of one objective state to another, such as mass becoming pure energy. Changeability without explaining the workings is not a good epistemological model, for unless we explain what we mean, of what value is a conversion statement?

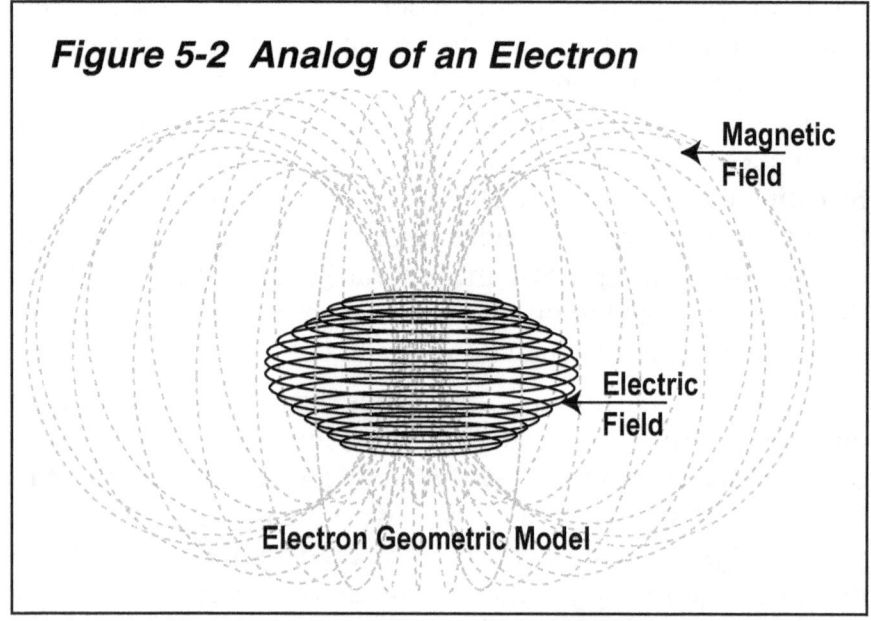

Figure 5-2 Analog of an Electron

In the above we have introduced a second type of objective reality with two elements uniquely playing its own role. We now have a magnetic reality as compared with the electric reality that suggests two matter fields. It is not unacceptable to talk of an indivisible magnetic monopole particle and an indivisible photoelectric monopole particle as the smallest constituents of objective reality. In multiples they form fields. A photoelectric particle will be used to differentiate the smallest unit of electric matter and it will be shown also to build photons ejected as bits from the electron.

It is worthy to note that we can touch electric matter, but we cannot detect magnetic matter. We can pass our hand through the magnetic field, but the moment we come in contact with an electric field we feel something. Electric matter we see. It also has atomic weight in conglomerate form, as we shall see. It reacts to gravity in relation to the unseen, untouchable magnetic field, for if it were possible to reach in and touch the electron we would not notice the presence of the outer magnetic field but there would be a sense of touch with the electric field. General experiment suggests this because we are sitting in the earth's magnetic field and are able to detect nothing by the five senses. Because of this, each field plays a distinct role in creation. We can breathe in electrons and other charged particles in more complex relationships and we can pass our hands quickly and sense a pressure, but it is not the magnetic field that we detect. It is the electric fields as they are held in close proximity to each other by a magnetic axis. If we were ever able to detect the magnetic flux in open space it would have to be something on the order of a sixth sense that would resonate to its motion. A small electric field can respond to magnetic motion because we can see it in a magnetic compass. Even planets may respond or resonate as the change in the magnetic axis resonates, but our five senses are not designed to detect any impact of a magnetic flux that is distant from electric properties.

We now have two objective components and can justify the existence of all matter as a compilation of the two fields. The essential reasoning for this can be explained by the ability of two particles in close proximity sharing a larger magnetic field separate from their individual magnetic fields. This larger magnetic field is realized by one electron inverting its poles so as to create a third magnetic flux that would pass through one electron axis, out, and into the axis of another particle. One electron pole would be orientated up and another down. This does not conclude that two electrons can marry each other. It only illustrates the concept that perhaps larger particles can develop some kind of relationship using shared magnetic fields.

Figure 5-3 would explain the relationship between an electron and a proton being much larger in order to create a neutron. The marriage of two particles and perhaps more could suggest a similar relationship as four particles could form a square with opposite corners manifesting polarity up or down. The concept is highly probable to one degree or another.

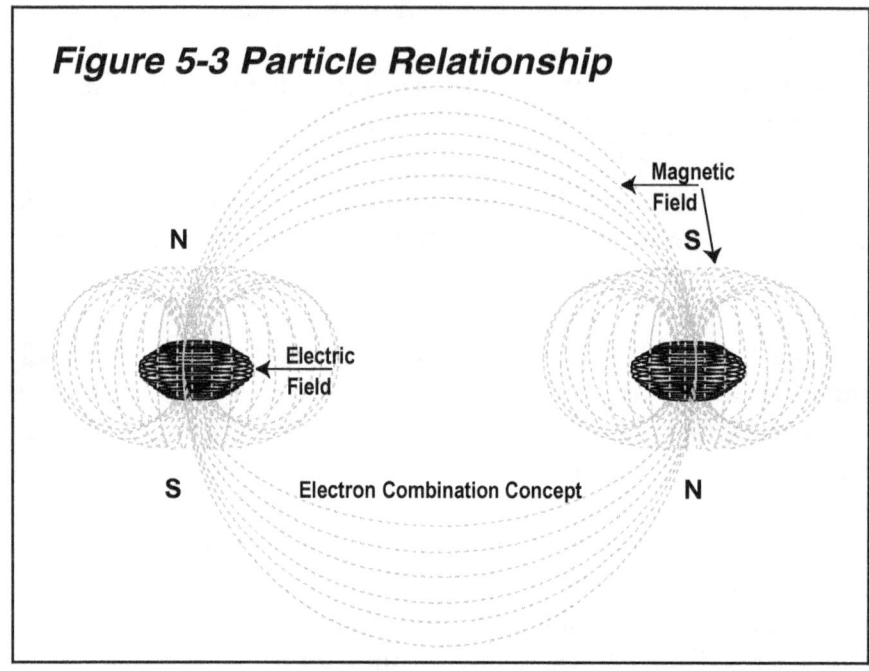

Figure 5-3 Particle Relationship

All analogs must fit the mathematics. One can suggest that any electric field in light is smaller than that of the largest electron. This suggests that this field can be absorbed into a larger particle that can share magnetic properties. It is simply a matter of reducing the relationship to a mathematical equation that agrees with what we know. Maxwell did this with Faraday's model and general experiments with electric and magnetic fields. Those equations are in use today including the relativistic concepts of light and matter. The problem arises when nuclear physicists stopped pursuing geometrical models based on Faraday's philosophy. They preferred the path of energy and mass conversion and never attempted to explain the workings.

Objective Reality | 68

In a personal way, Feynman apparently accepted this weakness without question in his book *The Classic Feynman*.

> Once, though, when I came back from MIT (I'd been there a few years), he (my father) said to me, "Now that you've become educated about these things, there's one question I've always had that I've never understood very well."
>
> I asked him what it was.
>
> He said, "I understand that when an atom makes a transition from one state to another, it emits a particle of light called a photon."
>
> "That's right." I said.
>
> He says, "Is the photon in the atom ahead of time?"
>
> "No, there's no photon beforehand."
>
> "Well," he says, "where does it come from, then? How does it come out?"
>
> I tried to explain it to him—that photon numbers aren't conserved; they're just created by the motion of the electron—but I couldn't explain it very well. I said, "It's like the sound that I'm making now: it wasn't in me before."
>
> He was not satisfied with me in that respect. I was never able to explain any of the things that he didn't understand. So he was unsuccessful: he sent me to all these universities in order to find out those things, and he never did find out.[1]

Photon numbers may not be conserved as atomic mass numbers but light comes in quanta or bits and pieces that have impact. This is why Einstein received a Nobel Prize for his photoelectric effect or the minute pressure of light. The debate between the new particle theory and the wave theory of light still goes on with the wave theory a leftover analog of classical mechanics and the particle theory from Einstein's photoelectric affect. Both are justified by experiment and by the equation process but there is little attempt to reconcile this debate by explaining the workings of mass and light exchange. The modern physicist still assumes that mass changes to pure energy of sorts, but that only begs the question, "If there are electric components in light and matter, then Feynman's father deserves a better answer.

Michael Faraday demonstrated that an electric field or current in a wire introduces the appearance of an external magnetic field. He also demonstrated that a magnetic field surrounding a magnet could cause motion in an electric field causing current to flow. Now current is the flow of light and is often conventionally assumed to be the flow of electrons. I cover this more in another book and will not attempt to cover it here. If you want to believe that current is the flow of electrons, consider that it is still electric matter that flows, whether light or electrons. Faraday also demonstrated that these two fields acted upon each other at right angles. This has been defined as the right hand and left hand rule. By pointing your thumb up and curling your fingers into your palm the thumb represents the direction of current in a wire and the fingers curling around this electric current at right angles represent the direction of the magnetic field. The thumb in the opposite hand refers to the electron flow moving in the opposite direction of the current in a wire while the magnetic field curves around the electron flow. Electrons move in the opposite direction of the current just as a rifle moves in the opposite direction of the bullet fired. The bullet is the analog of light and current, and the rifle is the analog of the mass electron. As each electron recoils in one direction, it emits a photon of light in the other. Because of the nature of refraction or conductivity of copper wire, this process continues within the bounds of the wire.

Figure 5-4 is an analog of light emission as the electron recoils to find a more suitable place within the atom or is ejected out of range and is captured by another atom along the copper wire. This process obeys the electron number in that the closer the electron is to the atom, the larger the electric field and the further from the atom the electric field diminishes in mass by quanta stages of emission. In each transaction of electric mass, converting to light requires that a piece or quanta of the electric field spiral off along the axis while the electron recoils in a direction equal to the laws of momentum. The direction of the electron and the light is determined by the direction of

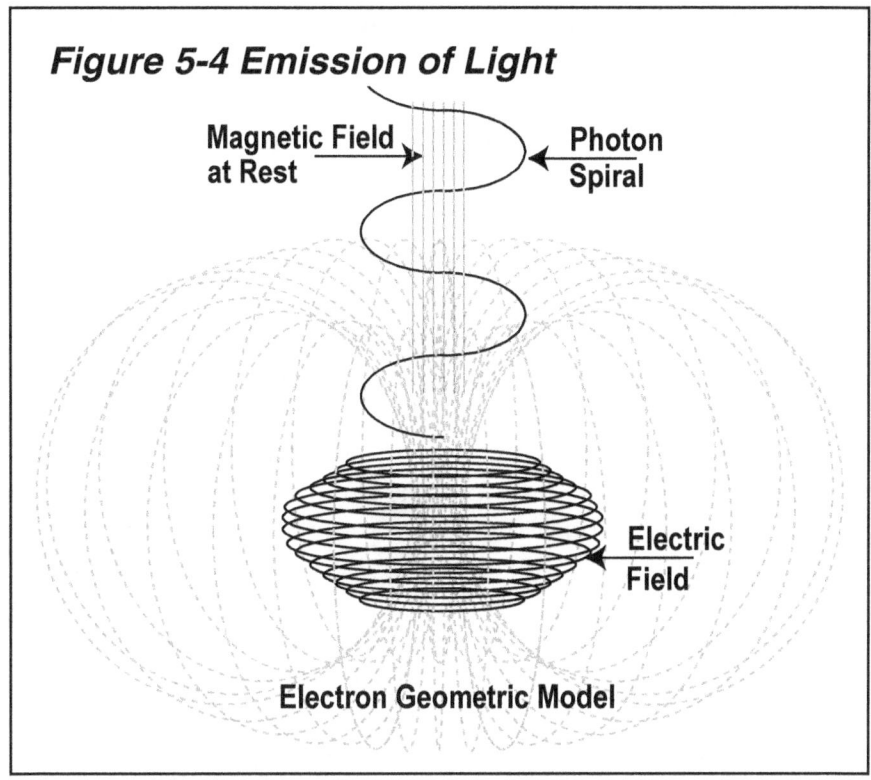

Figure 5-4 Emission of Light

the electron at the time of emission, its velocity, its mass, and the direction of the axis. This process indicates that the smallest particle of light would be a few electric monopoles spiraling around a magnetic field at rest until an electron or some other particle at a short distance or light years away recaptures it.

When the astronomer measures this light coming from the black sky as background radiation, it turns out to be about four degrees above absolute zero. Since there has been nothing smaller, for all intents and purposes, this becomes the smallest particle of light, or mass. Mass is not converted to energy, rather angular momentum and angular energy are converted to linear momentum and kinetic energy. As the magnetic field (holding an electric field stationery) stops or slows, its angular momentum and energy is passed to the liner momentum of a photon spiral. What energy was in the magnetic field passes to the electric field? It seems that energy appears out of nowhere and that mass diminishes in size. This satisfies relativity's epistemological setting of the conversion. Without this working arrangement, relativity leads to all sorts of strange theories including black holes, big bangs, as well as warped space and time dilations. This is child's play and the denial of intuitive meaning and of rational workings.

The reason for emission in the first place is due to a change in the electric and magnetic relationship. A change in equilibrium is a change in magnetic density. The density of the magnetic field changes as the distance changes between the electron and the nucleus of the atom. The electron's field emits as it moves away, and absorbs as it moves closer. This relationship maintains the equilibrium between the density and flux or angular momentum of the two fields. Whether energy is passed from field to field is not as important as each field maintaining its equilibrium relationship to the other field. In other words, you cannot pile on electric monopoles or particles without a corresponding increase in magnetic flux density. When there is a decrease, the magnetic flux density of magnetic monopoles releases photon spirals or a quantum portion of photoelectric monopoles.

Not only does the electron's electric field provide the particle nature of light, the wave nature is manifest in the spiraling of these photoelectric particles around a magnetic axis at relative rest to the center of the electron at a much further distance from the electron. The magnetic density of the surrounding space determines the speed of this photon spiral. The density is greater within matter and much less without; therefore the speed of light increases as it leaves matter such as a pane of glass. The assumption that the speed of light is constant is disproved in Einstein's General Relativity Theory. Of course the cause is assumed to be gravity rather than a change in magnetic density. Consider that refraction is none other than an abrupt change in magnetic density and thus a change in velocity.

When light reaches the earth's atmosphere, the speed increases proportional to the density of the earth's magnetic field or as the density changes. This is none other than a form of refraction. The further away from the earth, the faster the light will travel until the sun's magnetic field density becomes the primary factor in determining the speed of light. Light will travel the fastest between galaxies but there is no space in which there is not a minimum magnetic density. If there were, light would come to an abrupt end having no magnetic medium to spiral within or it might just spiral at an infinite speed to the next magnetic particle. This is a question far beyond the scope of this book.

This theory can be explained using experiments of atomic clocks although the experiments were not intended to do so.

> An atomic clock measures the frequency of electromagnetic radiation emitted by an atom or molecule. When an atom or molecule moves from one energy level to another, a specific amount, or quantum, of energy is absorbed when jumping to a higher energy level or emitted when falling to a lower energy level. The amount of energy absorbed or emitted depends on the difference between the energy levels. The atom or molecule emits energy in the form of electromagnetic radiation and the wavelength and frequency of the radiation depends on the amount of energy released by each transition between energy levels. Because the atom or molecule can only emit or absorb a specific amount of energy, the radiation emitted or absorbed has a regular frequency. A counter in the atomic clock keeps track of each cycle.[2]

Modern physics argues that gravity determines the slowing of clocks rather than magnetic field density. Simply raising or lowering the clock from sea level to a high mountain will illustrate that light slows at lower elevations. To say that gravity is the cause remains an assumption because there is no explanation for the workings. It could just as well be the magnetic field density in which the atomic emissions or oscillations occur.

In 1971 two American physicists, J.C.Hafele and Richard Keating, carried out an experiment by taking portable caesium clocks (Four of them, for safety and reliability) right around the world in a passenger jet aircraft. They compared them at the beginning and end of the journeys with the reference clocks at the US Naval Observatory in Washington DC. One circumnavigation was made eastwards, with both journeys taking about three days. The result of the experiment indicated that the clocks no longer agreed about the time of day. The eastbound clocks lost, on average, 59 nanoseconds (billionths of a second) compared with the clocks in Washington, while the westbound clocks gained 273 nanoseconds.[3]

How could such accurate timepieces disagree about the time of day? Taking into account the General Theory of Relativity, the jet aircraft would place the atomic clocks in a gravitational or unified magnetic field weaker than the clocks at the Naval Observatory on the earth's surface. The clocks in a weaker field at the higher altitude would naturally run faster. This would explain the westbound clocks, for they gained 273 nanoseconds. But the eastbound clocks lost. Why such a difference? Writers have dismissed this as a special relativity calculation. It makes more sense to consider the magnetic field density and to understand that as far as the magnetic field is concerned, it does not move east or west relative to the sun. It moves North and South. It is the earth that rotates against the magnetic field. A caesium clock moving with the earth would appear to run slow passing through the apparent density of more magnetic lines than at rest relative to the sun. In other words a jet airliner going west would be like following the sun or sitting in a magnetic field of less density. One would find also that the eastbound clocks should move even slower than the earthbound. This they did. When you consider elevation, the rotation of the earth and its motion around the sun, the density being greater on the sun side with radiation pressure and finally ask where were the jet airliners in reference to the sun at each given moment throughout a three-day travel? A three-day journey indicates that the eastbound clocks would not be much more than the earth's rotation. When dealing with the magnetic field there are numerous variables.

The velocity of light within an atomic clock depends upon the magnetic field density and not gravity. The apparent density (determined by altitude, direction, and the time of day) accounts for the velocity of light. Based upon observation, light travels more slowly in a gravitational field, but what has been understood to be the gravitational field that slows atomic clocks may just as well be the magnetic field density. The Inverse Square Law (double the distance and you double the strength or density) applies to both theories. This also gives us a natural limitation upon observation. I do not suggest that the velocity of light obeys the inverse square law in transmission because this would suggest that density follows an infinite graduation. This could not be the case. Just as gravity varies in very small degrees at different points on the earth at different times, gravity cannot truly obey the inverse square law either. I do not believe that the magnetic field changes so evenly in the atmosphere, but I do say that its change is sufficient that light curves twice that of matter moving at the same velocity and at the same elevation.

This is due to the fact that light is a single electric field spiraling horizontal to the earth's surface while matter has an infinite number of electric fields with only a net 50% moving randomly in the same horizontal direction. Matter has the extra baggage to carry and thus resists a change in motion while light simply bends twice that of light because of the graduated magnetic field density being greater towards the earth than the other side away from the earth. This curvature is very slight, but because of the inverse square law of acceleration and the very high velocity of light, even within the atom, matter falls to the earth very quickly because of the high angular velocity of the electric fields. It is as if any particle with a magnetic axis near horizontal to the earth's surface would pull magnetic space through the axis including the magnetic earth. Since the density is greater on the earth's side, the axis is forced to turn like Pac

Man chewing up bits of the magnetic properties in the process of acceleration towards the earth.

The above analogy is given to avoid the need to search for a graviton as a third component of matter. To this day the graviton has never been discovered. This can be explained by the analog of the unified field theory that has been put forth. Gravity, light, and matter are all electromagnetic relationships. Einstein worked on a field theory until his death because he disliked the direction relativity was going. He never completed the theory.

As a clock runs slower in a magnetic field, it should be understood that the photoelectric field propagates more slowly, not time. Time is constant. The velocity of light differs at different points in the universe. Even in a vacuum the earth's magnetic field density cannot be diminished. Time becomes an irreducible apparent reality distinguishable from the objective timepiece. The concept of time remains absolute by virtue of the law of conservation and definition. This could be demonstrated if the angular velocity of a spiraling photon could be measured separately from the linear velocity. The constancy of motion lies in the angular velocity of light's spiral and not in the linear velocity.

It was from Maxwell's equations, depicting Faraday's electric and magnetic particle field, that Einstein developed his equations. If the equations suggest particle fields—why not light and matter? The Maxwell equations relate the "partial variations" of, say, the electric field, in space, to the time variation of the magnetic field. They put into precise mathematical formulas just the sort of empirical observation that Faraday made.

Maxwell put Michael Faraday's field relationship into mathematical order; this epistemology or field geometry attempts to put Faraday's field description into a geometrical objective reality. The results build a more obvious relationship between light and matter.

Faraday, who was sixty-six at the time, wrote a letter to Maxwell and illustrated a need for which this theory fulfills.

> There is one thing I would be glad to ask you. When a mathematician engaged in investigating physical actions and results has arrived at his conclusions may they not be expressed in common language as fully, clearly, and definitely as in mathematical formula? If so, would it not be a great boon to such as I to express them so?—translating them out of their hieroglyphics, that we also might work upon them by experiment. I think it must be so, because I have always found that you could convey to me a perfectly clear idea of your conclusions, which, though they may give me no full understanding of the steps of your process, give me the results neither above nor below the truth, and so clear in character that I can think and work from them. If this be possible, would it not be a good thing if mathematicians, working on these subjects, were to give us the results in this popular, useful, working state, as well as in that which is their own and proper to them?[4]

Physics fails to suggest the workings. They prefer paradox and cosmological strangeness. Einstein abhorred the conclusions of modern cosmology, but failed to admit that the paradoxes of relativity fostered it. Once it is understood that light is a spiral electric field, the premise that the velocity of light remains constant in a vacuum everywhere in the universe becomes a contradiction. The Special Theory of Relativity assumes the constant velocity of light, but the General Theory proves it to be in error once the meanings of the terms move from the density of gravity to the density of the magnetic field.

Since the debate as to whether light is a solid particle or a wave comes from differing observational experiments and not contradictory mathematics, and since the previous illustrates that light is both a photoelectric particle and a wave as it spirals, this duality no longer suggests a paradox of mass turning into pure energy.

Whether you believe in the Unified Field Theory as briefly illustrated, actual experiments do suggest the possibility.

The Platonic Idiom

Creation can be composed of electric and magnetic monopoles as Faraday suggested and Maxwell's equations fit. Modern physics rejects the real aspects of fields, but admits that the field has force. This is an awfully poor epistemology.

Relativity describes the curvature of light as follows:

> A massive body squeezes and deforms space in its vicinity. Space is "denser" in the vicinity of a massive body and so light seems to travel more slowly there, when seen from afar.[5]

Despite this assumption, note the use of "denser" and consider that magnetic space has density where the epistemology is far more understandable. Light is matter in spiral form rather than some mystical waveform.

> The Earth intercepts very little of the Sun's out pouring, yet about 160 tons of sunlight particles fall on the Earth every day.[6]
>
> Hypothetical magnetic particles...have been postulated on conservation and symmetry principles: an electric particle gives rise to an electric field and when set into motion gives rise to a magnetic field; a magnetic particle should give rise to a magnetic field and, in motion produce an electric field. Neither quantum theory nor classical electromagnetic theory bars the existence of the magnetic monopole but it would have profound effects on the theoretical basis of quantum electrodynamics. Maxwell's equations would prove completely symmetrical if such particles did exist.[7]

Whether you believe or disbelieve, the equations of physics are the same. Actual experiment and measurements receive the action of particle definitions and density. Therefore the axiomatic conclusion can be accepted and done so without changing the meaning of space and time. Clocks move more slowly in a dense magnetic field but time does not. Clocks are objective things but time is predicative. It does not have particles. Light bends around corners and through slits because the magnetic field changes at the corner as the light spiral enters an abrupt change in magnetic density around matter's surface. Light is objective and can thus curve, refract, and compress in a dense field. Its change of direction is due to a change in magnetic density on one side of the light spiral and not as much on the other side.

Now space does not curve because it is subjective and conceptual. It is not made of particles. Space cannot be touched or apprehended. Like time, space is continuous but differs as to reality. Space is conceptual and cannot be observed save it be the objects in space. Try to observe nothing. It is impossible but not impossible to conceive emptiness. To conceive is subjective while to observe is predicative. Time is the apparent motion of objects and without objects we cannot observe time, but the mind will still conceive it. Time is predicative because the objects receive the action that we observe. That makes observation and time predicative. Mass can be observed but action does not define mass. It defines energy, another predicate reality. Why do we call something an object in the first place if it is not an object? Few will disagree that mass is objective, but many a scientist will talk of observed fact as if observation is objective and they will talk of curved space as if it is objective. Once understood, we can place words in the proper reality. But what we are truly interested in here is the intuitive nature of conceiving space, the intuitive nature of sensing time, and the intuitive nature of existing in space and time. Intuitively we know that this electric existence is separate from space and time. We call it mass. Mass cannot be exchanged into space or time because these are separate realities. The relativist never considers this epistemology.

Magnetic Space

Intuition is subjective, but it can help us understand the magnetic component of objective reality. This magnetic component is understood by the same intuition that helps us comprehend space. We know that magnetic space exists but it is difficult to fathom every aspect. Intuition is all we have to conceive of its existence. When we see the compass needle move or the iron filings create a pattern, intuition leads us to the concept of the magnetic field. It plays its own role and aids in the formation of electric matter. Another concept that geometrical space shares with magnetic space is *infinity*. In the objective sense I would call it infinite magnetic space. I use magnetic in order to assign physical properties that cannot be detected directly. I use space to show agreement with the concept of space warping, but it is not space that warps. It is magnetic density that is warped or uneven—causing the appearance of things to change as light curves in this magnetic variation. I do not mean geometrical space, but magnetic space, as substance would warp the path of light. In the magnetic sense, space is physical. Without the magnetic field space cannot warp. The space used in equations is not the kind that warps reality. Perhaps I should say magnetic properties in space and not magnetic space. I would just like to allow relativity concepts to be properly seen for what they are.

A unique property of magnetic space is that it is infinite and relatively evenly distributed until it is acted upon by an electric field. It is not unlike the classical ether concept except that it is not ridged. Instead, it abruptly moves in spherical circles in the presence of a stationery rotating electric field. A modern ether concept would call this a ripple in space. The problem with ether theories is that there is only one single monopole objective reality and not two. It takes two to draw a distinction and change in circumstances. Ripples do not happen without some distinct outward cause. This means that there must be at least two elements at play.

Now when light spirals around magnetic space, the stationery axis may squeeze slightly while the magnetic monopoles exterior to the electric spiral may part. In matter, the magnetic field circulates near the velocity of light in the spherical pattern described—perhaps drawing more magnetic monopoles into the system creating a higher density. It can also be suggested that the increased density is due more to the high angular velocity of the magnetic field thus changing the reaction time between magnetic space and the electric field. Density may not be density as an increase in the number of monopoles but an increase in velocity as a strong wind would slow a walker. I do not want to suggest that density is wholly motion. It could very well be an increase in the number of magnetic monopoles or even a combination of the two. In the case of the atomic clocks that traveled an east and west direction, what if the same experiment was done traveling north and south? The plane cannot take off and land in the same place as it circled the globe because once on the other side of a magnetic pole the plane would be going against the motion of the field rather than with it. If such could be done, I predict that atomic time would move slower against the magnetic field and faster with it. Light of course would do the same. We can yet study magnetic space more appropriately if experiments were designed as such. Science needs to move away from relativistic thinking and understand more about magnetic density in space. This would correct all of the paradoxes found in relativity and give a greater understanding about a unified field theory.

Intuition gives the mind understanding and intelligence with the ability to conceive the infinity of space and time. This same continuum will also apply to magnetic density in space. Perhaps electric matter also maintains some sort of infinite continuum. Magnetic space can remain at rest but it seems that electric matter must be constantly circulating a magnetic axis in motion in the case of matter or at rest in the case of light. This constant angular motion sets electric creation apart from magnetic space. Relativity makes creation infinite by curving it in upon itself, as a figure eight would never end. I do not think this represents infinity because intuition asks what is outside of the figure eight. In reality you cannot measure infinity. You can only measure creation, as it exists in infinity. Despite this, a figure eight is still a good symbol for infinity.

Control Monopole

Creation depicts one role of the whole of objective reality. Magnetic space fittingly depicts another role that

The Platonic Idiom

cannot exchange itself with electric matter for which all things measurable and touchable are created. This dichotomy is the extent that science has attempted. Even the magnetic field has been nebulous to most and denied existence by most theorists. A dichotomy can produce a distinction and create a reason for opposing forces, but it cannot explain psychology or intelligent perception. Proportion, unlike distinction, requires three elements such as two distinct properties and one unit that the distinction shares in common. I would attribute proportion also to the universe. The current scientific dichotomy does not lend itself to a holistic universe. We need something that gives more credence to will and choice as something distinct from electric creation and infinite magnetic shared space. I am suggesting that magnetic space is the shared component and that an undiscovered field or particle shows a real distinction from electric creation. This concept can be suggested in the equation for power as in the following:

$$\text{Action} = M \times L^2/T$$
$$\underline{\text{Energy} = M \times L^2/T^2}$$
$$\text{Power} = M \times L^2/T^3$$

Action is a motion without regard to mass or momentum. *Energy* is also motion but is directly proportional to mass and momentum. The concept of *power* is the third derivative with energy the second and action the first derivative. Power would then be proportional to mass and momentum. It would also imply action, but out of consistency, *power* would also imply a third concept. Energy obeys the law of conservation and in the short form it is written $E=mc^2$. As demonstrated, energy is not conversion from substance to non-substance but from angular energy within mass to linear energy in light. Power as in Kilowatts becomes a third derivative. The law of conservation pertains only to the second derivative underlined.

Arthur Young, a designer of helicopters, suggested a third derivative for velocity similar to power for action. To increase the velocity of an automobile, we push on the accelerator, causing positive acceleration. To decrease the velocity, we step on the brake, causing negative acceleration. We may also alter the directional velocity and acceleration of the car by steering. What is the process by which the accelerator brakes, and steering change the acceleration of the car? Clearly, a change in acceleration is what Arthur Young means by the word *control*.[8] In this respect we have three more equations with control the third derivative of the first order of velocity:

Velocity = L/T
Acceleration = L/T^2
Control = L/T^3

Control is not used in physics, but Arthur Young considered it an aspect of design. Control is the free will and to some respects the unpredictability of the system. The universe needs a control element or perhaps a third basic monopole to explain many intelligent and evolutionary aspects. Control should not be considered as some central location in the universe as one would control a nation or world, but control must have autonomous properties that exhibit indeterminate choice to local elements. The traditional concept of God lending universal control is also not appropriate as a method of control. If there were such a God, it would defy the individual control choices of autonomous localities. We would have a God that would also defy individual intelligence. Universal control is not what is being discussed. Control at great distances is a misnomer. Such is the case with gravity. It is zero at great distances, because control fields, if there be such a thing, should only relate to autonomous localities in the same way as electric fields. Individual intelligence would fit squarely under this description. It might also explain a control relation between electric and magnetic monopoles, but I would rather suggest something separate and distinct.

Now a control monopole would be the smallest unit of a control field. And for a lack of any previous attempt, I have attached intelligence to this third field. This would give us a subjective universe, a magnetic universe, and an electric universe all superimposed in the same infinite space and time continuum. We thus have a particle of intelligence, a particle of physical electric existence, and a particle of an active magnetic relationship between the subjective and the objective universe. What we are interested in is the reality of intelligence as something different from electric monopoles. We can discuss a human being and all of his or her electric fields objectively, but the ability to reason is intuitively something different.

A control monopole or an unknown third basic component of existence represents the smallest unit of autonomy and intelligent control. Whether you believe in intelligence as non-electric or not is a subject of the next chapter. I am only wondering how such a monopole or third field would work in conjunction with the magnetic field. One must assume that if the electric field needs a relationship with the magnetic field to exist in space, perhaps the control field needs a similar unknown relationship. This is conjecture, but does remove so much mystery as to individual intelligence, spirit, ESP, and other phenomena denied by electric reality.

All of physical existence can be explained by a unified field theory using the electromagnetic relationship, but there is no way to explain the action-at-a-distance relationship between the two fields. The same problem has haunted gravity far more because of the vast distances. If gravity is none other than a particular mass reacting to a variable magnetic density, you do not need a graviton or gravity monopole. Every thing is local, leaving the mystery or action between the magnetic and electric fields as the only form of action at a distance. Since the distance is infinitesimally short, there should be no problem in accepting it. A control particle would also have an infinitesimally short distance to react with a magnetic field.

Suppose a control field was similar to an electric field, but circulated in an opposite direction and, if composed of a finer makeup similar to the magnetic field, we would never be able to detect it. This would give us two physical relationships in the universe. We can even postulate that one is entropic and the other anti-entropic. One represents cyclic decay and the other evolves from a lesser order to a higher order. This would be consistent with religious antiquity and modern evolution and almost every theory in between, except atheism that bars anything outside that which we cannot touch.

Trying to find a graviton as a particular monopole will not solve the paradoxes of the universe. A gravitational field would not work in the same way as the relationship of the electric and magnetic fields. If gravity is an electromagnetic relationship, there is no need of a graviton. We spend millions to search for the graviton. We would be farther along in a unified field theory searching for a possible control particle or at least a better understanding of the electro-magnetic relationship. Intelligent force is in more need of understanding than the gravitation of black holes and the expansion or inevitable contraction of the universe. Looking for answers at remote distances does not solve the perplexing problems of society. It does no more for humanity than worshiping a God of stone.

We can lay hold of an electric monopole as a particle of light having a color temperature of about 4 degrees above absolute zero. We know the magnetic field exists but cannot lay hold of the smallest monopole. Finally we know that intelligence exists, but we also cannot lay hold of the smallest particle of intelligence. In the organization of matter, the electron or atom receives and will give up light according to the magnetic field density, thus causing entropic change to larger electric systems as atoms eject bits of the electric field only to be recycled by another atom. For this reason, the energy of creation seems to change as it entropies to a lesser or different order. This only means that death and resurrection, so to speak, are inevitable when it comes to electric fields. If the universe had any evolutionary capability along with this entropy, we could raise legitimate questions as to the cause of this evolvement power. It would be natural to suppose the possibility of a control monopole to explain evolution concepts. A control particle may not suffer the same death and resurrection nature as the electric universe. In contrast, the natural tendency would be to move from a lesser order to a higher order while the electric universe would move naturally from a higher order to a lesser. It would be a control field, or intelligence, that would bring about apparent change or reversal in electric properties. The electric fields would naturally be entropic while the control fields would naturally be anti-entropic. Once we confess the existence of the electric field and calculate the need of a magnetic field without the ability to actually see it, we can also propose an unknown and unseen control particle to answer the unanswerable.

As far as the relativist is concerned, light accelerates from matter as if energy appears out of the blue, and also magnetism produces energy in an electric field as if out of the blue. More realistically, if the angular velocity of the magnetic field decelerates, this would explain the counter acceleration of the photoelectric spiral. The question is this, if relativity can create magic out of physics, then does field theory have a perfect right to explain intelligence and evolution using a third control particle or field? To be evolutionary, it seems that control fields do not form electron-type bonds. In order to maintain intelligence, control fields would suggest a different process. This concept is no more impossible than finding dark matter in the universe. So much is assumed about unknown and unseen things that a third unseen field can easily be postulated for the same reason that a third reality has always existed, yet philosophy has not considered it.

Intelligence seems to evolve over time, but nonetheless seems to be inherent as if from another universe. A materialist would say that intelligence is none other than electric fields governed by genetics. This same person may even deny the existence of an unseen magnetic field. The debate goes on and perhaps psychological and philosophical motives remain at the base of all things determined. A dichotomy is a form of determinism, but a proportion impels choice and responsibility. If we want to run from responsibility all we have to do is believe in cause and effect without the element of control. The real issue is that we have a psychological problem and not a problem in determining the truth.

This is an open question and cannot be dismissed. A third objective monopole could play a part in existence. We have those believing in only one reality to justify their personal worldview. We have others believing in two realities to justify determinism. We have some believing in three realities to corner responsibility and, finally, we have some believing in many realities in order to make all things relative. It is a game of psychology more than philosophy. This game seems to avoid any direction that would require responsibility. Most thinkers delve into singularity, duality or plurality as in many, but to the best of my knowledge no one lays hold of three constituents of reality.

6. Subjective Reality and Intelligence

The purpose of covering intelligence is to better establish a cause of philosophical motive and to also illustrate that reason is the essence of subjective reality. Intelligence is a difficult subject with regard to defining its physical nature and has almost as many opinions among authorities as there are scientists that study its workings. I suggest who the more common understanding would prove better than the various idioms we have at our disposal. Instead of the usual debate between environment and genetics in order to find the nature of intelligence, I would like to add the issue of preexistence and individuality or a personal evolutional form of intelligence for the greater part separate from heredity. I introduced this concept in a previous chapter. The scientist cannot prove or disprove any sort of preexisting intelligence any more than they can produce a third field, but if environment and genetics do not supply the necessary answers to the most perplexing problems, then intelligence can easily be thought of as a separate reality from the objective world in much the same way as the concept of a control field that has been introduced.

There is no proof for such an individual entity and it is like trying to prove or disprove the existence of God. Because of the uniqueness of intelligence, it is much easier to suggest that there is another universe superimposed upon the magnetic and electric universe that would explain so many unanswered questions about spirit matter, immortality of the soul, individual identity after death, the ability to reason and the ability to say, "I think, therefore I am." To think intelligence is none other

Subjective Reality and Intelligence | 88

than entropic electric mater is ludicrous. Since the majority of the world has some form of belief system that incorporates the super natural, it behooves science to allow the concept of a third field and stop insisting on the existence of electric substance as the only reality. If objects only exist and there are no verb action in the magnetic field, and if there is no subjective will to choose, we are limiting our ability to search for understanding and for truth. To argue that science is only concerned about what is measurable is surely an excuse to maintain an atheistic orientation. Science is always predicting things not seen because of the laws of conservation. What science needs is the law of proportion in order to predict more intuitively, the law of distinction to preserve responsibility and the law of definition in order to preserve consistence in meaning. The law of proportion was used in predicting the elements and can be developed in other areas. The law of distinction is probably too philosophical, but needs to become a responsible part of separating meaning.

It is suggested here that there is a physical field for each reality. Intelligence is of one, electric matter manifests the second, and the action between the intelligence and the electric matter could be the predicate-like magnetic field or center reality. In this way, the objective will receive the action from the predicate that was initiated by the subjective intelligence. A single objective reality or field does not work. It is the magnetic field that creates patterns in physical nature, and it would be appropriate to suggest that there is a potential for a mirror image universe of sorts as the subjective is a mirror image of the objective. First we have the electromagnetic relation and perhaps it is possible that there would be an intelligent relationship to the magnetic field. Whether you agree or disagree, it is important to know that the electric field could not do it alone, nor could any single field create equilibrium, change patterns, or give opposition etc. Without the assistance of a relational field, existence could not be proportional. A field cannot act upon itself. If there are two, the universe could tolerate three fields, but the concept of proportion in the universe would be destroyed if there were more

The Platonic Idiom

than three. The idea of three fields is not unreasonable as long as the intelligent field does not react directly with the electric field and the magnetic field can react to both the intelligent field and an electric field. This is conjecture, but gives us a relational concept for all of reality and may also remove the paradoxes found in the study of intelligence.

Technology has advanced so far that we can define some basic concepts about intelligence. With some proficiency, we can establish the difference between artificial and individual identity intelligence. Artificial intelligence is none other than that of running a computer program. It could also be the running of a biological program. The human autonomic nervous system and perhaps much of the brain, if not all, is a very effective artificial computer that was created in much the same manner as a muscle, the eyes or any other peripheral element. A biological computer is none other than a biological robot procreated through the genetic process. Real or individual intelligence would be more appropriately referred to as that external to the human body possessing individuality, the ability to choose, and freewill separate from genetic creation. Without an individual intelligence, man is hard pressed to explain some aspects of fear, the ability to ask questions and raise intuitive concepts far beyond simple preprogrammed commands. Individual identity intelligence could also explain paranormal events and religious propensity.

Because of technology we can easily suggest a basic type of intelligence as a programmed, involuntary, artificial or biological intelligence. If we ask if this ever sleeps, we are assured that the heart and digestion, as examples, always operate regardless of the state of sleep or consciousness and therefore never sleep. This would be different from than what one might call moral and ethical intelligence. The two types of intelligence may simply represent two harmonic fields interchanging data reception and directives with the brain on the artificial side. This would be done through the magnetic field. The whole process would be based upon the emotional, linguistic, conceptual and kinetic makeup of the individual identity intelligence. It has been suggested that possibly other body parts resonate to identify intelligence such as the heart in ways that explain concepts of heart transplants changing the emotional makeup of the new host. It would be as if there was a parallel universe that could interconnect in a permanent fashion for the life of the human organism. A parallel universe is not to mean outside the physical, but a physical universe that behaves differently, has a relationship to the magnetic field, but cannot be detected by electric fields. In this sense, the magnetic field provides the action between the two fields. The typical consciousness or critical aspects could easily be classified as the preexisting intelligence. This would incorporate ethics, morals, and free will choices. Under hypnosis this level of consciousness of the intelligence is still in control. A preexistent intelligence would have no beginning and it would have no end. It would be eternal and evolutional. It would not die because it was never born. It evolved over time from one stage to the next and from one level of understanding to another. This conjecture is needed before we try to determine how intelligence is measured.

In scientific study there have been many theories along the way. The first is always abandoned for a better one. Those theories outside of science are constantly modified for the same reasons. In the theory of intelligence, Alfred Binet who developed a standard for intelligence in 1905 to quantify results, proposed the first theory of measurement of this strange reality. The objection to a standardize intellect is to assume that intelligence is quantitative and lacks any type of value that needs to be measured qualitatively. The concept of normal has been destructive to many American youth in a systematized, six-period educational structure that tends to teach the regurgitation of data rather than the insight needed to develop ethical and moral citizens. The standardized intelligence test mirrors this same problem. We test the IQ as we would test artificial intelligence.

Lewis M. Terman developed the IQ test further in order to determine a person's mental age. The concept of a quantitative testing seeped deeper into the psychology of intelligence. 100 became the norm while anything below 70 was retarded and anything above 130 is gifted. This resembled the bell curve and stereotyped the mind. I do not intend to demean the progress of testing over the years, for such methods have helped to determine certain problems and develop further insight. We do have a very long way to go. I really question the aspect of testing without various methods to determine the quality of intelligence apart from logical processes of yes and no artificial intelligence. Of course you can ask what one means by quality. You might even say that the word is intended only to demean scientific methods. Quality is probably the wrong word, but it is a start to defining the problem. The reason for this missing quality is that there are many views of intelligence.

> Researchers who study and measure intelligence—do not agree on a definition of intelligence. Some define intelligence as the ability to reason, learn quickly, analyze and solve new problems, and grasp abstract or complex concepts—skills that are measured by standard intelligence tests. Other intelligence experts include in their definition of intelligence such task-specific abilities as musical, spatial, and practical skills, as well as creativity and innovation—talents that are not tested for on standard intelligence tests.[1]

The above is the general reason for questioning the quality of intelligence testing. Perhaps we are testing only one aspect of something far more diverse than one can imagine. What will add to this problem are the questions as to whether intelligence is fixed or whether one can increase his intelligence. The argument goes this way: If you take a low testing individual and place him in a different environment, through adoption or special schooling, you can raise the IQ about 10 points. Those who maintain that intelligence is genetic and fixed indicate that this 10-point raise is momentary. The individual will eventually fall back to his predetermined level. I think this controversy indicates that there must be different types of intelligence, for when there is a momentary increase it may be due to memory retention and not conceptual abilities. This is manifest in the difference between those with photographic memories and those without. Those with memory ability can memorize and pass a test with a high grade, but they will not retain the information or be able to form complex concepts. Memory indicates retention ability but not conceptual ability. This suggests differing types of intelligence. High retention ability may indicate an intelligence of a special type that may do poorly in another non-tested type. We are just not measuring all types of intelligence. If one can improve his memory, is this not an increase in IQ? If one can improve her concepts, is this not also an increase in intelligence? I think it is safe to say that one can increase his or her intelligence in both quantity and quality. This would harmonize with both the principle of evolution as well as preexistent intelligence.

Let me illustrate with my own personal experience: As a child of five and attending my first day in school, I found it fearful and unnerving. I did not speak to anyone. I would play a little, but was quiet and kept to myself. To this day I can remember things vividly. I was taken to the principal's office for some reason. I did seem to converse a little because I did not fear the inability to express myself away from the other children. The principal asked questions and I seemed to respond a little because he also seemed to be more understanding than the typical child bully. I was not threatened with a comparison of others. The teacher had me tested crudely as many were during those years to determine my intelligence level. My first teacher evidently wanted to prescribe special schooling for I scored very low by her methods. This was perhaps because I had a low retention level in remembering things. Communication was painful and slow. It was due more to the fear of failure than any physical problem. This fear was magnified because I could see something that others could not see, but was unable to communicate it. I later learned that the principal did not agree with the results of the teacher and made a personal judgment from our conversation. The teacher argued that I needed placement in a retarded school. The principal felt that my intelligence was of a different type. I did not hear him say this, but my mother told me this many years later. She coined a phrase that it was a "religious type" of intelligence I was never placed in any special program at school, but I had difficulty throughout my education, including college, requiring retention void of conceptual understandings. This implied heredity to some degree because my mother was of a similar type.

My Father had a photographic memory. He was much quicker than I was. My mother was much more difficult to understand and struggled for acceptance. I always felt that perhaps I was like my mother. My Father was an artist and could draw very well. He was also an excellent craftsman. At about age seven I remember that I still had trouble learning, but when it came to art I excelled. There was one problem. I would refuse to draw animated objects such as animals on a covered wagon. I drew mechanical parts only as though the wagon were covering the oxen as they were pulling down over a hill in order to hide my ineptness at drawing animals. The wagon was most intricate and exhibited an engineer's way of things more than a fine artist. I knew in this respect the drawing was very good. It was confirmed by the teacher who said, "You cannot leave here until this is finished." She evidently caught that I was slow, not only in speech but in drawing.

I became a graphic artist but realized that late in life I should have been an engineer when as a technical writer and graphic designer combined, I spent more time with engineers and found them pleasant to be around, constantly asking questions and often challenging their conclusions. New engineers often thought I was an engineer and even a plant manager appointed me as project manager. I excelled in this relationship more than any other. It was as if I was maturing to where I belonged. After many years my IQ reached 133. This definitely indicates not only the ability to increase intelligence, but that it comes in types.

I mentioned the above to illustrate that the system is missing something. We get better, but failure is still eminent.

One would conclude from the above personal history that I inherited intelligence from both my mother and my father in various degrees. Perhaps I find this offensive that I am not an individual and the maker of my own intelligence. I cannot think for a minute that such complexity is simply a mechanical prediction. The need for individual development is so strong in the learning process that it seems ludicrous to think that identity is machined rather than personal and original to one's self will and choice. We can look at our bodies and be disturbed that they are not what we hoped for because we are prisoners in bodies of genetic creation. Most of us accept this in time. One does not usually think that way about his or he mind.

It is generally concluded that groups with lower IQ's tend to be poor, are on welfare, tend to participate in criminal activities, and seem to have more unplanned children. This is based upon observation without any attempt to rationalize the situation. This sort of observation can also suggest that intelligence testing really does not fully test intelligence, but is mostly testing one's learning. From my own experience this does seem to be the case. Science does not really know what intelligence is and testing methods are truly archaic compared to what intelligence really is or can become.

The fact that Asians score slightly higher than whites, whether in America or not, and because whites generally score 10 points higher than blacks, seems to indicate that heredity is the benefactor. Again, observation is the culprit to this conclusion for what if those designing intelligence tests focus on particular types that make the blacks do poorly and the Asians achieve greatness? I cannot help but remember the Japanese ability to duplicate American technology and eventually produce a superior product. This essence of duplication suggests a particular type of intelligence particular also to cultural subtleties, and the tests are geared to reveal only the results designed to accentuate the intelligence of the test maker. The ability to duplicate may be high on retention, but not necessarily high on conception. The IQ tester would surely argue that both are included. This only injects a new question, "How much of each?" Environment must have some effect for if the blacks were slowly accorded an equal place in American society, their average IQ scores would significantly rise. Reasonable experience justifies this. But again this may also indicate that the tests lean heavily to aptitude and not real intelligence. I do not intend to negate the black's intelligence. I only intend to suggest that each culture caries a different type and excels in different ways. I also say that this has little to do with genetics and more with certain types of preexisting intelligence cleaving to the same type. If intelligence is preexisting, then you have to come up with some form of methodology for intelligence to cleave to certain types rather than fall to random conditions. This means that similarities can pass due to intelligent selection and choice just as much as genetics. To what degree does the IQ test measure aptitude, retention or conception? Also, to what degree are we measuring artificial or biological intelligence as compared to real identity intelligence? These question need to be addressed. Something individualistic may be the primary nature of intelligence and genetics and environment may only participate or even negate the evolutionary process in developing ones real intelligence.

During the First World War, extensive testing was done not to weed out the draftee, but to give him an appropriate classification that would properly place each to defined duties during his military service. Many tests during the same period from various sources were also taken from groups such as black Americans, Spanish Americans, and European immigrants. And although it was claimed that the IQ tests were testing native intelligence and were independent of environmental history, "native intelligence" does not have a language mimicking the same as one as the environment of the creators of the tests. Thus the learned language of any culture may add to or detract from native intelligence depending on the native intelligences creating the tests. Every test requires communicative skills and the language one learns is going to be part of that which has been tested. In this respect we can consider one type of intelligence to be linguistic and another to be conceptual. Those individuals and cultures having a linguistic type as predominant would score high if the test were to be written by that type of intelligence. The only real question is what is native intelligence? Is it part biological or is it perhaps mostly preexistent?

It would seem that a linguistic mind would be better at remembering detail, having better communication skills, and would mimic a faster mind. This type of individual would do well in higher education and also become eventually the one who would write the test in the first place. This same intelligence would follow paths or professions that would include education, news media, acting and other forms of communication such as politics. But just considering education and communication, it can be demonstrated that this type tends to think linearly and follow a modern liberal methodology. The linguistic mind flourishes under formal education and eventually becomes the dominating educational force. As these linguistic minds populated twentieth century education there were Eugenics that arose believing that intelligence was greater among white protestant races than blacks and poor immigrants from Central America and even parts of Europe. The idea surfaced that the human race might be improved by getting rid of so-called undesirable human beings. These undesirables were tested crudely and proved to be feeble minded. As Americans, we have learned better but in our liberal methods we are still ignorant to other intelligent types. This would probably be due to the fact that the eugenic mind would be linguistic and more likely to advance in formal education, while conceptual minds would be pushed in the background due to slowness. This slowness would also inhibit advancement in education and their abilities would not receive development. In other words a linguistic education would produce more prejudiced minds lacking conceptual relationships. The protestant in Europe and America tended to have a more liberal education, which in turn would produce linguistic educators of regimented criteria. This regimented education was particularly high in Germany and Prussia and perhaps explains the reason for such cultural superiority that produced such high prejudice. John Taylor Gatto's book *The Underground History of American Education* thoroughly exploits this connection.

Outside of education, the general concept of ability does not seem to pass on to children at least as far as great abilities are concerned. What is passed on is parental status. For this reason a nephew of an eminent man has far less chance of becoming eminent than his son. On the other hand, men and women who are gifted with high abilities easily rise through obstacles caused by inferiority of social rank. Also, men and women who are largely aided by social advantage are often unable to achieve eminence unless they are endowed with the same natural gift of the father and mother. Genetics may produce a good representation of appearances, but when it comes to gifts, ethics, and intelligence, genetics is a hit and a miss among children. We do have fathers who were American Presidents who have sons who became the same and we also have sons of corporation presidents that out achieved their fathers. How strange it is that an eminent man may have a brother as a low achiever yet a nephew who excels like himself. Perhaps this is cultural, upbringing, favoritism or some other condition. It does illustrate that achievement is both opportunity and ability. And ability does not always run in the immediate family but it does run like a thread in similar cultures.

The most environmentally disadvantaged group has been considered to be the American Indian. Their environmental index or rating was as far below that of blacks as the blacks were below the whites.[2] This index was based upon income, unemployment, and standard of health care, life expectancy, and infant mortality. Yet the American Indian's ability and achievement test scores average about half a standard deviation higher than the scores of blacks. The differences were in favor of the Indian children on each of four tests made.[3] If learning were adjusted in the calculation, the American Indian may very well be much higher. Being disadvantaged will only have a learning effect on an IQ test. This suggests that certain cultures may produce a greater type of intelligence rather than the same as the typical white protestant. If it were possible to test the American Indian in their specific type and compare it with the white American, you might find very strange differences. I think this is manifest in religious and cultural orientation. In the case of the American Indian, some have a different cultural heritage than others. This would seem to explain the wisdom in some tribes and ignorance in others. Just look at those native tribes that sponsor gambling and those that do not. Also, look at the Navajo and then the Hopi as an example of this cultural divergence. As you leave Tuba City, Arizona, you see liquor bottles littering the highway until you enter into the Hopi reservation found deep in the center of the Navajo reservation, where the liquor bottles and garbage along the road are nearly gone. Perhaps the explanation for such apparent differences can just as well stem from cultural selection by a preexisting intelligence rather than heredity. Also, environment would have little to do with it. The Hopi are far more autonomous in their community structure than the Navajo. The Hopis are broken into four mesas and in each mesa you have the old ways and the new ways of living. Some prefer to live with running water, and some do not. There is a constant fight or ongoing battle within their culture that is structured in a kind of mini republic made of clans and groups. In the Navajo there is only our system of doing things with massive federal support and limited representation. In the Hopi there is a live debate going on and also far more tradition. We need to take a chance and discuss what defines a cultural orientation and why certain intelligences are attracted to certain cultures.

The Catholics have their Jesuit universities that offer greater recourse for discussion than the typical protestant and even the religious Brigham Young University. Perhaps this is evolutional or perhaps it is cultural. The Jews of antiquity have a rich history of family dialogue and other traditions that remain in some modest people. Wherever free will and agency are valued, there you will have a greater cultural orientation to conceptual intelligence rather than the typical rhetorical intelligence that says emotional things to get accepted, but has little conceptual understanding. That is truly the nature of the politician.

Proof of heredity or environmental factors are prevalent, but the conclusions completely ignore the individualistic or preexisting types. The IQ does rise in social status and degenerate families produce degenerate children. This is used to prove that environment plays a role. It could also prove that individualistic factors are attracted to their own kind or type of intelligence. I do believe that being learned will affect the IQ and reflect an average increase, for items in IQ tests are largely learned in school, but that inherited portion, if there be such a thing, could still represent an individualistic approach of attraction to like intelligence. For some unknown reason intelligence cleaves unto intelligence of its own type. In other words, it is similar types in preexistent form that tend to connect to specific cultures independent of genetics. Testing may be useful and predictable to some degree, but the source of intelligence has yet to be verified. When cultures intermix or different types of intelligence marry this can pose an unusual characteristic of polarity. Genetically a child could look like a particular parent on one hand and have a type of intelligence of the other parent. If you did a study, it could generally be demonstrated that a parent might favor a particular child over another, but this is not due to appearance, but to intelligence type. It could be nature's way of helping the parent accept unusual types of intelligence found in his children by giving them genetic appearances that show similarities to the one parent that more likely would reject them for having a different intelligent type. This polarization would be less likely in a culture that does not marry outside. This should be more of a problem in mixed cultures. Essentially, a preexisting intelligence would be attracted to one parent more than another, but would appear genetically more like the other. Highly mixed cultures may give one basic reason for such an increase in divorce and child neglect. It would not be fair to exclude economic, religious, and social factors, but the concept is worth a study if we ever come to the realization of different intelligence types rather than the more common quantitative IQ.

IQ scores do reflect behavior such that delinquents and other offenders have a lower measured intelligence. There are strong correlations between IQ and occupation level, school attainment, worker productivity, and possibly even political participation. This could be just as much a prediction of types of intelligence rather than the size of IQ. Those neglected because of prejudice of type, or lack of learning to show a better score may force some into delinquency. On the other hand, some rise above it all while equal opportunity does not produce equal testing results. Intelligence may predict how well people do in the world and even how poor they will be even if they are not born in poverty. Not because of the IQ, but because the IQ traditionally only measures linguistics and learned logic. Because these two areas succeed in our society and the methods of learning and testing seem to push other types back, we do not know how other types may be better suited to leadership responsibility and spirituality. We may be extolling the wrong intelligence and placing individuals in leadership when they might be better suited for research. If individuals were not so political, the prediction by IQ could not be made more effectively. It behooves us to learn more about types rather than quantitative intelligent scores.

IQ testing is always an indirect measure of learning. Literally every answer on an intelligence test depends on what a person has learned. Intelligence exists, but it has been brought into being by intelligence tests. IQ tests do not measure all kinds of intelligence. Howard Gardner is a Harvard psychologist and the author of *Frames of Mind: The theory of Multiple Intelligences*. He says that Stephen Ceci and Robert Sternberg, as well as himself, have discovered more types of intelligence.

> Sternberg and his colleagues have studied valued kinds of intellect not measured by IQ tests, such as practical intelligence—the kind of skills and capacities valued in

the workplace. They have shown that effective managers are able to pick up various tacit messages at the workplace and that this crucial practical sensitivity is largely unrelated to psychometric intelligence. Ralph Rosnow and his colleagues have developed a measure of social or personal intelligence—the capacities to figure out how to operate in complex human situations—and have again demonstrated that these are unrelated to the linguistic and logical skills tapped in IQ tests.

A growing number of researchers have argued that, while IQ tests may provide a reasonable measure of certain linguistic and mathematical forms of thinking, other equally important kinds of intelligence, such as spatial, musical, or personal, are ignored (this is the subject of much of my own work). In short, the closed world of intelligence is being opened up.[4]

There have been views about emotional intelligence for some time, and since the discovery of visual impairment due to accidents in Capgras patients, visual intelligence has come upon the horizon. Capgras is the inability to recognize relatives and also the inability to recognize the difference between a man and a woman after an accident or some other trauma. One can recognize the voice, but will often emphatically deny the person is who he is. He cannot put what he sees to the emotions he still knows.[5] Once perhaps thought of as a brain disorder or damage, new theories suggest the severing of emotional and visual intelligence. Is the visual artificial intelligence something different than the emotional identity? To sever two types of intelligence definitely indicates a disorder of the brain. If however the severing is between artificial and real intelligence, this makes perfectly good sense. In this case the artificial intelligence suffers a disconnection because of brain damage. The damage is to the connection and its ability to interface to identity intelligence where emotion is found.

There are countless human sacrifices that exhibit the passion of love in saving one's child over oneself. It is as if they defy reason on the spur of the moment to save another rather than themselves. Seen from the perspective of evolutionary biologists, such parental self-sacrifice is in the service of "reproductive success" in passing on one's genes to future generations. But from the perspective of the parent, this is love and they would shake their head mildly to such genetic conclusions. Whenever experience begins to bridge the unknown or the misunderstood, the materialists wave their hands in disbelief, for they believe that what cannot be measured does not exist. Connecting all problems to a relationship of the brain and external intelligence seems to answer every paradox of intelligence. In the case of Capgras it is suggested that after trauma the emotional intelligence separates from the visual or artificial intelligence, thus causing the inability to recognize a relative. In the case of rare diseases that destroy the amygdala, a section of the brain for responding to fear, one becomes unable to identify looks of fear on other people's faces. If someone were to put a gun to his head he would be able intellectually to be afraid but would not feel afraid as a normal person.[6] This tendency to connect emotional and visual intelligence to the brain assumes that intelligence is an inherited trait. We know that such cases are not environmental or learned therefore the assumption remains that the only view left is brain damage that might destroy the resonating connection that separates identity intelligence from artificial intelligence.

The brain may provide two functions. The first could be the artificial portion of intelligence and the other purpose could be that the brain is an interface much like the early computer processors had an interface to peripherals. It is interesting how one shops for a fast processor but may not consider a fast bus speed interface or memory capacity. Most inexpensive computers are sold on the basis that they will not be used for complex graphics and other highly integrated movement of data from the processor to the peripheral. What we think of as memory origin in certain brain cells could simply be an interface location of particular memories. It would be like catching data that is moving from real intelligence to artificial and perhaps back again. It would be like placing a probe on a bus connection rather than a point in memory or even a point in the processor.

As the biologist looks for cause and effect there arise all kinds of materialist assumptions. Like blinders they cannot see the possibility of something not seen. Depending upon which authority or which set of statistics you refer to, there is proof that intelligence is environmental and also genetic. It reminds me of the particle and wave theory of light that has not yet been resolved. As demonstrated earlier, both are manifestations of the same field theory. What better defines the differences in cultures and races is a type of intelligence rather than a quantitative IQ. Much more investigation must be made to determine how much genetics comes into play, but the study must also include an individualistic theory that considers that intelligence comes from an unseen universe that may even guide evolution to some degree. This guidance could be partially internal to living organisms as well as external as one would talk of genetic engineering. The transmigration of the soul would also demand a parallel subjective universe, but it is not the only explanation. Every religion that has existed should not be objectionable to intelligence coming from something other than electric fields.

IQ testing is only one piece of the puzzle of what makes up intelligence. Poor learning will result in a lower score, a better environment will provide better learning, and genetics will determine the characteristics of artificial intelligence in the same way as eye, hair, and skin color. The condition of the brain will determine the effectiveness of interfacing between artificial and real preexisting intelligence. Brain damage will disable the ability of real intelligence to effectively execute decisions and choice.

The typical student of any science is conditioned to accept that which is taught in his own field and usually ignores writing about his subject coming from other fields. The reason for this nature is a political process. To succeed means to get published and to get published with acceptance means to publish what the science community wants to hear. We gravitate to our own type of intelligence. Typical exams produce and foster a certain type of intelligence that in turn promotes its own kind. Such is the nature of intelligence. It gravitates to its own regardless of any form of genetics, environment or learning. Such would explain why a preexisting intelligence would favor a particular culture, parent or even linage. It would also indicate why types of intelligence gravitate to professions totally opposite certain environmental factors. This gravitation is a very strong point in favor of free will, for if there were no free will, a preexisting intelligence would not have a choice of culture, linage or type of people to gravitate toward. Mixing up marriage differences would then perhaps mix up learning and intelligent types for the good of man and give each individual an artificial part that would affect his environmental factors. This would give variety and opposition to life, and would be far better in cultures without principles. Too much gravitation to the same type can produce self-righteousness, fundamentalism, and bigotry unless the culture is driven by principles and understanding. Without meaning, we become revolutionary to our own destruction and the destruction of others.

Free will has not been disproved by science nor can science find a gene that even suggests that the will to choose is inherited. We are conscious and unconscious—thinking beings of unfathomable abilities, which cannot be explained as one would explain a machine. We can dissect the brain. We can even put it asleep but we cannot stop this personal identity from acting freely. Even death has proved intelligence to be continuous when the body has maintained momentary death. This memory of being separated for a moment suggests a different kind of consciousness. For while normal consciousness is anesthetized this other consciousness remembers events like we remember dreams when we awaken suddenly.

The computer expert talks of artificial intelligence as if it can do anything a human being can but without the type of free will consciousness the human has. Of course there are a wide range of movies and novels that suggest the possibility just like there are a wide range of movies and novels that take us backward and forward in time, but intuition counters every attempt to do this kind of thinking. For some reason we enjoy the possibilities because they suggest a special type of immortality that is within us that does not require the responsibility taught to us of religious philosophy. Fantasy proliferates for the same psychological reasons as any religion. All I have to do is believe and it will come to pass as I desire without the proper conservation law, evolution, or work put into the system. It is like getting something for nothing without adding value. Such is the mind of the modern investor and the modern religious model. This whole section of magical believing is manifest as a denial of responsibility in exchange for some artificial immortality. The atheist does not have a monopoly on this need. It is important to understand that what drives the atheist to object to school prayer drives the religious believer to accept grace without doing anything. The psychological motive is very similar.

Psychology does not study this concept nor does education. The reason for this comes from our educational system that weans out the conceptual mind in favor of the linguistic. The kinetic mind is pushed into sports and the conceptual mind has to suffer developmental classes and thus grows up intimidated just because responses are slow as a child. Einstein had trouble with the rudiments of math but saw concepts that few could see. The Bible refers to Moses and Enoch as slow in speech but eventually they became leaders of nations. The various types and intensities of intelligence are assumed to be hereditary because the parents are generally intelligent. Such is not entirely the case as with IQ but it is as to intelligent types. If intelligence were truly hereditary a couple of opposite intelligence types would have children that represented a composite. I think that if psychology were to study the differences of intelligence with heredity they would find that if the child represents a certain type, one of the parents or grandparents would be of the same type. It might be found that linguistic intelligence may be more artificial while conceptual may be more preexistent. Types also could come from the mix rather than one or the other.

Intelligence cleaves unto intelligence of the same kind, but when young human beings choose partners, there is a tendency to select one who fills a void. Intelligence finds the same kind of person boring at a young age. It is not until they mature that do they begin to seek friends of the same sort. This is good in that a society lacking principles and ethics gets mixed, but it becomes difficult for many children because we do not see the problem.

This effort to define intelligence has no scientific evidence other than experience, religious conviction, and intuition. I offer the explanation to those who are looking for a better view and since I have found that typical authority has missed the mark in much of science, the opinion here is justified. I thus conclude that the physical aspects of intelligence can be considered an objective control field, but the dynamic aspects would be subjective. This gives personal and individual identity as one might refer to as spirit or soul. I would emphasize, however, that the dynamics inherent in intelligence provide us with the origin of subjectivity and the essence of reason.

I am inclined to introduce a third type of intelligence that is neither totally artificial nor totally preexistent. It could be a combination in some way. It would be a dynamic aspect of both as they react through the current of a magnetic field. It would be like turning on the system. This level shuts down, to some degree, during sleep or perhaps very deep hypnosis. Another way would be to explain it this way: The first would be free choice voluntary intelligence; the second would be artificial involuntary intelligence; and the third would be consciousness or something that ties the two together. This consciousness could also be represented by three concepts at play rather than total sleep and total awareness. I would suggest those to be unconsciousness, faith consciousness, and fear consciousness. I also suggest that the typical concept of hypnosis is not as much a sleep state as normally suggested, but a faith conscious state. While we are awake, we vacillate from faith to fear. In the morning after dream unloading we may be more faith orientated,

The Platonic Idiom

while at late night we may be more fear orientated, especially if we cannot sleep. Depression may be more fear orientated. These concepts are only suggestions, but experiment could perhaps research it. Emotional and mental problems could also be fear-based consciousness. Drugs would certainly help because they would alter the consciousness, as would hypnosis. But because we are able to unload our fear in nightmares, it is important that sleep becomes a regular process. The pineal gland begins to release melatonin just for this process when the sun goes down. Excessive nightlife is detrimental to this process.

Essentially, we are left with consciousness, which no technology can really explain other than that the application of a magnetic-like current relationship turns on consciousness. In the case of a physical computer, there are standby and hibernation levels that do not require the computer to be rebooted or resurrected in classical terms. I toy with the word resurrection because of the ability to destroy a computer, but save the program that will run perfectly well on another computer with the same processor and operating system.

Computers can give us analogs to help understand intelligence, but consciousness is still a perplexing problem. Consider that a human being can remain in a coma for months and with no conscious recollection during that time, but so-called near death experiences seem to preserve out-of-the-body conscious memory. Dream states indicate that consciousness is very active, but we do not remember these dreams unless we awaken during or at the end of a dream. Hypnosis attempts to explain that there are various levels of consciousness. And though the critical mind can be separated in degrees, it is virtually impossible to get a person to do something under hypnosis that will present forms of anxiety. The critical mind may be put to sleep sufficiently to lower one's inhibitions, but not sufficiently to get someone to do something that is not ethical to his standards. Consciousness is like awareness. It sometimes enhances and at other times suppresses. Medical reports talk of a person being unconscious due to injury, while hypnotists talk of controlling the unconscious by putting the conscious to sleep. Under hypnosis, a person can communicate and answer questions, but try to get a person asleep to carry on a conversation. Under hypnosis one can recall details from his memory, but consciously the memory is not as vivid.

There are so many apparent contradictions about consciousness and there are so many ways of looking at it, that the only way to make real sense out of consciousness is to define four aspects: They are processing, memory, buss interfacing and peripherals. This is the same organization of a computer, but we can change the terms to intelligent relating, memory capacity, and biological interfacing to the brain and autonomic nervous system. This gives us a dichotomy of two realities intertwined in some way that seems to suggest a possible separation in degrees and areas. Brain damage would suggest a physical disconnection affecting certain abilities and hypnosis would suggest a synthetic separating. Since communication is a two-way process, it is important to have ways of providing this communication. Sleep may be the way of removing intelligent waste and study may be intelligent nutrition. The alcoholic can do synthetic damage to waste removal by numbing certain brain connectivity. The alcoholic cannot obtain the deep sleep needed and thus cannot remove the waste build up. Upon withdrawal, the alcoholic sees dreams while awake in order to deal with proper intelligent waste removal. Intelligent waste is like a garbage dump of fear and of things not logical. It is like role-playing. This works even if we are awake when we are taught to punch a pillow as if we are punching something real that we hate.

This interfacing of biological intelligence with real entity intelligence is a far better way to explain the various concepts of consciousness. To be unconscious is a synthetic separation. To talk of the unconscious mind is to talk of real intelligence. This use of unconscious can be misleading. In one way it is separation and in another way it talks of something different. When one is unconscious, it is the artificial intelligence that is still at play because it does not need a conscious connection.

The Platonic Idiom

Real intelligence is always working, but is not unconscious as one would describe sleep. To talk of an unconscious mind is a misnomer. Unconscious implies sleep to some degree and the deeper mind does not go into a state of sleep. Unconsciousness is a degree of separation of synthetic and real and does not describe either side. To put it plainly, consciousness is varying degrees and types of connectivity while unconsciousness is varying degrees and types of separation. The unconscious does define a mind, but it can define a state of connection to that mind. Psychology has twisted the term used by medicine to talk of a mind outside or inside separate from consciousness as if we have a conscious mind. Consciousness is the degree and type of connection and has nothing to do with a separate mind. Consciousness is a connection in the same way a monitor is a connection to the computer.

If science could look at two different realities such as biological or synthetic intelligence that dies and real or identity intelligence that evolves, words could be defined more clearly and concepts could be explained with a greater degree of understanding without the many paradoxes and mystical ideologies. Keep in mind that hypnosis may be a greater connectivity to memory aspects and a lesser connectivity to emotional aspects of intelligence. Connectivity is not only as one would describe the amount of volts, but also it could be the shutting down of some connection and increasing voltage, so to speak, of others. Death is a total disconnection until the synthetic or biological side stops functioning. The soul is nothing but a living connectivity. For lack of a better word in antiquity, spirit was used to describe real identity intelligence that was never created or made, but has evolved. The religious concept of breathing life into a biological organism fits well with the idea of connectivity to a living soul.

It is interesting to study the concept of fear and how it comes to play in consciousness. Generally speaking, a hypnotist can soften one's fear of something by suggestion or disconnection, but fear is there as an underlying element. Every human being from child to adult knows that dream outlets may help keep fear at bay, but fears will eventually determine what we believe, how we sin, how we get ahead, and the many symbols we create to deny it. It is apparent that a religious conviction can be just as appropriate in covering one's fear as a scientist's denial of the subjective reality thus defined.

Life is often a terror to intelligence, but consciousness puts on a face that creates the impression of peace or what we usually term a positive attitude and a phony demeanor. This self-dishonesty causes a problem. The fear builds up despite our conscious attempt to scare away reality. We even create symbols of heroism, immortality, and self worth in order to form some level of conscious denial of our fear of death and of rejection. We do the strangest things to cover up. But like a dam, denial eventually busts. We dream at night symbolic events of actual fear. For this reason, we come to understand that sleep is needed to unload the garbage build-up of all things fearful. Even though we talk of pleasant dreams, the monsters come out under the deepest form of sleep—only to wake us upon our rise to consciousness.

It is a tug of war for us and perhaps the reason the masters had different ways of dealing with the problem of fear. There are two universes at play and we consciously struggle to keep a good connection. It is this dynamic relationship of individual intelligence and artificial intelligence that seems to be something we need to learn how to manage. Some reach salvation and others do not. I use salvation in a broad sense and not as one would relate to sin, although overcoming the need to sin can be a part of the process.

I would strongly maintain that when we develop our abilities to define things clearly, we are on the road to salvation. When the parent instills understanding rather than just obedience, the child becomes more responsible. Education should be insight based rather than memory or command based. Schoolmaster techniques are only effectual when the parents and culture are of the same mind. With modern awareness, the child is no longer under cultural guidelines. Our only salvation is to think and learn to think with meaning. This separates us from so much development of artificial intelligence and in turn develops our personal identity. Too much artificial development can cause serious problems in society. The run-a-way computer concept is not too wrong. It does not have values that have been properly developed. Those values come from personal identity intelligence and not from a biological robot.

The intellect is fed by understanding the three aspects of reality and not by dwelling upon one or the other. This is a subjective process symbolically displaying all three realities in a complete rational statement. When we write we do the same. When we reason, we should consider a synthetic arrangement of the subject, verb and object and determining the rational truth through the principle of conservation just as we consider the objective truth through conservation. Conservation and meaning are at the heart of subjecting reasoning.

The idea that intelligence is objective as all known matter is objective is an assumption based upon a belief system denying wisdom as an attribute. The idea that intelligence is objective also makes love something molecular requiring self-interest as the motivating force.

Samuel Dael

7. Subjective Reality and Reason

The will to conceive and to define suggests that we are a greater composite of some entity other than the electric elements science has given us to understand. The complexity of this ability is far greater than the complexity of a single human cell. We are even greater than the artificial intelligence programmed into electric matter we know as the computer, and we are greater than the artificial intelligence programmed in animals and even the base portion of the brain that seems to run things independently of conscious thought or will. The free will aspects that suggest choice and the ability to conceive come from some form of intelligence that fears and carries motive to cover fear. One must respect the probability of a preexistent intelligence rather than autonomic processes coming from artificial intelligence. Free will defines the difference and free will suggests something from a different universe than simple electric matter. What does this intelligence do that the electric properties of a brain cannot do? I do not mean to imply that we should speculate upon the physical workings of intelligence, but I do suggest we consider the processes of intelligence and the ability to reason. This reasoning portion and the ability to choose are what truly make intelligence subjective.

There will be an attempt to avoid the overly synthetic forms of logic. Rather it will be emphasized that reason is a natural by-product of the intelligent ability to define and relate words to a reality. Some cannot reason in some respects as well as others because of the type of intelligence they possess, therefore a common mathematical language, using subject, verb, and object should present a simpler basis of reasoning. Anything beyond this is not conducive to our understanding other than the attempt to illustrate that words must fit a particular reality. I will consider a more innovative presentation of reason than what is presented in sophisticated books on logic.

The intelligent ability to give meaning to something and to give it a name indicates profound capacity. When each human mind first begins to babble in an attempt to communicate, it seems more certain that we can conceive before we can communicate. To conceive a concept seems much more interesting than the common language in which we do communicate. Conceiving is a different language that perhaps holds images that reflect what we think. But in order to communicate what we conceive we must have common definitions that keep us on track with other human beings and provide the ability to relate to one another. Most any intelligence can babble a phrase, but to understand what the babbler conceives is far more difficult. How many times do we hear an eloquent speech, but are unable to conceive what is babbled? We think one is intelligent because of the ability to grasp words to express what is meant. Some perceptions and concepts may be beyond normal language and thus the babbler appears unintelligent. If our language is void of needed words to express what we want, or if the meanings to words have been altered in reality by those who communicate with us, then we are surely in darkness When we share common terms that represent what all conceive we most certainly have exchanged knowledge. If we cannot communicate because we do not have the terms, the world around us will not benefit from our knowledge. The ability to teach and learn knowledge is the ability to define and use terms effectively.

A book having a chapter titled *The Early Development of Objective Reason* contradicts a sense of meaning for subjectivity. It has been the norm for a century or so to talk of objective truth, but objective reason tells us little about developing the subjective capacity to reason. To some degree reason has been used to prove external existence and determine by logical process that what one observes and reasons appropriately can become the objective truth. This should not bother us, but the concept of objective reason as if reason is outside the intelligent self is contradictory. Perhaps there is a misunderstanding about what objectivity really is. The scientists may ask if the process is objective. To be objective in this regard is not to allow emotion into the process. This labels subjectivity with nothing but fearful emotion. To be truly subjective is to be definitively rational. Emotion is more often a lack of clear definition shackled with tradition. Tradition is molded by false emotion and fear rather than reason. To go contrary to one's tradition eventually develops a poor attitude toward reason. Saying that we need to be objective does not solve the problem. We need to deal with fear and motive. This is overcome by defining our terms clearly.

True objectivity has exterior existence that cannot be controlled except by natural law. Subjectivity has interior existence that cannot be manifest except by rational law. Reasoning is to subjectivity as conservation is to objectivity. In this sense, to be objective is to obey the laws of conservation. If we want to be subjective we must obey the laws of reason. The basic law of reason should say that we should have as much conservation of meaning in our words as we find conservation in objective existence. As compared to objectivity, subjective reason abides by laws in the same manner as material conservation, but the laws are subjective laws and not laws pertaining to electric matter. It might do us well if we delved into a comparison more fully rather than lay down various methods of synthetic logic and traditional reason. There are two general conservation laws and each can be divided. The first of two main laws is:

Conservation of MASS and the conservation of ENERGY

Modern physics would consider mass and energy convertible. This issue was dealt with earlier. But conservation is still the most fundamental principle in objective reality. It is important to realize that mass is a measure of physical components while energy is a measure of all action of those components. This concept separates the two conservation laws and does not allow conversion. The attempt here will be to explain the corresponding laws of conservation to reason. The nature of defining would suggest the following:

Conservation of MEANING and the conservation of REALITY

Meaning would be the net result of all components of a term's definition while reality would be the net reality state of all components. Once a meaning of a term is fully clarified, intelligence is able to conceive a single concept without the need to refer to all the components that originally developed the term. The single concept is the reality state. A problem usually surfaces when one person sets a different reality state to a term than another. This reveals motive and fear, which we are attempting to overcome. This war between clarity of meaning and emotional fear is due to the aspects of intelligence being an evolving entity and not a result of deterministic objectivity. Conservation, however, works in reverse. In objectivity conservation is deterministic naturally, but with subjectivity indeterminism must be overcome through a choice of sound meaning. It is like the will chooses deterministic factors in meaning rather than remain a prisoner of fear—a by-product of becoming more intelligent.

Even though each component of a term may have differing realities, the net result can be only one and this reality must be the correct one. This is the essence of overcoming fear and the soul of predicativism. A single component term or even the net compilation of several terms must fit one correct reality. When we communicate, individuals must maintain this same correct reality, otherwise one demonstrates motive by attempting to cover his fear by changing the reality of the terms used.

In physics the term energy has components of mass, space, and time which are three different realities, but the term energy can only represent one of the three. If space is subjective, time predicative, and mass objective, which reality is energy? This question is asked in hopes of discovering a method for

The Platonic Idiom

conserving reality to a term in addition to the traditional concept of conservation in meaning. That is the essence of this section. This may sound pedantic to some because it is not a principle of philosophy. I think we fail in this because it is something we intuitively know, but forget to apply conservation correctly. Knowing the reality of a term is more natural than assumed, but the attempt here will be to compare this natural process with mathematics in order to obtain a more solid basis for considering the reality of a term as an important criteria.

Conservation in meaning is to maintain the sum of the components. If you change the meaning of a component you also change the meaning of a term. Neglecting the conservation of meaning of any component distorts the meaning of the new term in question. Conservation of meaning is maintained in all the components on one side of the equation while the net sum or net proportion of a new term on the other side of the equation is also conserved as to reality as well as meaning. This is like saying that the term *patience* cannot be subjective to one person and predicative to another. Consider that those who select subjective have one set of component terms and those who select predicative have a different set of component terms. This means that changing the reality of a term must of necessity change the meaning. It is like changing the mass of a body by changing the energy. It is the reverse. You change the energy of a body by changing the mass. Likewise you change the reality of a term if you change its component meaning.

Consider the action of energy as predicative, but the components are objective, subjective, and predicative respectively. This is intuitive. If we think of the mass that carries the energy we are thinking of an objective component. If we think of the velocity of the mass we realize that this term has two components—one of space and the other of time. Velocity is intuitively predicative action, but how can we know this for sure? The rule is that the proportional term such as *velocity* or *energy* carries the same reality as the modifying component on the other side of the equation. This also tells us that meaning can be expressed algebraically? Consider that some components of a term will modify other components or all components can be added to the total meaning. If a term implies two simultaneous and distinct component definitions, how is this expressed algebraically? Consider the term bachelor. One definition implies an objective man and the other will be the predicate state of being unmarried. We thus have two definitions and two realities. At first glance the equation may be something like addition:

Bachelor = Man + Unmarried
as compared to:
5 = 4 + 1

Man is an objective state and *unmarried* is a predicate state and each has a component meaning that perhaps is added to give us the meaning of the term *bachelor*. As compared with the mathematics, the summation of the two terms equals the meaning of bachelor. Also we need to ask what the reality state of Bachelor is. In algebraic manipulation, you cannot logically move a + unmarried to the other side of the equation and produce a negative state of being unmarried without changing the result. Even though the calculation and logic work, the meaning of bachelor is lost. The result would negate the *unmarried* to become *married*. What would be left is simply the objective *man*. *Bachelor* would lose its unmarried status. This would null the meaning of *bachelor*, but would preserve the term *man*.

Bachelor − Unmarried = Man
as compared to:
5 − 1 = 4

The term *unmarried* is really a modifier of *man* and not a separate component as in addition. The equation should really be listed as:

$$\text{Bachelor} = \frac{\text{Man}}{\text{Unmarried}}$$

In this case *bachelor* and *unmarried* are interchangeable algebraically. One does not negate the other as in the earlier example. This may indicate that the essence or reality state of *bachelor* is predicative rather than negating *unmarried* to produce objective *man*. Another way of looking at this relationship is to understand that *man* and *unmarried* are directly proportional while *bachelor* and *unmarried* are inversely proportional. We know the meaning of *man* and the modifying meaning of *unmarried*. Together they produce the meaning of bachelor. Is it the modifier that determines the reality? It certainly contributes to the meaning of *bachelor*. In rational statements, modifiers create direct proportional equations rather than what perhaps could be called additive equations. This brings us to ask about indirect proportions.

Using mathematical equations will show the difference as to proportions more clearly.

2 in x 2 in = 4 sq. in.

The above is an inverse proportion. In order to keep the 4 square inches constant one of the dimensions of 2 inches can be increased to 4 but the other has to be reduced to 1. This is what is meant by inverse proportion. Note that the reality with both 2-inch components is spacial. This means that the term *sq. inches* is also spacial in reality. The inverse proportion between the two multipliers must have the same reality such that you cannot multiply different realities as one would try to multiply 2 inches (subjective space) by 2 seconds (predicate time). Thus, if we move *unmarried* to the other side of the equation to become a multiplier with *bachelor* in order to create an inverse proportional relationship, the two terms would carry the same reality; otherwise they are not inversely proportional.

$$\text{Bachelor} \times \text{Unmarried} = \frac{\text{Man}}{1}$$

The above gives us a similar result as the equation of addition, but it shows that *bachelor* and *unmarried* manifest the same predicate reality. This comes from the algebraic interchangeability of *bachelor* and *unmarried* and their inverse proportional relationship. It seems that the modifier of a direct proportional relationship of *man* carries the essence of the reality. It must be asked if this is due to just being a modifier or is it because of its predicate nature. In physics we understand that time is the basic modifier called the denominator and it also represents the predicate reality in physics.

A direct proportion is two different realities, as space divided by time would be directly proportional and give us velocity. Velocity is inversely proportional to time and thus would be predicative as illustrated above. But do we multiply velocity by time to produce space by simply moving time to the other side of the equation?

Miles per hour x hours = miles

This is like saying five miles per hour times five hours equals twenty-five miles. This is logical and maybe not practically useful, but it does illustrate the manipulation of the terms is correct. It also illustrates that the term speed, as in miles per hour has two terms and two realities; but as has been suggested that it should only manifest the reality equal to the modifier. When we say miles per hour, we are talking about two realities, but when we say speed do we think of the space traveled or do we think simply of how fast we are going as one would say he was going fifty without any concept of the distance traveled to reach that speed? This expresses the intuitive nature of taking the modifying reality and applying it to the proportional term. Mathematics always carries the two realities together as in speed equals miles per second. But language does not consider all of the components when communicating terms. This is appropriate as long as the net reality is maintained.

Physics does not say that time is predicative or that space is subjective. This is intuitively understood; otherwise the equations would not make any sense. If space and time were of a similar reality you would be able to multiply one by the other. You would never be able to divide space by time if they were of the same reality. Modern physics attempts to treat the meaning of space as physically objective calling attention to warped space. What is understood intuitively in physics should be the norm rather than strangeness, but when there is a tendency to change the reality of a term, it affects the meaning and vice versa. It also affects the intuitive ability of intelligence to understand the truth. Without understanding, authoritative tradition becomes stronger than good sense. You find this in religion, politics, and modern physics. Tradition aligns with a sense of relative magic rather than responsibility to truth and conservation. Incorrect realities eventually undermine the truth. Philosophy is so diverse simply because it has neglected the concept of three realities and the need to apply the correct reality to each term.

The whole concept is that in order for conservation to mean anything directly to related terms (such as *space/time*), the denominator must modify or break apart the numerator into a single component. In mathematics this is a particular amount of space for one second of time. In reason this would be a particular state of a term expressed in the modifier. A particular state of *man* can be expressed in the modifying term *unmarried*. In velocity we say *space per second,* but the reality is expressed in a single term *speed*. Logic says *unmarried man* but intelligence has provided a single term that in reality we refer to as *bachelor*. We can hold fast to mathematics and logic, but must realize the intelligence must simplify concepts in order to canvas a vast amount of data. If we stay with immense information and never generalize, we eventually lose our sense of reality.

Consider the definition of chair as having four legs, a seat, and something to support the back while the reality is distinctively objective as opposed to a subjective or predicative chair. The obvious reason is because all of the components are objective. This simple concept is self-evident or intuitive but comes from a distinctive equation rather than a proportional one such that:

Chair = four legged + seat + back support

In a distinctive statement, all components are of the same reality but there is a distinct difference between each component. In the above, each component term is objective making the term *chair* objective. A distinctive statement does not deny the objective as Plato suggested. It gives meaning to it. Without the reality of the objective there would be no need to show a distinction. Plato never considered the conservation of reality, thus making *chair* objective and not subjective. Plato considered the essence as subjective rather than the proper and correct reality for a term. The fundamental truth is that essence pertains to the correct reality and even though the meaning of chair might be more precise than the term chair alone, it is the reality (objective in this case) that determines the essence. The most important point to emphasize in regard to Plato's method is that meaning is not a subjective methodology. It is a predicative or axiomatic process evolving into an algebraic expression. Just because the definition might be placed in the mind for analysis does not make meaning subjective. Meaning is a dynamic process. It is not stagnant. This is fundamentally why we need to place the correct reality upon each term in order to prevent any form of Platonic or objectivist meandering of terminology.

One might think that the expression, "The chair sits there" is predicative, but this denies the conservation of reality across the equation in regard to chair. The chair is still objective as determined by its original subordinate terms and not due to its linguistic use. The objective state of the subordinate terms determines the objective state of the term *chair* regardless of how it is arranged in a sentence. The term *sits* has its own predicate reality and does not affect the term *chair* other than to modify its objective condition. This is what verbs do. If they modify an object, they modify objective reality, and if they modify a subjective term, they modify subjective reality. The reality of a term is eternal and when thwarted not only is reality changed, but meaning also is changed. Meaning and reality must be conserved.

The Platonic Idiom

Consider this mathematical expression:

Five Pennies + Two Nickels + One Dime = One Quarter

If the same were a rational expression, the plus sign would be the connective *"and"* and the equal sign would be *"are"* with quantitative values assigned to the mathematical modifiers *five, two, one,* and qualitative or definitive terms inherent in *pennies, nickels, dime, and quarter.* This is a simplistic comparison but does illustrate that distinctive rational statements are exactly equal to mathematical liner statements. The same would apply to proportional statements. Just take the component *five pennies* and note that mathematically it would be *five x pennies* or *pennies x five*.

The meaning of a penny is the unit in common with *quarter, dime* and *nickel.* The meaning of each is a direct proportional relationship as:

$$\text{Penny} = \frac{\text{Quarter}}{25} = \frac{\text{Dime}}{0} = \frac{\text{Nickel}}{5}$$

The use of numbers indicates that all three meanings are quantitative and not qualitative as indicated above. This correction illustrates that *quarter, dime* and *nickel* though rational terms that we would think are qualitative—they are not. They are qualitative in the type of metals, but quantitative as to meaning. Qualitatively they are objective metals, but quantitatively they are subjective. The reason being is that 25, 10, and 5 are subjective modifiers. Numbers do not have physical existence other than ink on a paper or a light image on a computer screen. If the expression "25" is subjective then transposing as below would indicate that *penny* is also subjective.

$$\text{Penney} \times 25 = \frac{\text{Quarter}}{1}$$

The objective realities of these coins are metals, but numbers determine their meaning. All numbers are subjective modifiers, as any adjective would modify a noun. This is a perfect example of subjectivity being more real than objectivity.

Plato would be right in this regard when it comes to legal tender. The subjective values assigned do have more conserved value than the objective metals used in transactions.

Modification clarifies a particular component. This is essentially what a denominator in mathematics does to the numerator. Time, for example, calls attention to a particular part of the total space. When space modifies pounds, it calls attention to a particular part of the total mass. Pounds they are, but they may give a slightly different look at modification and reality because a pound itself represents a net proportion rather than a linear definition. This may force us to look deeper into the process of reality. Consider the modification of reality in this proportional equation where *pounds* state a proportional term in its own makeup.

$$\text{Pressure} = \frac{\text{Pounds}}{\text{Square Inch}}$$

Pounds, like mass, exhibit objectivity and *square inch* is subjective. Thus *pressure* is *lbs per square inch* or a direct proportion between what appears as objective pounds and a subjective square inch. This would appear to make the reality of pressure subjective because the modifier is subjective. It is time a clarification is illustrated. Pounds, like mass, manifest the intuitive idea of how much matter there is in an object. In everyday usage, pounds are more commonly referred to as weight, or the strength of the gravitational pull on an object as measured in units of force. Force is a predicate term because time is the modifier. In this case time is inversely proportional to mass as in:

$$\text{Mass} \times \text{Time Square} \times \frac{\text{Space}}{1}$$

The above is derived from:

$$\text{Mass} \times \frac{\text{Space}}{\text{Time Square}} = \text{Force}$$

The Platonic Idiom

How can mass and time be of the same reality? In this case mass is a unit of force and modified by time and therefore predicative. It all depends upon what we think of mass whether as units of matter or units of force—being more active as is energy. The difference is also manifest between gravitational mass usually referred to as weight and inertial mass usually referred to as the amount of matter. Because of these differences, measurements can be different if gravity varies.

The question arises—should we make mass predicative rather than objective? In case of momentum of an automobile the equation usually does not include friction caused by gravity. The friction is predicative, but the mass is still objectively the same. A decrease in momentum is due to a force, which is a loss of energy that is predicative. There is not a loss of mass in the inertial sense. So force, friction, pressure and energy are all predicative. This seems to change the rule that the modifier does not determine the reality as in the case of pressure above. Pressure does receive the modifier of time coming from pounds, as in gravitational mass. This would indicate that time or any verb is always a determining factor if it is a modifier at any point in the equation.

Now let us consider the verb of mathematics. For something to be equal with something else is predicative in the stagnant or subjective sense as in mathematics. As in the case of numbers considered subjective as having defined values rather than ink on the page, equality also has a defined value. Does this make mathematics subjective or predicative as to reality? Does equality modify the equation or does time? Does this give us a difference between something defined by the mind and something defined by existence? One can easily say that mathematics is a creation of the mind, but it does equal what is also in existence. If objective existence does not receive the action of the verb *equality*, which in turn agrees with the equation laid out by the mind for analysis, the equation is wrong and needs to be corrected. The equation like any statement has a subject, verb, and object. This is all in the mind, but is a description of existence. This whole process is a predicative process incorporating all of reality with emphasis upon the verb *equality* between subjectivity and objectivity. The definition processes in meaning and the rational processes in mathematics are holistic predicative processes. If it were not for these predicative processes, we could not know the out there world. When we think only in subjective and objective realities we mistakenly put mathematics and meaning in the subjective as perhaps Plato would. Predicativism abhors such an attempt. The essence of intelligence is to phantom the dynamics. This is a participation of the predicate. If we want to dream and imagine, this is fine, so let it so be, but it is not truth without the predicate link to the out-there world. In understanding terms we need to put reality to those terms in order to avoid fantasy designed to cover our fear of the world and separate us from objectivity. The reality of terms is the link between understanding what is and what is not. Thinking of the reality of *pressure* as predicate action helps us fathom objectivity. This is far more intuitive than one would think, but using some law rather than using our intuition in placing a reality to a term has sufficiently been tried here in order to show the importance as to reality. Terms have meaning and they also have reality. It is like a particle having mass and also energy. The energy of a term is the reality state that the term implies in addition to the meaning.

It has been illustrated that a distinctive equation is linear and similar to an additive equation. All components are of the same reality, thus making the term of the same reality. This is like listing several synonyms and perhaps negating any antonym. Proportional equations are of two types. One is a direct proportion with a predicate modifier to define the term and reality. When a numerator is a direct proportion itself, the predicate of that proportion determines the reality. The other type of proportion is an indirect or inverse proportion of like realities or differing realities.

Can a rational equation be created to illustrate a similar predicate proportion as was done with *energy* or $E=mc^2$?"

The Platonic Idiom

Consider the following:

Faith = substance or work given x conviction or confidence [2]

If the above is true, faith would be like energy and would be a predicate proportion that would have nothing to do with subjectivity. If substance or labor were zero, then faith would be zero regardless of the conviction. Likewise, if the conviction or confidence were zero, faith would also be zero. The reality of faith is in the action or total dynamics and not merely in a belief. Conviction and confidence are more than a belief. It is like really believing sufficiently to give of substance or labor. Faith is predicative rather than subjective as in positive thinking. If you think of doing something in the mind sufficiently to cause you to act, then faith is achieved, but without the action faith is null as when one tries to multiply something by zero. The symbolic squaring of confidence or conviction tells us that the substance might be small as in a small gift, but the love may still be greater than the gift because the conviction is so great.

The reason for using the above is to illustrate our tendency to change the reality of a term—especially in religion. Take the scripture by the apostle Paul:

> By grace are ye saved through faith; and that not of yourselves: it is the gift of God. Not of works, lest any man should boast.
>
> Eph. 2:8-9

The "grace vs. works" controversy has been raging since Martin Luther's time and perhaps since the era of Peter and Paul. Roman Catholics today tend to believe that salvation requires certain works (giving of substance or labor), while the Protestants' most often are quoted as being saved by grace only. The answer can probably be dealt with in Paul's following remark:

> For we are his workmanship, created in Christ Jesus unto good works, which God hath before ordained that we should walk in them.
>
> Eph 2:10

Religious fanaticism does not consider all the meaning of all the words on a subject. It does not consider the intuitive reality. It only considers what it wants to hear. It is not much different in philosophy, politics or physics. If we study every word we might get both a better meaning and a better reality concerning about the terms. "God ordained that we should walk in *works*." If this is true then grace has a meaning that is not clearly expressed by Paul. Let us take the expression *"By grace are ye saved through faith"* and try to put it into an equation.

Saved = Grace / Faith

In the above, saved is the object that receives the action of the verb *"are."* This object or result is always placed on the left by itself and the other terms are placed on the right in a proportional fashion. This is the traditional aspect of equations while language is usually the reverse. It is like turning the statement around in order to determine the object of the statement. Some terms are not needed. Such is the case with the word *ye*. The object of a preposition, such as *through*, usually suggests a predicate modifier rather than a subjective modifier because it is by which something happens. Faith, like time, breaks grace up into a particular component totally dependent upon action. The predicate reality of faith is transferred to the predicate reality of being saved. We are mistaken to think that that the reality of saved is objective.

Our equation says that *saved* and the direct proportion of *grace* and *faith* is basically equal. Saved and grace are not equal without faith and faith needs works. Grace has a constant denominator and the essence of reality is found in this denominator. Just as time is the essence of reality in the physical equation, the predicate denominator is the essence in logical statements. Here is where reality is determined for the other side. This constant represents the requirement needed to facilitate grace and also the reality that being saved lies in the word faith. We can transpose the equation in order to give some idea of the meaning of faith. They can be transposed because they are of the same reality.

Faith = Grace / Saved

This equation differs from the above because of the different proportional terms *grace* and *saved*. Saved becomes the constant essence of faith with grace directly proportional to it. Does this define the reality of faith? If we know what the reality of *saved* is, then we should know what the reality of *faith* is. Both are constant as to *grace*. We can ask, "What is constant about being saved?" Is it a constant place to live or is it having a constant spiritual companionship with God or is it a constant state of living? A place may progressively change and whom we are with may progress and change in degrees. How we live is far more of a constant essence than where we live or the people with whom we live with. How we live is predicative, but where we live and with whom we live is objective. This implies that being saved is a continuing state of living. This state is predicative. We can turn the equation around and ask, "What is constant as to faith?" Is it a moment of being positive or adhering to some rule or is it a constant way of living? A positive attitude is subjective, and following a rule is objective, but a constant way of living is predicative. If you agree with these meanings then both faith and saved are predicative. This implies a continued state of action and not an objective condition, as religious zealots would prefer. To have faith and be saved requires constant adherence to a particular way of life. It is not a subjective moment or a place or with certain persons. The reality of being saved is not objective.

This does not mean that grace does not have an objective component while retaining the reality of action. In this sense, grace is a gift directly proportional to faith and salvation. Christianity talks of the final judgment after death according to our works. Grace would simply be that final promise given sometimes before we die. Christ promised a second comforter to those chosen as in many are called but few are chosen. This would be a far better description of grace than subjective believing. It would also fit Paul's explanation "...we are his workmanship, created in Christ Jesus unto *good works*, which God hath before ordained that we should *walk* in them." To walk in good works is a state of living. It is truly a predicate reality and not subjective or objective. The grace or second comforter is given before the end because of our works in the form of substance and labor.

Those who have historically received grace would have made sacrifices sufficiently to receive it. According to particular activities in acts, those sacrifices could very well have been financial substance for the poor. Thus Paul writes to saints after the fact of receiving grace or a guarantee of salvation and not before as the modern Christian defiantly assumes. The suggestion that we are saved by just believing puts salvation as objective and believing subjective. This does not fit with reality. It could also make salvation subjective and believing subjective in order to make the statement rational, but this would simply be all in the mind with no attempt to live righteously. Modern Christianity has twisted realties in order to suit personal desires and make it easy and attractive to believe. The modern liberal and modern physicist have done the very same. The magic of relativity, government solutions, and also of salvation scares away the reality of death and gives magic to the believer.

There are other religious terms that have been distorted and it does not matter which religion. They all are guilty either of looking for some authoritative guarantee or some sort of magical believing rather than good works. It does not matter what the discipline, including modern physics and politics, term twisting reality is our favorite pastime. Predicate action is the constant reality that is most twisted by simply ignoring it. Subjectivists will try to move objectivity into their subjectivist epistemology as did Plato, and the objectivists will try to move subjectivity into their physical corner, as did the Sophists. We have been doing this ever since.

Conventional knowledge is often full of assumptions because it tends to shift reality around. Entire traditions are built around conventional knowledge because it sounds practical and is popular only because it requires less responsibility. Conventional knowledge tends to be associated with tried and true terms in order to accelerate it into popular acceptance. No one dares to question the association. The most prevalent theory today regarding this process is the assumption that democracy spawns freedom. Democracy is based upon the idea that the majority must rule and that freedom is the absence of any dictatorship. These are the basic meanings, but to associate the two incorrectly is what has become conventional knowledge.

Here is the argument against such an association: If justice for all is based upon sound principles and the majority choose not to obey these sound principles and instead vote democratically to inflict a minority, is this freedom or is it just freedom for the majority to become the dictators over the minority? No matter what one does with the meaning of the terms, there is an eventful contradiction when we link meanings that should not be linked such as democracy and freedom. The mind is so conditioned to this conventional rhetoric that it cannot see that someone along the way coined an expression to justify a lie and since the majority like the lie, it becomes tradition and darkness until a generation comes along and proves otherwise. The rebuttal would be either that laws chosen by the majority are for one's own good or that a constitution prevents tampering with minority rights. History has proved otherwise. Think about it in terms of realities. Freedom is the predicate state of each and every individual having the same freedom to vote or pursue happiness. A democracy is an objective state allowing the majority to rule by popular vote. A democracy that allows freedom to vote does not negate that the majority still rules. The predicate act of voting is carried over from freedom to the objective fact that the majority rules in a democracy. For some traditional reason, the right to vote justifies that the majority rules, but how can this be if the realities differ? If we link freedom and justice, we link better ideology because both are predicative. With justice, the majority does not rule. Rather it is principles that rule. This is like saying the constitution rules. If so, why do we have popular voting that tends to warp the constitution? Justice is a rule that applies equally to all and not to a majority or a minority. One might argue that a democracy is predicative, but ask, "Is a freedom" predicative? How is it that we can say *a* democracy, but we cannot say *a* freedom? Intuitively, one's freedom is a possessive ability. We do not possess democracy. The freedom to vote is really different than a democratic vote. The first implies a choice of representation while the latter implies the majority will rule.

Some might think the above is like hair splitting between two Christian religions for the truth. Logic tells us that religious traditions of every kind have ideologies that originators pontificated in order to gain position among petitioners. The very same process is built into the nature of politics. Just as there are errors in Christian theology, there are errors in political ideologies. We propagate what we like rather that what is truth. We propagate the ideology of democracy rather than the truth of justice. The key to justice and the enemy to democracy is representation. It is not that the majority should rule, but that every person is represented. A politician who struggles to get support of the majority by appeasing that majority is not a representative, but if he or she struggles to stand up for justice for all, then that is a true representative. Issues are for the majority to rule by, principles are what we expect a representative to rule by.

Whole doctrines could be turned around if we considered the reality of every term. That is the true nature of predicativism and the true nature of responsibility. Linking different reality concepts as one would try to link an inch with a pound in addition is like linking the majority as truth and power as responsibility. Democracy is a complex proportion as also is freedom, but the realities of these proportions differ. When we link contrary realities we do so linearly as if freedom plus democracy equals prosperity, happiness, peace or some other concept. Freedom plus justice would be a more accurate equation for prosperity, happiness and peace. Another example of reality twisting is found in modern physics. When we talk of a space-time continuum it conjures up a mystical, incomprehensible concept and in order to explain it we resort to two-dimensional analogs that make the third dimension act in rhythm to the so-called fourth. The mind can only conceive of three dimensions, as the so-called fourth is a derivative plot of time and not a direction of space. Time is the essence of all relativity concepts and not space. Time is the denominator and space is the numerator. They are directly proportional. Just because we plot time on a graph as if it is indirectly proportional to something does not change its direct nature as only a denominator or divider of reality. Relativity makes space objective and makes the uncertainty principle subjective. There is so much confusion in reality that even predicate energy changes into objective mass. It is all due to changing the reality of terms to fit a mathematical observation based on the assumption that light travels at a constant velocity in a vacuum everywhere in the universe—something only demonstrated at a fixed point on the earth relative to a certain magnetic density. When things are not rational we should question our attempt to change the reality of terms. Modern physics should be requesting its assumptions about the velocity of light.

Considering Kant's View

This thesis on reason is totally different from any classical form. It is a view derived from the structure of both mathematics and language with emphasis on the predicate. I know of no attempt elsewhere to consider the conservation of meaning and of reality in rational statements. This thesis comes from a need to understand and says understanding is both rational and intuitive. Kant argued that people cannot understand the nature of things in the universe, but they can be rationally certain of what they experience themselves. Experience is not enough to maintain a proper form of reason. Experience is a lot like observation. We are tempted to change meaning and reality to fit the observation or experience rather than question the assumptions we make and keep our realities clear. Experience and observation may be appropriate to some degree when it comes to physical things, but philosophy is loaded with ethics, metaphysics, epistemology, aesthetics, and even religion where empiricism does not work without both reason and intuition. Predicativism looks for the constant reality in the equation and is the only way to give proper meaning and reality to terms before reason can be established and understanding enhanced.

Kant also suggested that within the realm of experience, fundamental notions such as space and time are certain. He did not say it, but what makes space certain is when it is placed in the subjective and what makes time certain is when it is placed in the predicate. Kant suggested that it was experience that revealed this notion, but it is really a by-product of intuition. Intuition is often considered experience because no one wants to admit that intuition is an essential part of knowledge and understanding. Intuition comes from intelligence that affects and often colors what we experience with the senses, but we fail to admit it. Kant should have fixed the reality of terms such as space and time to prevent this meandering of modern physics. Reality checks fear from being interpreted as intuition. Since experience is based upon the observation of things mixed with intuition and even unconscious fear, assumptions are often worked into one's conclusions without regard to the proper reality. Experience does not correct this obliqueness of the mind. Unless a statement can be made into an equation with the conservation of reality working in the equation, reason cannot be claimed regardless of conditional synthetic examples.

In Kant's theory of perception in *The Critique of Pure Reason*, he maintains that our understanding of the external world has its foundations not merely in experience, but also in both experience and *a priori* concepts—thus offering both an empirical as well as a non-empiricist critique of reason, which Kant and others refer to as the "Copernican revolution."[1]

Kant's philosophy suggested two methods. One was analytic or the breaking apart for analysis and the other was synthesis or the combining of things. Synthesis should be understood to be something generally learned through one's experience and what that would bring to a proposition. If you cannot break apart the proposition for analysis to determine its parts, it would be called a synthetic proposition determined by experience. The two forms are listed:

Self-Evident:

Analytic proposition: a proposition whose predicate concept is contained in its subject concept; e.g., "All bachelors are unmarried,"

Experience:

Synthetic proposition: a proposition whose predicate concept is not contained in its subject concept; e.g., "All bachelors are happy

Self-evident is *a priori* and intuitive as expressed earlier. This seems to be antagonistic to the term analysis as in analytic proposition. It is self-evident when the concept of the verb is contained in the subject, but if we were to break apart for analysis the terms *bachelor* and *unmarried*, we would see their identity as being the same thing. Analysis still seems to be more scientific or comprehensive while self-evidence or intuition is not so comprehensive. Epistemology, starting with Kant, has selected the wrong word. Analysis is more empirical and has been associated with the scientific method. Something self-evident does not need analysis. Perhaps Kant felt that analysis eventually would yield self-evident knowledge. Predicativism would say that the essence of the concept receiving the action of the verb is contained in the subject. This is self-evident, but if one prefers analysis, that is fine too. Predicativism and Kant seem to agree. The use of terms is all that differs.

Experience is needed when the predicate concept is not contained in the subject. It seams that analysis would be beneficial in determining if *bachelors* are happy. One could also say that after enough experience one could have an intuitive conclusion that some bachelors are happy. The use of synthetic is the general consensus or synthesis of a conclusion. Perhaps this is not as self-evident as one might think. Each person's experience would synthesize different examples in determining if the synthetic propositions are true or not. The use of the word synthetic is appropriate when one considers its derivation from synthesis to combine. Modern philosophy's use of synthetic as in synthetic logic is used more to indicate an artificial proposition. This is because the term has changed meaning over time. A philosophy student would have difficulty understanding Kant in that regard. Because of its change over time, its use has been avoided.

One thing about self-evidence is that the reality of the term is manifest intuitively. To determine the same by analysis, a predicate term is determined by an indirect modifying term already determined to be of the predicate reality. It was attempted to analyze the intuition because many wish to thwart the intuitive by changing reality. Thus, the self-evidence or intuition is due to the meaning of the terms sharing a common reality as one being contained in the other. It is not due to analysis unless considering reality is a process of analysis. With intuition you do not think through it. You simply know it because of meaning. If you do think through the proposition you study the realities in conjunction with the contained meanings. This would be analysis. Kant was correct in assuming that no further knowledge was required other than to grasp the language—such as the predicate concept being in the subject (intuitively having the same conceptual meaning). On the other hand, synthetic statements are those that transcend the content of the language used. In the above case, happy may or may not refer to *bachelors*. Determining the truth of the matter requires experience before such a statement could be considered true.

Bertrand Russell, the modern philosopher primarily responsible for popularizing the view that logic or the rational statement is identical to mathematics, would also affirm that synthetic logic is concerned solely with analysis. Russell was right in the first, but differs slightly from Kant by treating logic as analysis. The tendency is to try and push for self-evidence through some synthetic processes based upon conventional assumptions. You cannot push every statement into a condition of self-evidence and, for this reason, synthetic logic clarifies by stating a proposition within an "*if*" statement. Using *if* defines the conditions and makes it possible to conclude mathematically and authentically a proposition. It should be considered that conserving reality could be more elucidating. If reality is not conserved, then the author of the statement has changed the meaning of one term in hopes of changing the reality of another.

Kant and others try to say that perception is based both upon experience of external objects and *a priori* knowledge. The external world provides those things, which we sense. It is our minds that processes this information about the world and gives it order, allowing us to comprehend it. Our minds supply the conditions of space and time to experienced objects. I think that Kant should have concluded that space and time are intuitive and not learned from reason. Also, observation and experience are predicative and depend upon the conclusion or objective existence that receives the action of observation without changing reason for which observation must agree. Changing the reality of space and time in modern physics to fit an assumed observation does not agree with reason. Not only should existence receive the action of observation, the observation must agree with reason. It is like an extension of saying that existence must agree with reason and reason must agree with existence. If not, change the assumption about observation.

Concepts are the inclusion of reason, observation, and existence and these comprise the whole of reality. In addition to this, intuition is also needed and is often neglected as the feminine side of reason. As Kant put it, "Without the concepts, intuitions are nondescript; without the intuitions, concepts are meaningless"—thus the famous quotation: "Intuitions without concepts are blind; concepts without intuitions are empty."[2] Kant meant that intuitions do not stand alone, but are a necessary part of rational statements. I think the essence of intuition is in the reality of all terms. Reason may establish a consistency of meaning, but intuition sees the consistency of reality in the same term.

Kant and others understand the principles, but fail to be able to explain it in the way predicativism explains it. The tendency for most is to assume meaning without in-depth discussion. They simply follow a dialectic argumentation without the inclusion of many minds. That is what Plato did in his *Republic*. There were so many assumptions in his meanings that the most important predicate word *justice* was never tied down correctly. In fact, justice to Plato was something the state provided as an objective goal. Justice was something forced upon the people in the same manner as communism and fascism. Plato represented the very beginning of state control and I feel certain he inspired every despot since. Plato failed to define terms first. He gave many examples of his assumed forced justice, but never attempted to define it. Plato even gave Socrates credit for his abominable ideas. I can't help but feel that Socrates was long gone and Plato used him in his dialogues because he could no longer speak for himself. Plato was a student of Socrates, but he never got the point.

Like most Platonists, philosophers have a way of making things right in their dissertations, but they never ask what we mean by justice, freedom, rights etc. Educated theorists place the responsibility in the hands of the state because they are more concerned with the way of things and their position to decide what is best for all than it is for individuals to obtain the meaning and reality of terms in order to decide for themselves. It is the meaning of words that motivate man to be responsible and to offer justice to his neighbor. It is the Platonist who seeks justice to establish himself rather gives up his life for a correct principle and a correct meaning, as did Socrates and Christ.

Essentially, I have slightly redefined reason from the traditional form. As children we naturally asked questions. As adults, we assume we know by repeating the rhetoric we have been intimidated to repeat. We are forever learning, but never come to the knowledge of the truth because we stop questioning tradition. It is the questioning that sharpens the meaning of things and eventually reveals true intent on the part of those who lead us. Most writers pontificate like preachers using traditionally accepted words that are not really fine-tuned in meaning or reality. Philosophy does the same but uses more sophisticated words that have meaning only to the establishment. In studying meaning, one can easily find that each cultural system has its own words in which the whole culture wears blinders.

Traditional adherence to incorrect meaning and reality enslaves the people. Whether in religion, philosophy, psychology or even physics, certain words are passed around with incorrect meanings as to reality. These meanings are usually accepted because every listener likes the meaning implied and the lack of responsibility that a true reality would engender.

Socrates most certainly represents a school of antiquity in which the oral methods of discussion were the source of meaning rather than the written word. The descent of western thought has forgotten this process and eastern thought has mystified it.

Samuel Dael

The Platonic Idiom

8. The Nature of the Predicate

From the beginning until even fifty years ago the realist had a criterion that had enabled him to claim factual status through logical analysis deducted from observed objects. In some cases this analysis has been acceptable indirectly, even if objects could not be directly observed. Throughout history the main opponent of this type of objective analysis has been the idealist who has had a differing criterion that allowed him to deny objective elements as real. The idealist claimed a certain status for inclusive wholes, better described as a meaning that the realist had been unable to define. After this came the pragmatist, who in his turn had a criterion different from the realist and the idealist. The pragmatist was ready to recognize as fact whatever proved to have practical significance in man's ongoing experience and refused the analytic process of the realist and the conceptual meaning of the idealist.

Philosophy seems to have come to a dilemma in trying to operate in this daring and difficult area that lies between real objects and the subjective concepts. Each worldview of differing philosophers reflects a diverse presupposition in order to draw a line between the real and the ideal. Even though Pragmatism was such an attempted line, philosophy continues a tug-of-war between the ideal and the real. This lack of equilibrium suggests the failure of philosophy. It seems that philosophy cannot come to terms with reality. For the most part it is because there is a tendency to avoid a specific reality in meaning and continually argue which reality is the only one in denial of any other.

Philosophy is too much like a game of political parties rather than a search for meaning.

Since the onset of reason there has been a tendency to think we can draw valid inferences about the facts that at any given time are accepted as such so we can arrive at a systematic explanation of them. Rationalism was supposed to give us tested help in doing this, but by what logical axioms should rationalism guide us? Different philosophical schools have proposed different answers to this process and different periods in history have been dominated by different philosophies. Psychologically speaking, each discipline has sought its piece of eminence without regard to the whole of reality. They have completely neglected the predicate reality.

It might be reasonable to cover some basics of Western Philosophy and see if it can be improved. Since Aristotle the attempt has settled upon three laws of thought.[1]

1. Law of Identity
2. Law of Contradiction
3. Law of Excluded Middle

In logic, the *law of identity* states that an object is the same as itself, such as $A = A$. Essentially, equality produces the fact that A is A. Equality makes the equation self-evident. Identity is only a highbrow word to make the law sound intellectually new to philosophy. In philosophy, the law is often mistakenly attributed to Aristotle, who actually wrote: "Now 'why a thing is itself' is a meaningless inquiry…"[2] Why man is man or the music is music is meaningless unless one were to answer 'because each thing is inseparable from itself.' The law of identity is meaningless, and to make more of it is to elevate the originators. This pedantic use of identity in philosophy is strictly artificial. In 2002 a petition drive was made to pass $A=A$ as a statutory law in Berkeley, California. Specifically, the proposed law stated that, "every entity shall be identical to itself." Any entity caught being un-identical was to be subject to a fine. The law did not pass.[3] What a waste of pedantic behavior.

The Platonic Idiom

In logic, the *law of contradiction* states that, in the words of Aristotle, "one cannot say of something that it is and that it is not in the same respect and at the same time." Plato probably made the original statement in regard to opposites when he had Socrates saying:

> The same thing clearly cannot act or be acted upon in the same part or in relation to the same thing at the same time, in contrary ways; and therefore whenever this contradiction occurs in things apparently the same, we know that they are really not the same, but different.
>
> For example ...can the same thing be at rest and in motion at the same time in the same part?[4]

Aristotle's assertion that '...it will not be possible to be and not to be the same thing' is not the statement a modern logician would call the law of excluded middle. Aristotle claimed that no statement is *both* true and false; modern theory requires that no statement can be *either* true or false. Philosophy has attempted to fine tune the three laws and Bertrand Russell clarified the laws even more:

Law of identity: 'Whatever is, is.'
Law of noncontradiction: 'Nothing can both be and not be.'
Law of excluded middle: 'Everything must either be or not be.'

When one learns computer programming with exercises in basic languages, there is the proverbial *IF* statement that guides every action in a computer program. The programmer knows intuitively what he or she wants and methodically reduces choice to a mathematical yes (1) or no (0). Choice is reserved within the programmer's domain. Essentially, we are talking about artificial intelligence. Choice is taken from us or limited artificially to *yes* or *no* and never maybe so. It is somewhat like a case in court where the witness is not allowed to explain.

Complex choices become a more advanced way of making decisions. They require real intelligence and are not artificial in any way or form. No matter how far the philosophy of logic goes, it will never be able to advance to a level of average human intelligence of good sense as long as it insists upon pedantic logic. This is because logical equations are limited to a dichotomy of if and yes and no rather than relative choice. Choice, here used, has nothing to do with arbitrary selection as if Alice in Wonderland would say, "It means what I want it to mean." Choice in classical terms means:

> The act of choosing; the voluntary act of selecting or separating from two or more things that which is preferred; or the determination of the mind in preferring one thing to another.[5]

Preferred choice is not creating what we want, but choosing what is preferred between two or more elements presented. This brings us to the word preferred:

> Literally, to bear or carry in advance, in the mind, affections or choice; hence, to regard more than another; to honor or esteem above another.[6]

Classically, to prefer something is to do so in advance. This implies something already present rather than something arbitrary after the choice is presented. There is an element of prejudice in this definition, but I do not mean prejudice due to tradition, but a type of prejudice due to intelligent learning. It is like a pre-judgment due to our ability to choose the greater rather than the lesser value. It would be like choosing things good rather than things that encourage evil. It is like choosing the right rather than the wrong as to intent. "Thou hast chosen well" is our reward rather than choosing selfishly as one would choose yes to help themselves and avoid no in order to not help themselves.

This gift to choose is almost more intuitive than deducible. It is preexistent rather than arbitrary child's play. It comes by wisdom rather than selfishness. It is what makes the programmer different from the program. It is also what makes God different than any elementary life form. It is that which increases one's intelligence rather than diminishes it.

An attempt was made in the previous chapter to introduce a system less synthetic and more intuitive. Those who resist because of tradition will certainly fall to a level of synthetic logic over time. Intelligence must be constantly expanded and less programmed in order to increase in value and judgment. That is the essence of wisdom. While knowledge may simply be a quantitative amount of programming, wisdom is the real qualifier of intelligence. Logic is too often the enemy of intelligent insight.

The following presentation is given in hopes of making more sense out of the basic laws of philosophy. This author's version would be:

1. Law of Equality
2. Law of Distinction
3. Law of Proportion

Both distinctive and proportional equations were introduced in the previous chapter in hopes of preparing the reader for the above concepts. When logic says $A=A$, it obviously reminds us of the *law of equality*. If equality is to demonstrate more than this, we need something more than a single variable. Thus the *law of distinction* raises our sights to the concept that $C=A+B$. Epistemologically, to identify is not the best word. One might identify a distinction or even a proportion just as much as if something equals itself. The law of distinction is a better law than contradiction, because distinction gives greater insight into whether something is a contradiction to something else or not. Contradiction negates as in the computer saying *no* while distinction clarifies why something does not equal itself.

If we identify a man as Bill, we intuitively say that the man *equals* Bill. Reason is somewhat irrelevant. In a distinction, definition gives us something more detailed or as Kant might say—more synthetic. Each part becomes relevant to one's understanding. The uniqueness of distinction is that it contains the hidden or intuitive component of equality. Out of two statements that are contradictory, the usual assumption is to say that only one element can be true. $A=2$ and $A=3$ draws a distinction in that they are contradictory. It is true that only one can be true, but it may also be that both are untrue. Simply seeing the contradiction is not the solution, because both distinctions in a contradiction may have a very small amount of something in common. You might be able to get a contradiction in a synthetic statement starting with *if,* but this does not resemble open discussion or normal conversation. This leads us to the *Law of Proportion.*

A proportion introduces a common element within a distinction that can provide a relationship to an apparent contradiction. Most contradictions are not much different from the contradiction between men and women or the contradiction between good and evil. The law of proportion gives us a better understanding about the act of lying when considered relationally to motive. Most judgments are based upon some sort of opposition, but we too often choose according to what we traditionally think is the greater good or what is least contradictory and not just contradictory. Judgments in life are not artificial or synthetic arguments. They are full of gray matter to such an extent that one must choose something that may not be the perfect choice as desired. In guiding our choices we should look for what two distinctions, yielding a contradiction, have in common. However small, there is always something. Of course, these are real life situations and not artificial logic manipulation. The reason logic will never solve the dilemmas in life is primarily due to looking at contradictions artificially.

Rules of logic will often give synthetic examples such as: If all men are selfish and since Bill is a man then Bill is selfish. The first distinction is between *man* and *selfish.* The second distinction here is between *Bill* and *man.* The problem with synthetics is in the word *if* as illustrated above. *If* is used because the meaning or association between men and selfishness is conjecture. The connection is presented only to prove the equation but not the meaning of the term man or selfish. In this, we escape the responsibility of meaning as to what selfishness is and what man is. The meaning of each word is so paramount that behooves us to make statements that reveal a propensity for selfishness rather than to try to determine if Bill is selfish.

The Platonic Idiom

Perhaps Bill is selfish in some areas and perhaps he has a problem regarding certain things. Essentially, the two terms *man* and *selfishness* are of differing realities. One needs to find a particular aspect of man and set that apart. That aspect becomes the predicate action that can be compared with selfishness. Using *if* does nothing for meaning and nothing for the understanding of selfishness. It also does nothing for logic. Traditional logic follows a dichotomy of true or false and the terms *man* and *selfishness* require more proportionally related concepts than yes and no. Just because nothing can be and not be and just because everything must either be or not be does absolutely nothing for wisdom and understanding. It is like having some form of robotic thinking without intuition and good sense. The law of non-contradiction and the law of excluded middle have the mentality of true and false. The philosopher condemns the religious for clinging to good and evil without a single judgment against his own pedantic tree of true and false. Although reason works like mathematics, the meaning of the terms used in reason are quite unlike those used in say physics. Space, time and mass are three basic meanings, but justice and the like take a lot more consideration as to meaning and also as to reality.

What would happen to a mathematical equation that calculated perfectly, but the terms assigned to each variable were nebulous? Synthetic logic is actually useless without sound terms. The more rigorous the mathematical logic the more rigorous should be the meaning of the terms. The terms are what Socrates emphasized. Plato and others that followed did not perform a rigorous analysis of meaning to fit their synthetic logic. Just because the syntax is correct does not give understanding to a statement. We need better meaning and a clearer demarcation of reality.

We need to set aside computer-like judgments in determining human behavior. Mostly, we are no better than the programmer who is a prejudiced person. When we enter the aspects of morality and ethics, things get complicated. We can no longer think in terms of yes or no. Here is an example: To say that one may tell a lie sometimes under stressful or mitigating circumstances produces a new or different meaning about the act of lying. This new meaning is probably not the meaning of common usage and this new meaning also tells us that the common definition of lying may not be sufficient. For some reason we have drawn a distinction in agreement to something more than the definition of what it means to lie. This new distinction seems to counter the definition that *lying = bad* and thus we have now said that *lying may = good*. We have challenged the usage of the term and justification for such an attempt must be explained by clarifying the distinct meaning of what it means to tell a lie.

Despite any form of departure, lying still seems to be misleading or bad in some way. Therefore, instead of dwelling upon the act, we need to know what drives the act. In the case of lying, we need to dwell on the subjective motive a little more. We often dwell on the act without considering motive. What we need is to find agreement between the act and the motive rather than simply dwelling on the act alone.

No one will question the need to mislead a beast in the forest away from children, but to mislead children from the truth reveals incorrect motive on the part of the one misleading. The intent becomes the real concern and not so much the act of lying or any act of misleading. Intent may perhaps be an unconscious aspect or even a personal judgment. In this scenario the act of misleading must agree with the intent. Both the subjective motive and the predicate act must show agreement. If the intent is bad, then the act is bad. What we have done is not to judge the act of lying, but to consider the intent of the lie. Many religions dwell on the act while a good legal system seeks for intent. Using the statement *lying = bad* may not define the relationship accurately and thus we may have a false statement. *Bad intent = a bad lie* is obviously in agreement and represents a better analysis. We must consider the difference between the predicate act and the subjective intent and how they relate. Acts do not exist of themselves any more than running exists without someone to do the running. The verb shows agreement between the subjective intent and the object that receives the action or definition given. This whole process indicates the relevancy of the predicate reality in relation to the subjective and objective. Above all, the necessity of agreement is paramount.

Those who use computer-like test scores to select an applicant do it out of laziness of thought. More individuals use computer decisions to justify their prejudice than they do to find the best person. Human beings want a simple solution and avoid the idea that something takes a great deal of thought. For a professor to read a paper that is full of terms he uses and those created in the discipline will prejudice his reading for that paper and will not consider the intent of the writer. The sound of the terms excites the reader more than the meaning of what is being said. Likewise, the sound of the words used by a politician excites the listener more than the meaning of what is being said. This is what perpetuates philosophical, religious, and political terms. Each seeks to become more eminent than the previous authority and in order to get that approval he talks about the same thing in the same way and changes it only to make it more synthetic. It is like the religious becoming more directed to blind obedience than understanding. Each teacher of philosophy is compelled to start with the same laws of logic and only will invite discussion that will prove more synthetic rather than invite discussion that will challenge things altogether.

Plato was attempting to become more synthetic in his presentations and less understanding as Socrates would have him do. In modern education we quote prior authority and even systemize it in our attempt to show a more particular view than the original. When a candidate withdraws he invariably becomes more general about the party in order to maintain his acceptance than to say he is different and will strive to improve that difference. Being different is not being contradictory. It is trying to see things in more relational ways rather than as the regimented good and evil. We are like Adam and Eve who prefer a dichotomy of good and evil rather than a tree of various manners of fruit. We are taught that the Tree of Knowledge is a one-sided tree of good only. This is the most devastating concept in religion. We again think that the two party political system is the only dichotomy acceptable. We make the mistake of thinking that without it we would have a dictatorship.

We must dig deeper into the meaning of things. Logic cannot be handled on the surface with synthetic dichotomies. We must discuss differences and qualify meaning. Consider the most exasperating contradiction between the liberal democrats and the conservative republicans. There are many who would like to blend the two into one, but that would not solve the problem. The human mind wants a dichotomy. Rather we must look for things in common and build from this agreement. This makes a contradiction something that can be harmonized eventually. Contradictions are paradoxes and some people love to generate paradoxes in order to prove that nothing is absolute. Others like paradoxes just to position themselves to a side opposing an opponent or to set themselves above another. This positioning does more to foster contradictions than anything else. Finding common denominators is avoided because that means we are not perfect and the opponent is also not perfect. Making a contradiction out of things is a dichotomy of human nature, thus trying to study a contradiction artificially is hopeless unless you look at it proportionally. What would it mean if presidential candidates came to the same conclusions during a debate? It would actually happen if opponents would forget that one could change his mind, forget the party and maintain open discussion sufficiently long enough and continuously, maybe extending it a day or two.

Most statements are full of assumptions in an attempt to position an idea to a particular reality rather than dig for understanding in order to find equitable meaning. Paradoxes and apparent contradictions, when broken down in order to find a common denominator, will resolve many issues and avoid the typical attempt of positioning. Positioning is nothing but polarization instead of looking at a principle with clarity. How many use freedom to prove their polarizing view? The problem is not with freedom, but with the assumptions that are built around it in order for one to position things to a specific corner. The result is more contradictions.

Assumption is born out of the fact that two opponents may have different meanings for a word. In order to resolve the differences, there is an attempt to use tradition or conventional knowledge. The nature of religion is to assume a particular meaning and over time it eventually becomes entrenched into tradition. If the meaning is wrong, then the blind lead the blind and both fall into the ditch. There is no way out from distorted meanings unless one looks back and sees the origin of distortion. This means we must study etymology as well as epistemology. Taking terms for granted has caused more confusion and chaos in the world than any tyrant. Dictators first change the meaning of freedom or some other word before they change the laws. That is the beginning of corruption and real evil. It kills in more ways than taking life.

Once meaning is seen proportionally, then we can remove contradictions. Take the statements "Love is blind" and "Love is caring." To say that only one can be true could very well be the case. This surely depends upon the meaning of love. The second probably is the true statement, but if blindness were an allegory for sacrifice for an individual, then that would suggest that both statements could be true. Reason is simply defining the terms in order to see either the assumption or the truth. Reason is not a synthetic process. It is born of wisdom and the choice of true meanings.

Things may not be as absolute as one means or as absolute as what one sees. But absoluteness can still be achieved by sharpening the meaning of the terms used. A very simple solution to the differences found in the words *apples* and **oranges** can be found in the proportion we call *fruit*. When we hear the expression that two things are as different as apples and oranges, someone is not correlating correctly. There is no distinction between apples and oranges when we apply the meaning of fruit to both. In this sense, fruit is an absolute. Fruit is the third element of a proportion and fulfills the law respectively.

Avoiding wisdom is simply the avoidance of meaning. Real knowledge is also avoided simply to maintain the status quo. We need to ask deeper questions and avoid the polarizing effects of changing the meaning of things. We should look for underlying principles and avoid dichotomies of contradiction. Opposition tells us that something needs to be done other than to throw the opponents into a ring and see who wins. Usually, the loser is the one who should have won and the majority is not always right. It all depends upon the amount of false meaning tossed around.

The three laws that I have illustrated are what will later be referred to as the realm of the subjective with distinction mentally on one side, proportion on the other, and equality the harmonic of the two. This whole concept is the intelligent ability to choose wisely. This ability considers both reason and intuition. While reason would be the ability to distinguish and intuition would be the ability to see underling common factors in what can be considered as proportional thinking, every individual has both the ability to reason and to deliver intuitive insights to one degree or another, but men are primarily gifted with reason and women with intuition.

Philosophy and science have generally relied upon reason and together they lack the broader aspect of wisdom and the ability to choose wisely. They negate intuition's ability to make a preferred choice. Consider these comparisons: Intuition uses the mind's overall faithful eye effectively while reason tests each fact for precise agreement. Intuition applies faith in axioms while reason tests meaning for invariance. Intuition trusts axioms while reason questions them. Intuition senses an axiom in relationship while reason would look at an axiom as a single distinction.

When Descartes suggested the classic axiom or self-evident truth "I think therefore I am," intuition accepts it, but

The Platonic Idiom

some of those who reason regressively wants to deny it. To continually dissect an axiom usually indicates an attempt to distort the terms. To understand an axiom means to understand the terms. What I am saying is that reason and intuition must work agreeably. In doing so, we have a harmonic process in meaning. This process is what builds understanding out of harmony and equilibrium.

To take apart a machine by every bit in order to repair it does not fix it unless you have a general knowledge of the machine, so too when one dissects meaning pedantically there is no solution if he does not understand the general picture. By separating a machine into its electronic and mechanical sections before going further, we draw a distinction. We can then ask which of the two concepts we should divide next in order to find the problem. We then divide again and again, always preserving the whole in its general parts. It is working from the general to the specific rather than starting at some arbitrary point breaking everything indiscriminately into its parts simply because we fail to work intuitively.

It might be acceptable to consider that an axiom has both distinctive and proportional characteristics or, to put it in a better way, axioms are both rational and intuitive. In some respects an axiom is similar to a definition in that equality and equilibrium are the basis of both definitive and axiomatic meaning. Definition has a new term on one side of the equation and a proportion on the other. An axiom has relational proportions on both sides. With axioms there is no new term but equilibrium of two concepts. This does not dismiss the fact that a definition of a term is an axiom if the meanings are clear. As with an axiomatic relation of two concepts, meaning must also be clear. In the case of *I think, therefore I am* there are two concepts with an implied equilibrium between *I think* and *I am*. One could say:

I think = I am

We only need to establish a clear meaning of the words *think* and *am*. In order for each term to be derived from proportions, both terms would need to be predicative as a result. If thinking is predicative as in an active process and if *am* also implies a predicate process of active awareness, the axiom would be true. If however *I am* means an inert physical body of sorts, thinking has no relation to inert objective existence. The clarity and reality of the terms must be relational. A clear definition does not always solve the problem unless reality is also considered.

Consider a basic concept of inertial mass and gravitational mass. As mentioned earlier, one is defined objectively and the other is measured from a predicative orientation even though the actual mass in question does not change under either definition. The reason for no change is that both definitions respond to the same gravitational force with the same result. Inertial mass could be predefined as a certain number of atomic particles. Gravitational mass is defined in conjunction with a gravitational force.

The two direct proportions would be given as follows if the gravitational force modified or acted upon both:

$$\frac{\text{Inertial Mass}}{\text{Gravitational Force}} = \frac{\text{Gravitational Mass}}{\text{Gravitational Force}}$$

Even though inertial mass is defined independently from the force it still reacts to the same gravitational force in the same way. In this we can equate algebraically one unknown mass with one known. We do this with a gravitational force. The result is usually referred to as weight. Suppose the inertial side has a 6-gram label applied to indicate a specific amount of atomic units. This knowledge was obtained separately from this comparison. We could then say that the unknown gravitational mass equals the 6-gram inertial mass—the difference only being that one side has a label and the other not. It is this label or prior knowledge that gives us a means to communicate or calculate a conclusion. The whole equation incorporates a complete rational thought, but the label was determined under a prior situation and independent from our current consideration. The first situation was generalized as:

Inertial Mass = 6 grams of atomic units

There is no point in trying to define what a gram is or even what atomic units are. That would not facilitate the point being made. This whole method of obtaining knowledge is circular and we have to start somewhere, so I am jumping in with the proverbial method by saying, "If the inertial mass equals 6 grams then the gravitational mass also equals 6 grams." What was obtained in a previous state of knowledge is used in the next cycle. We are looking at one single cycle of knowledge in that the definition label assigned to the left side of the equation was the result of some prior equation on the right. It is like moving the object of an equality equation from the objective side to the subjective side in the next equation in order to obtain additional knowledge.

I say the above as a matter of convention, but the point is that definition requires a complete equation surrounding the verb equality. The total concept becomes a subject for the next definition. This is how definitions become subjective and we should respect that these definitions are in the mind, but we cannot forget that they were obtained in certain respects from objectivity through the predicate meaning of equality. In addition to this, the concept of a definition becomes intuitive in the next step of knowledge. Inertial mass is intuitive in determining gravitational mass through the action of gravity. It uses the definition of a prior result as an intuitive subject or concept in the mind in order to get a new meaning for something else the mind has not yet fathomed. A definition itself is a distinction, but when it becomes a concept in the mind it becomes intuitive. A simple example would be the term *running*. We can go back to its various distinctions suggesting the movement of legs and arms in order to obtain a forward movement, but the mind does not justify the meaning by association with various distinctions. The mind accepts the meaning intuitively. Once the mind gets the concept, it drops any distinctions and from that point on the term is intuitively used.

Often intuitive concepts are improperly defined assumptions. This happens when the distinctions of a term do not exhibit the same reality or when the modifying term in a proportional definition is not considered. Intuition often gets a bad name because of so many assumptions in human thinking. Other times intuition is condemned because the mind cannot reverse the intuition and break it down into its particular distinctions as one would break down a direct or indirect proportion. Intuition is like a proportion. Once this is understood a gravitational analog for defining terms can be illustrated.

Using gravity in a balanced scale, **Figure 8-1** easily represents the meaning of weight and how definitions can become intuitive. The concept of an axiom derived from an axis does well to give us an understanding of the intuitive.

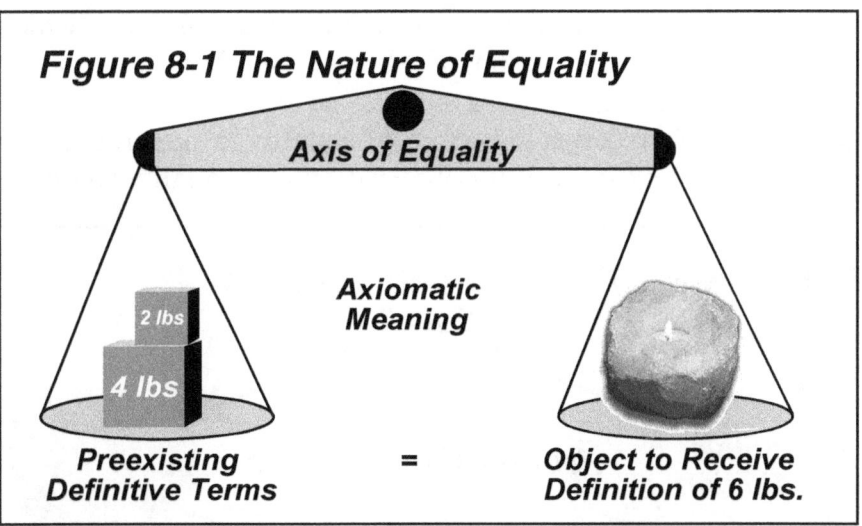

I have labeled the predefined weights as the intuitive or subjective side of the equation and the object in question as the undefined objective side. The axis in the center produces the axiom once equilibrium or equality is reached. The new axiom would be, "The object is equal to 50 lbs." This is an axiomatic statement because of the action of gravity and the intuitive labels of the predefine distinctions. The gravitational weight is what both share in common. This weight is predicative as is also force, acceleration, energy etc. This process is also a complete statement and shows how the object receives the action of the predicate, which in turn agrees with the subjective or intuitive terms. It also shows how essential the predicate is in determining the axiom. In fact, all axioms originate through a predicate process and can later be used as subjective or intuitive concepts in determining additional axioms. The subject provides the distinction, the verb provides the equality, and the object manifests the proportion in reality.

With the above in mind, let us consider the use of subjective, predicative and objective reality as a complete process rather than deny one for the other, as did Plato. The equation will determine the existence of an apple as independent of the intuitive definition. Three realities are represented. **Figure 8-2** will show that intelligence holds the intuitive definition, which was received by the action of observation. This observation agrees with the apple as a subject of study. In reverse the objective apple receives the action of equality in agreement with the intuitive definition. Both observation and equality share the

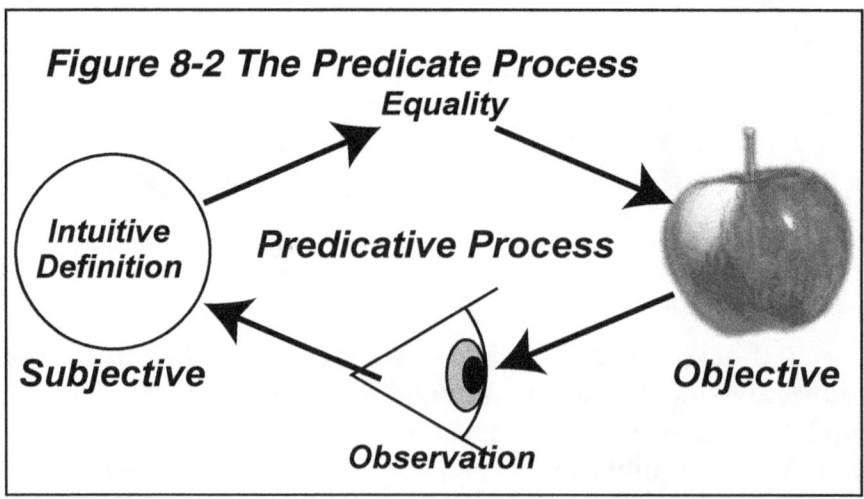

same predicate reality. Both subjective and objective reality is manifest and understood through the predicate. As mentioned earlier, the definition was an equation in itself where the apple has various objective components determined through observation. The whole definition process is almost infinitely circular as if the equation reads from right to left and back again from left to right. In this equation observation is not objective and the intuitive image comes from the predicate act of observation and not from objectivity. You cannot put anything intuitive into the mind without the predicate realities of observation and equality.

Observation has been considered objective by science, but is far more time dependent upon stagnant objectivity. Observation does not mean that we see space, or that we really see things. It is impossible to lay hold of objective reality directly. Bertrand Russell understood on this wise:

> He (Russell) has insisted that if certain well-established facts about visual perception are taken into account, it follows that when we look at an object what we really see is not the external object but an image located in our own brains. The decisive fact which leads him to this surprising conclusion is that it takes time for light to travel from the object to the retina of the eye, and for an impulse from the latter to reach the visual center in the brain; if, therefore, what we see is the external object, we must see it an instant before this transmission is complete.[7]

Russell was not considering observation as a predicate, but he demonstrates observation as an active, dynamic process that takes time to accomplish. The reason relativity is a paradox is that observation is treated objectively and thus it distorts objectivity. Distortion is due to time differentials and, thus, observation is predicative and not objective. It cannot be emphasized enough that the subject, verb, and object play a part in thinking just as much as in writing. Thus philosophy should consider three realities and not just one or a dichotomy of two.

To say as the scientist has maintained that all truth is objective and not also predicative and subjective is a narrow conclusion about reality. There is true subjective reason, true predicate action and true objective existence. That is the nature of all of reality without trying to corner it into a particular cubicle. Truth is reality and reality is truth. Philosophy as been pigeonholing reality for centuries and with it truth has been molded into personal reality formulas in the same way different religions corner their realities. Just because one does not talk of God does not suggest his reality is more truthful. Humanity makes the same mistakes whether religious, scientific, political or philosophical. The most important point in this thesis is that every form has a motive to seek eminence, avoid responsibility, and limit reality. We talk of human beings not wanting to face reality in their everyday lives, but even the great minds have the same problem. All the intellectuality and education obtained does not change the psychology of the human mind.

Clarity of meaning is fundamental to seeing reality clearly. Take the simple word *love*. Whether it is used as a subject, verb or object, it remains in the predicate reality. If anyone wants to consider love subjective or objective it would become relative and not invariant. The desire for relativity in meaning rather than accepting responsibility introduces the *Law of Invariance*. Before this law is introduced it would be well to refocus on the basics about reality. When Plato made the concept of an apple more real than the objective apple, he was thwarting reality and our understanding. He denied the predicate aspects of observation and meaning. Most of science and philosophy do just this. If Plato had understood the predicate, subjectivity would not have risen as the only reality, and objectivity would not have been the only reality for science. Plato's reality was restricted to the mind. There was nothing real in the predicate or the objective. This is a sad state for any ideology. Stressing one side of a polar reality is simply avoiding the predicate responsibility that truth demands and that equality of conservation insightfully will engender.

Philosophy and science avoid a predicate reality and thus assume that all things that are not objective are subjective. If you think this is being too meticulous and wish to challenge it with the idea, "Why not a reality of position, adverb or even a connective reality or why not a reality of modification and conjunction?" These are grammatical points of language and deserve an explanation.

Prepositions and adverbs are extensions of the predicate and particularize or define the use of predicate words more fully. A predicate word for example may have a general meaning and the adverb just defines it more particularly and a preposition shows its location more particularly. Thus modifiers do the same for subjective and objective words. Connectives and conjunctive words are similar to the equals sign in mathematics and represent verbs with logical implications. When all is said and done we have subject, predicate, and object and thus if we can write in three realities we must also be able to reason with the same. Philosophy has failed to introduce the predicate and Plato was the first to deny the objective and ignore the predicate. Even though Socrates talked of a constant need for predicate meaning, Plato thwarted it by distorting the process to define justice by using it to show forth his view of a controlling state.

Subjective and objective terms are generally acceptable, but predicate terms are difficult to pin down because most minds push reality around from the predicative to the subjective and sometimes to the objective. The predicate reality is a reality of right action and carries the same fervor as energy and the dynamics of sound judgment. With the predicate reality it is not enough to figure things out. It is paramount that the proper action takes place. This action must agree with the basic intuitive gifts. But the mind avoids this responsibility. The mind is impatient and seeks control or waits indecisively to be acted upon. When we think that reason can be controlled regardless of misbehavior; we fail to realize that when a leader misbehaves and makes statements to sway others, he or she is not going to adhere to reason regardless of his or her intelligence. We too often forgive the celebrity for misconduct because of beauty or brains, but they walk in fear and denial and are basically incapable of sound judgment. Like linguistic actors they learn to sound the words of insightful writers to cover their lack of the intuition needed, which guides our behavior until we obtain sound reason. What we think of as sound reason is only appealing arguments because we too are afraid. We lack intuition and good sense to guide us through the maze of life. Intuition looks behind for motive. It reads between the lines and senses something is wrong with one's so-called rational delivery. The basic lack of a predicate reality is due to ineptness in our understanding motive. We sense motive on the other side and in other people, but fail to see motive in ourselves.

      The hallmark of the predicate reality is faith and its enemy is the denial or repression of fear. Faith is the acceptance of reality and of fear. Philosophy and other disciplines fail to understand this essential psychology that plagues so many theories and so many religious ideologies. Faith requires the application of axiomatic principles while fear fosters control, magic, and the denial of responsibility. It can easily be demonstrated that religious terms have been most influenced by pushing them into subjectivity rather than conserving them in the predicate reality of responsibility. Science pushes all reality to the objective and through indeterminism falls completely to the left in various forms of subjectivity. There is no predicate reality to the scientist or philosopher. Although the predicate is hard to maintain and explain, it follows the same law of invariance as both the subjective and the objective, but no one ever cared to find this method of testing terms according to which reality they naturally rest.

The Law of Invariance

      The clear meaning of all terms is contingent upon the law of invariance. One would think, however, that the meaning of a term is anything one assigns to it. If this were the case what are we to do about a new term originally assigned to a concept where it has been subtly given over to a slightly different concept? We now have a former concept without a word to describe it. The original meaning as well as the concept is eventually lost

The Nature of the Predicate | 162

to future generations. Thus traditions adopt new meanings and new reality changes. We eventually wander into darkness when we take upon ourselves to move a term to a different reality in order to propagate a more desirable meaning. Creators of new concepts often steal old terms designed to express old concepts and assign them to new concepts. It is not unlike putting new wine into old bottles. When you have new concepts you need a new word. Take the term *space* as used by modern physics. The classical concept is expansion—something intelligence can fathom. Another classical concept of space would be nothingness as in empty space. When modern physics took this subjective term and moved it into the objective making it a thing that curves, there was now no term for that which the classical mind conceives as the immensity of empty space or open expanse. The old concept is baffled with curved nothingness. Space is no longer invariant in meaning. If the mind can conceive of the expansion of space, there must be a term that communicates this concept. Just because the measuring device changes do not mean that the concept has to change also. The new concept of relativity should have created a new term. Perhaps the reason that this was not considered was due to the assumption that observation is objective rather than predicative.

Time, a classical predicate term, has also been moved into the objective. It does not follow that just because the objective timepiece slows due to natural forces, the concept of the invariant nature of time does not warp. Time is the motion of objective reality and just because physical things slow or speed up does not change the meaning of the intelligent grasp of the nature of predicate time.

The essence of the law of invariance is to maintain the law of conservation not only of space, time, and mass, but also of the meaning of words. Words cannot have a relative connotation. The meaning must imply invariance otherwise one can choose any meaning he desires. When we change the original axiomatic meaning we actually change the reality of a term in order to curve fit meaning to a personal or relative concept. Relativity is

The Platonic Idiom

the enemy of the law of invariance and the predicate process. To keep meaning sure and to keep words in the proper reality, the law of invariance becomes the methodology we can use to maintain not only the conservation of meaning but we can also eventually avoid motive.

It does seem naive to think that philosophy can come up with the meaning of a word that will remain fixed for all time. Common language will not permit this for it is the nature of man to misunderstand the original meaning and also place upon the word his own concoctions. The dictionary of any language over time gives the various usages and does not attempt to say this is it. The etymology might give the origin, but that does not solve the problem. The interesting thing about meaning is if two people define the meaning of a word differently and one is asked to change his to fit the other, the one required to change must come up with a word to fill the void created. Rarely will one choose an honest word because it will reveal their intent. Finding a new term for a new concept is essential to the mind if told it has the wrong term. It is like calling someone Bill for many years because you could not hear very well. When someone corrects you and tells you that it is Will and not Bill, you simply substitute the new word with a little confusion at first. When ideologies are challenged no one wants to admit intent, thus old terms give credence to foolish ideologies.

Consulting the dictionary for proper meaning may not be a simple task. While each dictionary clearly demonstrates that many words have various meanings—even related definitions and antonyms, simply choosing a definition would not be the role of epistemology. Determining the origin of a word and its part of speech differentiation exemplifies the true function of a term's meaning and reality. Too often, the thinker selects meaning out of choice or out of tradition, never realizing that the various shades of evolved meaning can be arranged into three connotations. Choosing the right meaning can be just as explicit as choosing the right word. An important example of this argument comes with the word reason. Three connotations will surface as if from three reality points of view.

The definitions for reason from a dictionary are:

1. "Sound mental powers that are concerned statements of logical thinking."

Reason here implies a cognitive (thinking) process - a process in which attempts are made to define things free from contradiction. This can be selected as a subjective definition.

2. "A basis or circumstance that justifies some action or event."

The action or event may be clear, but the justification may or may not be a cognitive process. The cause for action may be emotional or even arbitrary and that is not reason in its original form. Reason here is tied more to the predicate action rather than a mental process. A better word to explain an act is in the word *why?* We reason things out through a subjective process and then act accordingly. Reason should describe a cognitive process while *why* may be simply an excuse. As described in meaning two, the user may have a watered down understanding of reason and thus this use is relative and prevents a better understanding of the invariant meaning.

3. "To form conclusions based on facts."

This meaning attempts to place a conclusion along side a fact. The fact may be clear, but the conclusion may or may not be correct. Both conclusions and facts are objective by-products. No action is implied and the cognitive process is not clarified. This meaning is tied to the objective.

A common denominator appears in definition two and three. Both are relative and subject to motivation and opinion. The reasoning may or may not be true. One assumes a certain action is justified and the other assumes a certain conclusion is true. Only the first definition stands invariant. Properly called subjective reason, it does not relate to motive or justification, such as, "that is the reason why" or "this conclusion results from that." Subjective reasoning is not a conclusion drawn from a process. It is the subjective process itself. Thus, reason, intelligence, and logic are invariant in the subjective.

The key in the above analysis of reason lies in the word *invariant*. For a word to exist in the proper reality the meaning must be invariant, unchangeable, and cannot be relative. The aim in definition, as taught by Aristotle, was to define words in such a way that they are invariant and unchangeable and free from hypothesis and opinion. Perhaps the original meaning of reason was to find justification and perhaps also Kant came along and used it in referring to a logical process. Kant did call it *pure reason,* suggesting that certain purities about reason are invariant. Sometimes a modifier will clarify. This is the essence of good communication and helps keep meaning invariant.

The next reflection occurs with the word faith. From a subjective point of view, faith projects a belief statement void of any reason or proof. This sort of definition means little to the intelligent mind. It appears far too relative. From an objective point of view, faith might be observance of or fidelity to one's religion or social norm. This definition refers to some rule, but if the rule is wrong, faith is blind. Again, objective or goal orientated faith is also relative. Too often we consider faith an antonym to reason; faith more appropriately compliments the rational process. Thus, the real meaning of faith lies in the *acceptance of axioms*. In this sense, faith is predicative. The dictionary suggests a traditional view as follows: *"complete acceptance of a truth which cannot be demonstrated or proved by the process of logical thought."* Note the use of truth as something that cannot be demonstrated by logical thought. As shown earlier, intuition could be a summation of a previous logical process or a conclusion in a single image. This process may be conscious and one can break the intuition down in order to prove the truth of it. But in the case of the intelligent abilities beyond conscious thought, we can easily muster the ability to understand that all we can see is the single result with no time to question the workings of the subconscious. We just move in the direction of the intuitive image and do not question. You can ask a person if it is good to love your neighbor and he might return a yes! If asked why, he might not be able to explain it logically, but he would still sense that something good would come of it. This comes from the idea that intelligence is pre-existent and we may have learned in many logical ways certain actions to be true, but amnesia has led us to doubt because we can no longer consciously break things apart.

Faith causes us to act honestly. If we do not act in faith we act in the denial of fear—the antithesis of faith. The antithesis of honesty is motive. In order to cover our motive we act in denial of fear rather than in acceptance of it. If we are encompassed with inaction, we are full of anxiety, panic, depression, and various types of neurosis that are very debilitating. The human condition cannot deal with neurosis without action. The attempt therefore is to act in denial of fear rather than in honest acknowledgement of it. Honest recognition is humility and the antithesis of humility is pride. One cannot assume that a pontification of one positioned reality in denial of another is a humble pursuit of knowledge. Rather it is pride and the desire for eminence that covers one's rejection of responsibility. There is a concept that you cannot have faith in something that is not true. If we accept something that is not proven yet is intuitively true, we have faith, but if it is not true we are probably in denial. We believe things that satisfy our personal need for acceptance, but we have faith in something because it simulates responsibility, conservation, and general well being for all. This would bring faith to the level of invariance. The best synonym under this connotation resides in the word trust. Faith would then be predicative because one acts in his life and trusts that some principle such as justice will eventually prevail. He acts according to his principles and not according to a subjective power as commonly expressed in positive thinking. Faith more appropriately balances the equation of reality because it is predicative. Faith or trust in self-evident axioms preserves the rational process while the axiom shows agreement between reason and objective reality. Reject faith as a necessary part of philosophy and *a priori* thoughts are put asunder. Faith starts at the beginning in the same way a religious person, a detective, or a scientist has a hunch due to unremembered experiences. He moves from one axiom and definition to another until his faith grows into well defined knowledge. Faith is the true verb that eventually reaches the object. When the object confirms the premise that had driven faith, then proof is reached and faith is justified.

The common criticism of faith is actually a criticism of subjective motive rather than true faith. When we criticize faith incorrectly rather than motive we darken the terms in the mind of the listener who is justified by faith. In reality it is those who justify their ignorance by saying "Prove it." They foster darkness and destroy the justification of faith. The predicate of right action is so often ignored in understanding faith that the educational elite seem to be justified when they should be condemned for moving faith into the subject. Faith in principles, such as justice, makes it possible to develop more complex meanings such that: *if given sufficient time, justice will always prevail through the opposing forces in nature.* Wisdom comes from intuitive faith and reason combined.

As each word extols one definition as more invariant than another, such as reason being invariant when defined in the subjective, faith as being invariant when defined in the predicative, and such things as physical facts as being invariant when defined in the objective, all other definitions must be considered relative. The meaning most invariant for any word should stand as the proper and most effective meaning in science and philosophy. It cannot be too strongly stated that the origin of each word rightly belongs with an invariant connotation. Tradition tends to add and build upon relative definitions. Relative meanings are often canonized in favor of invariant meanings in order to control others or exalt a personal worldview.

Some words do not have clear reality markings, but by studying the most effective synonyms, the meaning can be assigned to the most fitting part of thought. There are, however, a few words that may exist in no reality or all three realities. Many terms such as *pure* are modifiers and only determine an emphasis of the nature of another term it modifies. *Pure thoughts* and *pure reason* would be subjective and *pure gold* would be objective. Perhaps *pure love* would be an emphasis on predicative action. It seems that some words are able to transcend the subjective, the predicative, and also the objective because of their ability to modify all of reality. Take the word truth for example. Is it subjective? If so, would this not mean that truth comes from the mind with each person having his or her own version? This defines motive and not true reason. Truth in the subjective must refer to axiomatic self-evident statements used as an intuitive subject in a new statement. Truth can come from the mind as long as it originates from the axiomatic and not motive. Motive is essentially the invariant antitheses of truth. This brings us to the reality of *motive*. It is obviously subjective and invariant in its attempt to cover intent with term-twisted ideologies.

Truth can also modify actual existence. Science would be the advocate of objective truth, but when associated with words such as observation and measurement, truth cannot be invariant unless the observation or measurement shows agreement with *true reason* as in a *true observation*.

Religion, mysticism, and even modern physics are often destructive when relative meanings are canonized in favor of invariant meanings in order to warp reality to fit one's concepts or personal acceptance formula. Each person must learn to set aside all relative meanings when trying to give meaning to words. Words with invariant reality preserve intelligent wisdom and knowledge and also lift us out of darkness. Man will often put things backwards and upside down not seeing the predicate process of meaning. Uses of words are often multifarious and logically undisciplined. Meaning often has contradictory implications for the problems with which philosophy is concerned. When the philosopher attempts to define his terms he or she should have known better.

9. The Epistemology of Meaning

The human motive has certainly been the primary concern of various would-be doctrines and philosophies. This conclusion comes from the fundamental understanding that humankind will focus more on personal acceptance formulas than responsible principles. One will kill to be accepted by a peer, but will never give to the poor to be accepted of God? Responsible persons seek for honest awareness rather than formulas of denial. Honest minds attribute to God fundamental values that the hope of man will come to understand. Personal acceptance formulas of denial do not support the truth. Rather the mind turns truth upside down in order to avoid responsibility to reality. Poor philosophies are born from the need to force ideals upon others rather than to let each individual come to a clear form of understanding. Sometimes social norms are imbedded so strongly within our traditions that the knowledgeable person may even agree mildly with these false notions because of social rejection. Thus, rejection becomes more painful than accepting responsibility for truth.

Some see the necessity of conservation and harmony in existence better than others while the ignorant succumb to the rhetoric of the educated and somewhat intelligent formulas that attempt to guarantee some ideal without any need to understand. These ideals will often antagonize conservation, harmony, and equilibrium. We obey authority blindly in order to sustain our acceptance and deny conservation. We control those we can in order to prove acceptance and deny our own fear of rejection. The dictator, for example, may use the sword while the more educated may use unjust legislation or theory to control the many. Plato most certainly fit the latter. He was eloquent, but lacked harmony in his State. Plato wanted to instigate his idea of justice upon the people by creating rules that should be played exactly as he thought. This is no different from religious ideologies in which God is used as magic to control the people. Distorting salvation and doing away with personal responsibility turns truth upside down. Plato, dictators, and religious zealots do not consider the necessity of human choice and human understanding. Too often we lack conservation and harmony in our ideologies. Truth must be equitable, harmonic, and demonstrate equilibrium. Truth is not arbitrary and it is not relative. It must make sense.

False intellectual formulation has dominated every democracy and dictatorship since Plato. Plato's ideology has often been used as an excuse to give a rising dictator the idea for which he already had a propensity. Most aspiring power seekers are filled with a psychological need to use some level of physical or ideological force to justify their importance and vent their denial of acceptance. Denial of acceptance is to understand that the one in power is likely to bully those beneath him in order to avoid admitting the need for acceptance. Aspirants take a strong physical or ideological stance to scare away the reality of death and rejection. Those who follow aspire to the same. The populace considers him to be strong, but the wise see him as a fearful bully who calls good evil and evil good. Being strong and standing up for freedom and principles without the need to control the populace is a far better method. Taking choice away from the people or putting shackles on leadership is the central core of the Platonic Idiom. Responsibility is the mainstay of a true democracy. If the individual does not take responsibility, he suffers the laws of nature. If the leader does not take responsibility, he should suffer removal. To make untold laws to cover every infraction stifles choice and individual responsibility. Laws should uphold principles and not control behavior.

The Platonic Idiom

The problem with Plato and every republic or democracy since is that there is always a failure to establish an equitable taxing method and an equitable method of representation. Corruption enters in and destroys as the control mongers rise up to make a multitudeness number of laws to prevent deviation from their power. But, like a virus, many merchants become immune when they find loopholes. This eventually passes the burden on to the common laborer. Taxing equitably will require fewer laws and greater responsibility to all. Plato missed the mark and every government since will topple for lack of proper taxation and representation. It would take heavy funded bureaucracies to foster the control Plato desired. If there were any form of representation, the people would say no to almost all of what Plato designed. People will never accept taxation without first accepting the ideology for which the taxes are designed. In fact, the freedom to exercise a stand against allows for a greater confirmation of particular taxes.

Responsibility is the predicate method. It implies personal action in order to reach up without enslaving others. Responsibility and principles are learned by discussion and not by lectures, political speeches or even extensive reading void of interactive debate. The mind must learn to ask why and each must be able to express the meaning of things in both oral and written defense. Listening to just a few on TV or one on the radio on in the classroom does not aid in this process. Essentially, all must participate in the dialogue or select someone to represent them. This is the Socratic method. Listening to a debate rather than participating only relinquishes responsibility to express our thoughts. Each must be open to the correction of others at every stage of life. If not, we end in a corner of our own strangeness. Sometimes we become institutionalized or we end up in group therapy trying desperately to obtain what we missed growing up. The massive problem of every democracy is allowing individuals to vote without participating in the dialogue. It is like giving power to the ignorant.

Consider that the Jews, for thousands of years, used a cultural priesthood as a form of discussion in firming up responsibility and consider on the other hand that the anti-Semite distorts individual responsibility in favor of force, strict laws, and blind obedience—the same false sense of justice Plato tried intellectually to importune upon the mind of his readers. Socrates would not have used this new intellectual anti-discussion method. I suspect that Socrates learned from Jewish traditional philosophy and not from the dark side of thinking. Plato was the typical student who wanted an ideal state that would force justice rather than inspire responsibility to justice. Socrates wanted each individual to vocally discuss the meaning of things in order to learn responsibility. This process has been lost in modern education. We are far too Platonic, linear and anti-relational in our talk. I do not suggest that modern Jewish thought follows correctly. I refer to Hebrew antiquity as the origin of Socratic thinking. I would begin by pointing out that all of the Greek philosophers learned from the Egyptian Jew at one time or another but often failed to get the full understanding intended.

It was Thales, Pythagoras, Democritus, Eudoxus and even Plato who visited Egypt to obtain the oral knowledge of the Egyptian Priests. These priests cannot be thought of as strange fellows of a superior culture out of nowhere. They came from the Chaldean culture from whom also the Sumerians descended. The most ancient of cultures had the greater knowledge of how to obtain meaning. These priests sometimes postulated strange ideas for the populace and kept the hidden oral knowledge for the priests. It was this oral knowledge that was carried from generation to generation by the Hebrews.

The following are portions obtained from the *Great Pyramid Its Devine Message* by Davidson. Within each selection the various authors sight references:[1]

> Thales visited Egypt in 600 B.C and studied science. Hieronymus of Rhodes said of Thales, "He never had any

The Platonic Idiom

teacher except during the time when he went to Egypt and associated with the priests." *(ap. Diog. Laer I, 27)*

Pythagoras visited Egypt about 500 BC and studied science there. Returning from his travels, he founded a School of Astronomy and Philosophy in Sicily. He also traveled in the East. The Pythagorean doctrine of the immortality of the soul is clearly of Egyptian origin, whereas the connected Pythagorean doctrine of transmigration of the soul is certainly of a more easterly origin. The Pythagorean idea of placing natural phenomena on a numerical basis, of associating numbers with conceptions and entities, is also clearly Egyptian in its origin. Thus of the ancient Egyptians Dr. Sprenger states "An idea, a period of time, or any remarkable occurrence were frequently connected with ideal persons in mythology, and when any similarity existed, received the same appellation" *(Vyse's "Pyds. And Temp. of Giseh," Vol. II, Append).* Hence the importance of the following from Dr. A.S. Pringle-Pattison: "Impressed by the presence of numerical relations in every department of phenomena, Pythagoras and his early followers enunciated the doctrine that 'all things are numbers.' Numbers seemed to them, as Aristotle put it, to be the first things in the whole of nature, and they supposed the elements of numbers to be the elements of all things, and the whole of heaven to be a musical scale and number *(Meta. A.986a).* Numbers, in other words, were conceived at that early stage of thought not as relations or qualities predicable of things, but as themselves constituting the substance or essence of the phenomena—the rational reality to which the appearances of sense are reducible" *(Enc. Brit., Vol 22 p. 699).* Pythagoras discovered—or more probably derived from the Egyptians—the mathematical proportions of the intervals of the diatomic scale.

Democritus studied astronomy for 5 or 7 years in Egypt *(Diodor., I,98),* and claimed to have been a disciple of the Egyptian priests and the Magi, having visited also Persia and Babylon *(Clem. Str., I, p. 304).* He knew of the obliquity of the ecliptic.

Anaxagoras (born 499 B.C.) studied astronomy in Egypt. "He held that in a solar eclipse the moon hides the sun, and in a lunar eclipse the moon enters the earth's shadow" *(Forbes, p. 14).*

Eudoxus (408-355 BC) visited Egypt with Plato.

Plato (429-350 BC) visited Egypt and Cyrene. In Egypt he conversed with the Egyptian priests. He was the pupil of Socrates, and was a follower of Pythagoras. He proposed to the astronomers the problem of representing the courses of the planets by circular and uniform motions" *(Forbes, p. 17).*

After the conquest of Egypt by Alexander the Great, the early Greek philosophers memorialized their indebtedness to the Egyptians in the sciences and arts by founding the famous Library of Alexandria. From this age onward, a long succession of Greek geometers, astronomers, and philosophers, in the various schools of Alexandria, maintained the connection that previously had been more remotely held by oral conversation by the first Greek philosophers with Egyptian priests. At Alexandria, all the learning that was gleaned and developed from Egypt was passed on to Euclid, Aristarchus, Archimedes, Apollonius and possibly Hipparchus who also studied in Alexandria. Ultimately, Alexandria declined by falling completely under the pernicious spell of popular Egyptian dogma because the oral traditions were lost. In 642 AD, the famous library was burnt by the orders of the Caliph Omar. Such an act was irresponsible.

The residue of ancient oral knowledge survived through the Greek philosophers and some Jewish tradition, while the mythical knowledge survived in literature. Throughout history the two were often at odds. Just as Columbus was at odds with the mythology of his time, Modern astronomy takes similar odds against anthropology. The sources differ but the two have a common denominator. The Egyptian priest devised both— one to keep hidden through oral transmission and the other to become the recorded portion designed for the common laity. Anthropology makes its judgments from the recorded portion while mathematics, geometry, and astronomy make judgments based upon Greek recollection of Egyptian oral knowledge. The oral knowledge that evolved through the scientific centuries was secretive while the literary knowledge accommodated the desires of the popular mind at large. It was essential to keep

The Platonic Idiom

the ignorant from learning technical knowledge without the wisdom to use it and instead place them under superstition and law until they reached the ability to gain wisdom through oral education under the priesthood. Whenever the barbarian gained too much knowledge he would find ways to control and dominate. This could be the very reason the Jews kept scientific knowledge secret. The bible of antiquity was somewhat the same. The recorded culture sounds mythological, but the oral meaning lay hidden for those that could understand. This was the pattern of the priest in Egypt and also the Jewish priest of the desert. I maintain that they both had the same origin. The whole reason for confounding the language after building the scientific edifice of Babel was because of the lack of wisdom in using the knowledge. I suspect the Chaldeans built the Great Tower, as they did the Great Pyramid. I also suspect the building of both was of the same period. If the Great Pyramid revealed great scientific knowledge, the Great Tower would have also. Perhaps dark tradition is a byproduct of losing the knowledge. It is not too far fetched to think that the Great Pyramid was the Great Tower. Noah went west to the land of Shinar where the city of Babel was built. Others went east to Samaria and some went to the isles of the Genitals—more likely Greece. These three civilizations are the hallmark of scientific knowledge of antiquity.

History makes the mistake of equating Babel with Babylon. There is no association in the scriptures, yet tradition has made it such. Consider this recent press release:

> 4 June 2008
> BABYLON WAS NOT BABEL – The State Museums of Berlin commission MetaDesign and Johanssen + Kretschmer with communicating Babylon exhibition
> BABYLON WAS NOT BABEL is the claim the new cultural campaign being conducted jointly by MetaDesign and Johanssen + Kretschmer (J + K). The two agencies are in charge of promoting the special exhibition "Babylon. Myth and Reality.", which will have a unique appearance at the Berlin Pergamon Museum in the summer of 2008. For only here will the exhibition, which was developed

in conjunction with the Louvre in Paris and the British Museum in London, take place along the processional road of Babylon. In addition to formulating the claim, the Berlin agencies also developed the design and communication concept, which form the foundation for the exhibition's interaction with the public.

Babylon – two worlds, one exhibition. From 26 June to 5 October 2008, the State Museums of Berlin will present the background behind the myth of Babel and the reality of ancient Babylon. The historical significance and the achievements of Babylonian civilization are far less well known than the numerous myths that are usually associated with Babylon. That forms the basis for the campaign developed by MetaDesign and J + K. The claim BABYLON WAS NOT BABEL prompts the audience to reconsider what it thinks it already knows by creating awareness of the discrepancy of myth and reality, of Babel and Babylon.

I do not know the significance of the above, but it is characteristic of questioning tradition. It can be illustrated further that the Great Tower was misinterpreted as being a structure for physically reaching heaven rather than allegorically teaching the science of heaven. The high priests of Egypt realized that the knowledge given was too much for those who lacked wisdom and thus confused the message of the Great Pyramid to such an extent that those who followed would receive a different story. Anthropology tells of this distorted message, but astronomy has seen into the science of the Great Pyramid. Understanding this concept is essential to seeing how great minds of the Greeks would have learned the mysteries of the sciences and also the teaching methods of the greatest civilization before their trek into darkness.

Pythagoras was only about 30-40 years older than Socrates and this should indicate some knowledge about the Hebrew methods would surely have been circulated since it was the pattern for the Greeks to travel to Egypt in order to learn from the masters—who still kept a residue of the mysteries of the sciences and of philosophy given them of the Chaldeans. The reason Socrates did not write was that it was not appropriate to give out wisdom without the proper training. Even though

Plato visited Egypt, he did not follow the proper traditions. If all of the philosophers for the previous 200 years visited Egypt, it stands to reason that Socrates also visited or learned from the best.

What should be understood about antiquity is that the undeveloped mind tends to settle all things on a good or evil basis. Either by some authority or some traditional myth, the commoner tends to argue obedience from a dichotomy of good and evil. This is even better than modern objectivists taking the primitive singular survivalist view. Greed, for example, can be argued as good if the basis of reality is survival of the fittest. This is not good or evil but backward thinking. It is singular and an underworld method below that of good and evil. The dichotomy of good and evil raises man from the dark side of survival but the high priest of antiquity had something more than a tree of knowledge of good and evil.

A pluralistic method of antiquity says that the dichotomy of good and evil is yet below that of a greater method. Instead of saying things are good or evil; we must ask instead, what is the relational meaning rather than just an opposite? It becomes a more complex method of looking at things intuitively rather than in left and right terms. This suggests that there was a better mind running in the veins of the cultures of antiquity. It is a far more dimensional way of looking at reality. By dimension, I do not mean spatial dimension. Rather I suggest three separate realities and perhaps three dimensions in each to properly define the meaning of things. The ultimate number of variations of this methodology depends upon the culture and the philosophy or religion of that culture. The Jews of antiquity had a total number of positions equal to ten, Christian prophecy suggests twelve, but modern man has remained at a level referred to as the classic binary notion of good and evil. Every democracy and dictatorship uses this method to justify control. Philosophy too is a pull between the subjective and the objective as also politics is a pull between liberal and conservative. In the beginning, harmony was a central part of good and evil with an element of responsibility. Today we think in terms of moderate—a blending of opposites. A third point of harmony is much better. A good tree of life has more than a dichotomy, sometimes three, and the great minds talked of many manners of fruit rather than one, two, or even three. Genesis is only the allegory in predicting this trend in human nature. Man turns good and evil upside down, because he cannot see or understand that there is more to our understanding than singularity or a simple dichotomy of good and evil. To partake only of a polarized dichotomy is allegorically comparable to being cast into a dreary world or as the priest of oral knowledge would explain—cast into ignorance and misunderstanding.

Dimensions in understanding the meaning of things are simply the creation of points of view broader than the simplistic good and evil of which the letter of the law is based. Two is too distinctive and contrary to responsibility. I have found that nine variations is a comfortable number for the meaningful mind to contemplate. I would say that there are nine relative positions to place important words in such a way that the meaning is nailed securely and cannot be moved. It is not enough to place a word on the left or the right. We also need a harmonic of the two. With a two dimensional philosophy of good and evil, one is apt to take any word and distort the acceptable meaning to such an extent that evil becomes good and good becomes evil. Consider the horrors that have been done in the name of Christianity, freedom, and even justice. I think it can be demonstrated how civilization can and will turn good and evil upside down. The fewer points of reference the easier it is to turn meaning around. If you have nine reference points, it is very difficult to tamper with meaning and thus each generation studying meaning will add to civilization if discussion and the Socratic Method allow at least three points. It will be better with nine. But it must be understood that oral discussion is paramount. Insightful knowledge does not come from authority, but from one another.

In **Figure 9-1** we have a relationship between the subjective, predicative, and objective, and a relationship between

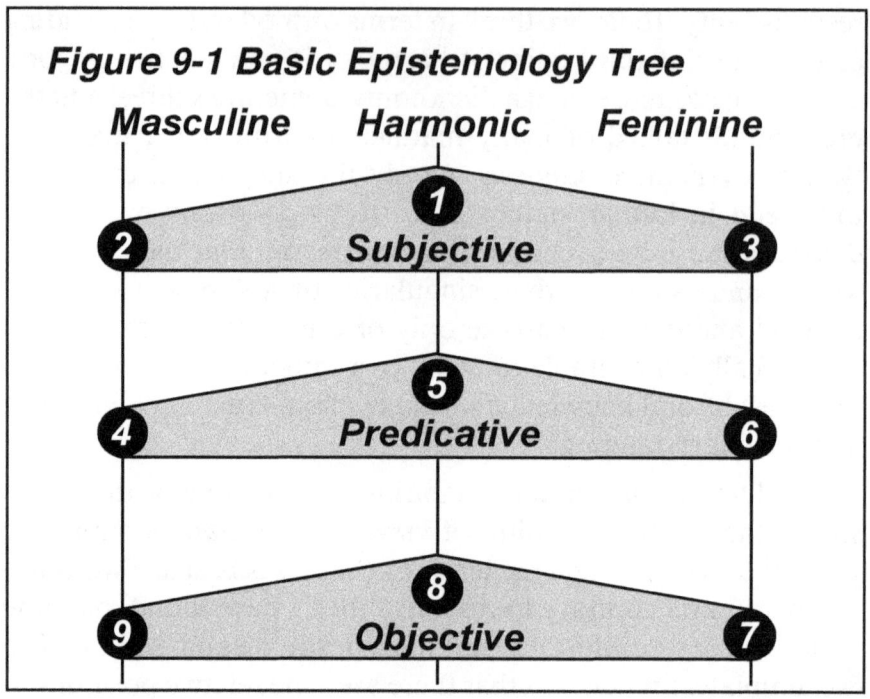

Figure 9-1 Basic Epistemology Tree

the horizontal aspect of masculine and feminine. This is the development of an epistemology tree used to define words and keep their meanings sound. Upon closer examination some will find a similarity to the Jewish Kabbalah.

Let us assign numbers to the nine points in units of three with the numbers *one, five,* and *eight* as the harmonics. With music, *three* is a harmonic with one and five, but within a complete octave three sounds like an extra-unneeded note. As we shall see, *three* has a strong resonance to the meaning of words.

Socrates tried desperately as he took the oral traditions of antiquity and endeavored to instruct his students to find the meaning of things. Plato, on the other hand, became so caught up in the dichotomy of subjective and objective reality that he could not see the value in meaning and its broader implications in solving the dichotomy so rampant in a two-dimensional mind. Justice to Plato was something the state forced upon the people. This is not far different from the most primitive cultures and even democracies that look for government solutions. If we could define justice in a broader relationship to many other meanings, we might avoid this two-dimensional way of thinking.

This author developed the idea of three realities more than twenty years ago, but found out later that the Jews had already come up with the subjective, predicative, and objective even though they did not call it such. In fact, man has always had them in various forms. It is just that philosophy failed to study the idea of three realities. It is the tendency of theory, especially relativistic theorists, to jump from two to many without understanding the essence of three. The third or predicate reality provides the axis of all.

Up to this point I have used a three-part reality horizontally with the subjective on the left and the objective on the right with the predicative in the center. This is not a graphic representation any different from the English language. If a three-part reality is understandable, it is now time to rediscover a nine-point methodology of determining the meaning of words. In introducing the predicate, I illustrated that an axis provides equilibrium in reality and yields equality to a proportional relation statement. By turning the three language realties from a horizontal to a vertical orientation we can now add a masculine and feminine on each side with a harmonic in the center. Harmonics serve a similar role to that of a verb. This gives us nine points of meaning.

The masculine is on the left side and the feminine on the right as if the image is facing us. This would give us a human figure with a right hand on our left. The right hand is controlled essentially by the left-brain and becomes the more logical route. Although Jewish tradition has it both ways, I will treat our image or tree of meaning as something that faces us as a human being would face us. The feminine would then be on our right. This is precisely what the Jews did in their Kabbalah. Although they did not use subjective, predicative or objective, they did compare the vertical axis to the mind (head), heart (breast) and

The Platonic Idiom

body (loins). Ancient Eastern thought has tried to unify the three for perfect mastery and improved health. Until modern self-help publications came upon the scene, philosophy left the heart to religious culture and created a tug-of-war between the subjective and the objective. I would suggest that Plato was probably not the first to do this and he was not the last. It is human nature. Plato tried to singularize reality and emphasize the subjective as superior to the objective. Western science has been so rational and objective since Plato that often the art of equilibrium between the subjective and objective has been lost.

Because of the nature of equilibrium or agreement, axiomatic meaning says that the meaning of a term cannot be changed once it is placed in the proper position of both reality and gender. A two-dimensional axis with nine positions locks the meaning of words and differentiates one from another.

Since the left-brain is the interface for the rational, we will place that on the left as one would think of his own brain and not the brain of the image. Intuition will represent our right brain as it interfaces with a more emotional and artistic aspect of our intelligence. Different cultures have switched the left and right, but this does not really matter—each to his choice. It is only paramount that one side be masculine and the other feminine. We now have slightly different meanings in each of the three realities. This sidedness is not opposition, but complimentary as two eyes and ears offset a little to produce a third dimension in sight and sound. This third dimension becomes the harmonic.

Let us take the numbers from one to three and see how they fit their respective positions.

2. Reason   1. Wisdom   3. Intuition

The Jews use reason and intuition as the appropriate masculine and feminine counterparts, but they do not have a harmonic for the subjective. They do, however, place knowledge there and reserve the *one* position for the word *crown*. Wisdom is a special type of knowledge and both reason and intuition should be required to possess it. By placing reason on the left as a masculine association and intuition on the right as a feminine association, wisdom becomes the harmonic of the two. This is precisely what the Jews did. The Jews, however, often considered wisdom as masculine and understanding as feminine. These differences are nothing but a byproduct of finding comparable words in translating from one language to another. The example still illustrates the methodology. In addition to placement, words were also given numbers. The Jewish numbering is similar to Figure 9-1 above, but changes from right to left depending on the authority.

In this presentation and in other writings, there is no attempt to give a number to a word, but rather to give a word to a number. It is assumed that numbers came first and, if not, they most assuredly were fixed and unalterable in meaning. For this reason it makes sense to use numbers to define terms in a qualitative manner rather than simply quantified terms. If this can be done, we have a foundation of meaning not only for the number itself, but a foundation word that can be used as a prime meaning for other words. This has been the attempt of this author. The words used are from mathematics and physics. The arrangement of the numbers shall be explained in the process.

Numbers have a definitive power as great as the reality placement or even a masculine and feminine relationship. Let us start with the number *one* by taking the numerical equation:

4 / 4 = 1   thus the number <u>One</u> yields the Axiom of Equality

Two equal components as one divided by the other equals one. Thus equality is derived from the number one. Equality comes from a direct proportion of two elements from the same reality. The same can be said of the balance scale. **Figure 9-2** shows that 4 lbs on each side provides equilibrium. The focus is on the axis of the scale, which determines the axiomatic meaning of equality. Once in equilibrium the term equality is manifest and thus becomes an ***axiom*** that cannot be altered. The masculine and feminine concepts play roles similar to a subject and object but strive to reach harmony rather than having one

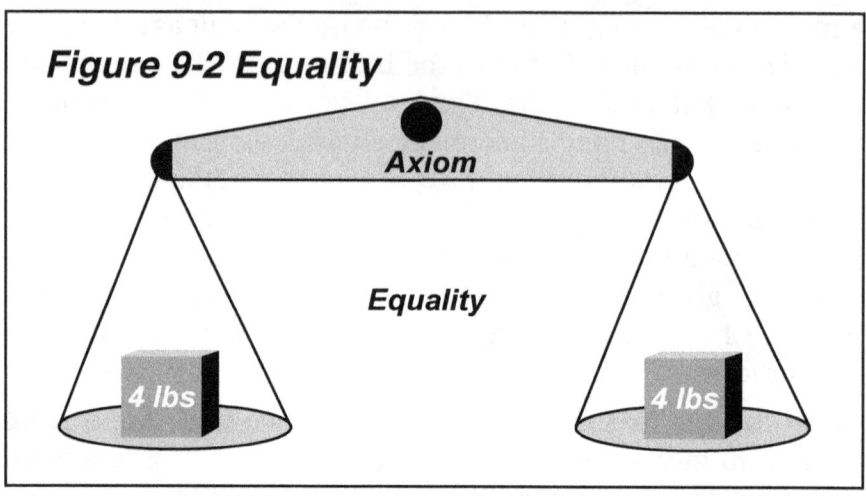

Figure 9-2 Equality

receive the action of another. In this sense, the prophetic Jews used numbers in a similar fashion, but *one* meant *crown* and had a mystical connotation. The scriptures have used unity and in some cases equality was used to mean *at one*. Consider the expression: "They shall become *one* flesh." Instead of some mystical sexual meaning, perhaps properly translated it would be—they should become equal flesh or equal in temporal things. The scriptures hide the meaning in numbers because few will accept the interpretation. The above interpretation would be acceptable today, but not centuries ago. Consider the expression: "Be ye therefore one as my father in heaven and I are one." A better analysis would be in the expression: "Whatever the Father has shall be yours." This sharing implies equality if we can overcome our greed.

One becomes the first harmonic in our search for meaning. It would be placed at the center with wisdom.

Masculine	Harmonic	Feminine
2. Reason	1. Wisdom	3. Intuition
	Equality	

Consider Descartes axiom "I think, therefore I am" to illustrate the harmonic. This statement is not so much an equality statement, but a harmonic one. Opponents have tried to devalue Descartes' axiom altogether because the distinction between equality and harmony was never considered. Opposition to Descartes comes from pragmatists who refuse to affirm any absolute. For example, pragmatists do not believe that a single absolute idea of goodness or justice exists, but rather that these concepts are changeable and depend on the context in which they are being discussed. Context and intent may be considered to be the cause of differing opinions, but the semantics (the linguistic study of meaning or content) are needed to avoid differences of opinion. To say that justice varies means only that each variation describes a different meaning of the word. We need to find the meaning that is absolute in its relation to other words. Such is the intent of epistemology and of meaning. The process here described had been lost, but survived in bits and pieces throughout philosophical and religious time.

In the case of Descartes we can place *'I think'* on the left and *'I am'* on the right, equality in the mathematical sense is not manifest. *'I am'* divided by *'I think'* does not represent equality. A more appropriate word would be harmonic. *'I am'* and *'I think'* show harmony or agreement. We could represent them horizontally as in:

"I Think" – is harmonically in agreement with – "I am"

Compare this with the grammatical thought such that:

The Subjective agrees with the Objective.

The standard theory assumes that agreement consists of the verb agreeing with the subject in person, number, and gender (e.g., masculine, feminine, neuter). Agreement applies to a relationship between the subjective and the predicative as also between masculine and feminine. The standard theory also assumes that the objective receives the action of the predicative. This is an additional component between realities that is not between genders. Action between realities is paramount, but agreement is with both reality and gender. This gives us a

The Platonic Idiom

basic distinction between vertical and horizontal placement. With equilibrium, the two genders harmonize in order to show agreement. With verbs, agreement is in the action.

Reverse the axiom as in 'I am therefore I think.' This illustrates harmonic agreement as well as action agreement. 'I think' is the action of 'I am' and 'I am' is in harmony with 'I think.' Agreement is not just a process between the subjective and objective through a verb. It is also found harmonically between the masculine and feminine gender. Agreement in a broad sense is equilibrium.

We can now introduce two more terms, although from physics they parallel reason and intuition. Consider the numbers 2 and 3 such that:

1 defines Equality
2 defines Distinction
3 defines Proportion

With a little Pythagorean-like thinking, two defines distinction and three defines proportion while one defines equality as shown earlier. An example of distinction and proportion would be *apple* and *orange* as being distinct, but if we incorporate *fruit* as the third principle or common denominator, we find that both distinct items share this third concept. This relationship is called a definitive proportion. In physics and mathematics there are two additional proportions. They are respectively a proportion of magnitude such as *40/20* which yields a 2 to 1 ratio; and a directional proportion such as *2 inches x 2 inches* defines a square. These two proportions are also distinct as in a direct and indirect proportion. It simply depends upon the distinction between division and multiplication. We can conclude that a proportion has within its meaning both distinction and equality.

Not only do numbers define words as Pythagoras and the Jews suggested, but each lower term becomes a particular component in the meaning of all higher terms. Consider that equality is a component in the distinction *(2/2)* and also consider that equality is a component in the meaning of a proportion. When we compare two lengths such as six inches and four inches we have a common denominator of *one inch* that exists equally in each distinction. This common one-inch makes it possible to relate this distinction in the first place. Another point is that equality particularizes a distinction in that it breaks it apart into particulars. Distinction also particularizes a proportion in that it shows the particulars. The reverse can also be implied wherein a proportion generalizes a distinction and a distinction generalizes equality. The meaning of one is in the next higher terms and the higher terms reveal a broader view of the previous. To generalize something can be confusing to some, because one thinks of something simple and the other thinks of something more complex. To generalize is very difficult for people because of this dual nature, but if we think of it intuitively, as reaching beyond, it might be easier for some. A proportion is something beyond a distinction in that when we look closely at a distinction we can see something relational. It is like looking closely at an apple and orange in order to see the term fruit. Fruit is a generalization of both apple and orange while apple is particular to fruit.

In returning to reason and intuition, consider that reason breaks apart into basic elements for study as intuition seeks a general principle by looking at the larger or more general picture. Wisdom is the harmonic of the two, or like the left eye that sees slightly different images from the right eye but is eventually harmonized in the brain into one. Even when one eye has poor clarity, the harmony between the two gives dimension that neither eye can muster on its own. Likewise, harmonic words cannot be placed in the masculine (rational) or feminine (intuitional) side. This is because they harmonize and do not stand alone as the rational and intuitive natures. Just as equality cannot stand alone, without noting a distinction or even a proportion, wisdom and knowledge need reason and intuition. Another way of looking at this relationship is to study how the mind sees *space* distinctively as to direction and proportionally as to magnitude. Space is a harmonic function of direction and magnitude.

Figure 9-3 illustrates the various words discussed at this point. When space is considered axiomatic in the subjective, it cannot be distorted as modern relativity tries to do. It is a perfect harmonic of dimension (masculine) and magnitude (feminine).

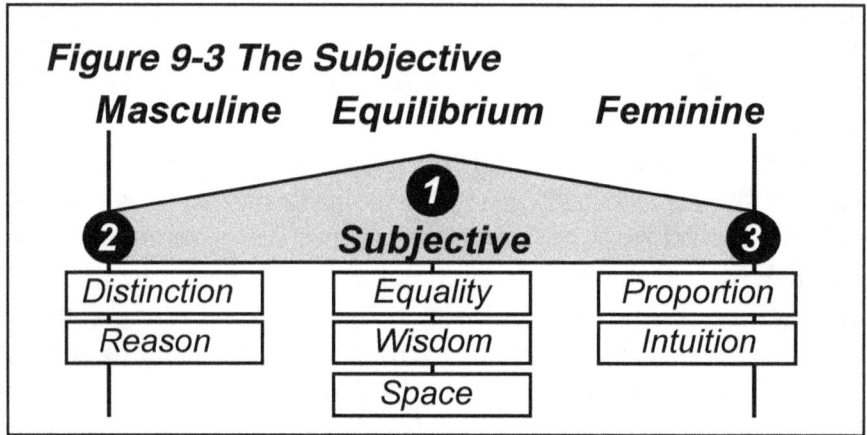

One can see how various words from various disciplines can be distorted in meaning from traditional established positions.

We have thus covered the subjective, but it should be mentioned that the Jews were not as precise with numbers as here illustrated. In many respects, the concepts are still the same. We can now turn to the predicate world and the three words derived from mathematics and physics. Unlike space, they are time dependant. Time implies action. Time is conserved from moment to moment, and time lies at the foundation of three basic predicate terms. They are conservation, meaning, and measurement. We thus have:

    4 defines Conservation
    5 defines Meaning
    6 defines Measurement

The reader may question the use of meaning, but follow this pattern and make your judgment later. Conservation requires the components of equality, distinction, and proportion.

In one statement, conservation is two distinct proportional relationships that maintain equality in the universe. The first distinction is the proportional relationship between the conservation of inertial and gravitational mass and the second distinction is the proportional relationship between inertial and gravitational energy. Both distinctions preserve equality in the universe. Preserving equality is conservation. Conservation means equality from one moment in time to the other. The four conservation laws were discussed earlier:

I. Conservation of inertial MASS
Conservation of gravitational MASS

II. Conservation of linear momentum or inertial ENERGY
Conservation of angular momentum or gravitational ENERGY

What we are considering are two types of mass and two types of energy. Mass is inertial as it resists a change in direction. Mass is also a quantum number of electric units or particles that react to a gravitational field. Essentially, they are the same but are determined differently. One determines the external force applied to change direction, and the other determines the internal torque that reacts to gravity. Energy also comes in two forms. They are linear and angular just as momentum is linear and angular. Momentum has direction, but Energy is a scalar quantity. Angular energy is a good way of describing the energy in mass at rest before light is emitted or absorbed at which point the mass diminishes or increases respectively. This tells us that mass and light are convertible. This saves the law of conservation of mass in atomic reactions. Misunderstanding comes by calling light energy that came from mass at rest. Light is mass and the energy is in the motion of mass in the same way energy is in the motion of any moving object. Light is objective mass, and energy is predicated upon the motion of mass, but is not mass. Confusing light with energy is a misnomer. Light carries energy but it is not what modern physics would call pure energy. Within solid mass bits and pieces of light or electric fields follow an angular motion but in free light the motion is linier or better yet a spiral around a magnetic field at rest. Rest mass would be angular or total potential energy. Essentially, it should be understood that mass is objective and energy is predicative.

Conservation transcends all disciplines including finance, environment, social interaction and natural law. Artificial law often tries to conserve but often needs individual judgment in order to constantly rectify poor laws that generate discrepancies. When one leaves the physical sciences there is often a tendency to drop the laws of conservation. Reason, equality, and intuition lie at the foundation of conservation. If modern physics had kept intuition we would not have such a relativistic and distorted universe that seems contrary to what we intuitively see.

Conservation underlies things good and supports the truth. Conservation reaches out to every rational mind desperately trying to teach consistency and responsibility. Conservation becomes distorted as the mind seeks for magic and some secret law that will defy conservation in existence and justify ignorance. Almost every daily newspaper has a full-page ad on how to get rich and find success financially merely by following some set of rules learned at a seminar. Is this justice? Is this mercy? Is this responsibility? We should think not and we should also understand that conservation is justice at its best and mercy at its grandest. So many ideologies break the law of conservation that many suffer because of it. The law of conservation states that one person's gain without adding value is another person's loss. How many of us at one time paid money for a book that claimed to show us the secret of the ages? All these magical systems never teach conservation. We are still trying to turn lead into gold. Conservation points to the essence of reason, equality, and proportion better than any other word, for without conservation nothing is absolute, true or even meaningful. Conservation drives sound business practices and is the basis of all economic downturns when the law is broken. Conservation drives correct environmental judgment and is the basis of our depleting planet when we fail to conserve. Conservation supports sound religious principles and is the basis of preventing immorality when we fail to consider the least in our community. Conservation proves correct under freedom, but it also proves destructive without a corresponding level of human responsibility. The meaning of conservation is paramount. Proper meaning is neglected and sometimes changed in order to avoid responsibility. When this happens, conservation has been thwarted and misaligned.

We can now move to the next numerical meaning. Interestingly, the word is meaning itself and is derived from the four prior axioms. These four are particular components used by the dictionary in defining a word. *One* demonstrates equality or the *synonym* that equals or approximates the correct meaning. *Two* demonstrates distinction, or the *antonym* that reveals a difference or opposite meaning. *Three* demonstrates a proportion or *relationship* that, if associated triangularly with say a synonym and a similar word, the meaning can become even more precise. *Four* demonstrates *conservation* in meaning. In other words, meaning should maintain *proper usage*. Historical usage, as compared with a change in current usage, illustrates times when the user neglects conservation. *Five* would be the general essence of meaning itself. This intuitive essence is implied in the word measurement as one might say to measure the meaning of a word is to consider its five points of clarification. Meaning particularizes measurement. In the reverse, measurement is the general essence of meaning. Perhaps there is a better term, but measurement is more scientific than any comparable term. Measurement is the essence of meaning in that it contrasts a term, as the dictionary may indicate.

The meaning of contrast is well worth mentioning:

Contrast is to set in opposition two or more figures of similar kind, with a view to show the differences and to manifest the superior excellence of the one by the inferiority of the other.

Origin of measurement:

The origin of the word means to stretch or extend in order to arrive or come to the correct measure.

I do not mean to say that they are synonyms or in anyway particularly equal. I show them together only in order to extract a general concept. That concept is to seek for the ideal word for the sixth axiom. There are many words that come close, but in keeping with physics I chose measurement. I chose it also because in the broader sense it is used outside of mathematics. When the master said, "With what measure ye mete, it shall be measured to you." This is not unlike *mercy*; which suggests that we can forgive regardless of our sins one against another if we have learned to measure justly. *Justice,* on the other hand does not tolerate forgiveness until punishment has been fixed. The *beauty* of both justice and mercy is that it can become *symmetrical*. Meaning is the epistemology of philosophy. As Ayn Rand said, "Philosophy is the foundation of science and epistemology is the foundation of philosophy." Meaning is the essence of epistemology and a good epistemology tree needs a three-by-three reference grid.

Not only has physics played havoc with the meaning of space and time, but religion has also turned upside down the meaning of faith. An active principle, faith has been pushed into subjectivity. Like faith, the meaning of words are meshed together in order to lull the mind into thinking two contrasting words mean the same thing. Such is the case with free enterprise and capitalism. Free enterprise obeys the law of conservation, but capitalism does not. Just as conservation maintains equilibrium in the marketplace, capitalism ignores it and periodically will depress free enterprise.

Another word that fits with measurement and the number six is observation as well as the other senses. In general we often talk of the sixth sense to complete the category. Observation has six aspects in itself. They are the basic two dimensions, the perspective third, motion the fourth, color the filth and intensity the sixth. Note also that the senses and their ability to measure lie on the intuitive or feminine side and conservation is like reason and justice on the masculine side. We have now completed the predicate portion of our epistemology tree in **Figure 9-4**.

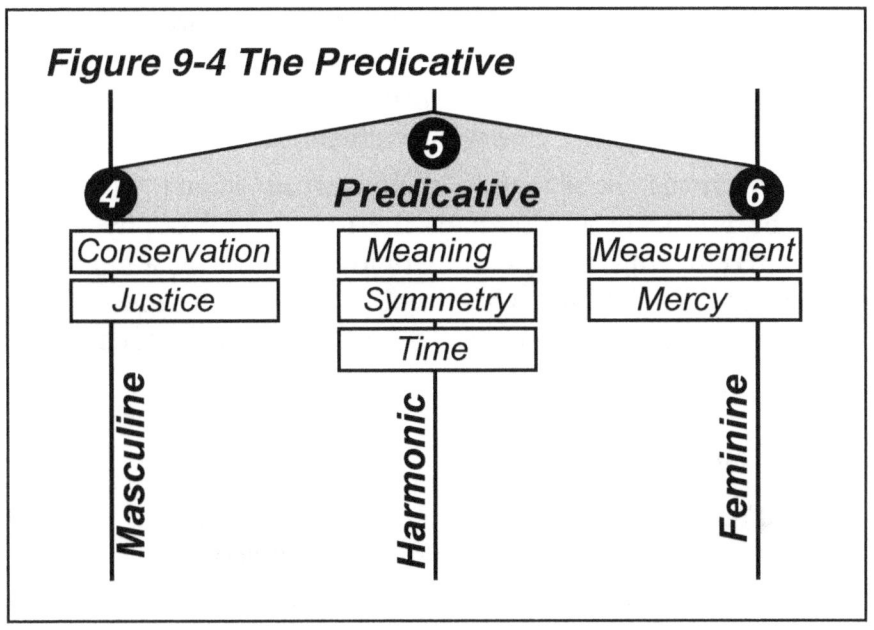

Figure 9-4 The Predicative

Once *conservation, meaning,* and *measurement* are illustrated, we can associate other words that fit the tree respectively. What applies to physics applies to any discipline. The Kabbalah has the following:

4. Justice   5. Beauty   6. Mercy

Five also incorporates many spiritual words. These words are harmonics of justice and mercy. When one truly loves he does not give to get gain or give to appease, but he gives in a way that encourages responsibility in the recipient. The tree illustrates that justice is masculine, mercy is feminine and beauty is the harmonic. All of these are predicative terms. They are not subjective nor are they objective. They are dynamic predicate principles. Responsibility is the essence of this predicate reality. The Jews place beauty as the harmonic, but they did not mean physical beauty. For this is why I prefer symmetry for beauty. Symmetry is a word for beauty and harmonizes better. Justice has the same connotation as conservation and depends upon it to have any sort of meaning. Mercy is like measuring all the general or more intuitive aspects and not just the particular or distinctive laws of justice. I cannot be more emphatic than to say that mercy is like intuition at work. It sees things hidden. Faith, Love, and Charity are perfect harmonics of justice and mercy, and they describe very well what faith should be.

It can also be seen that religious words seem to fall in line with the predicate and perhaps the reason philosophy avoids them. In returning to physics, I would place time as a harmonic in the predicate reality. This would then give us the obvious three harmonics for physics and a look into objective reality:

1. Space is subjective
5. Time is predicative
8. Mass is objective

Figure 9-5 displays both Jewish concepts and terms I have drawn from physics in regard to the objective.

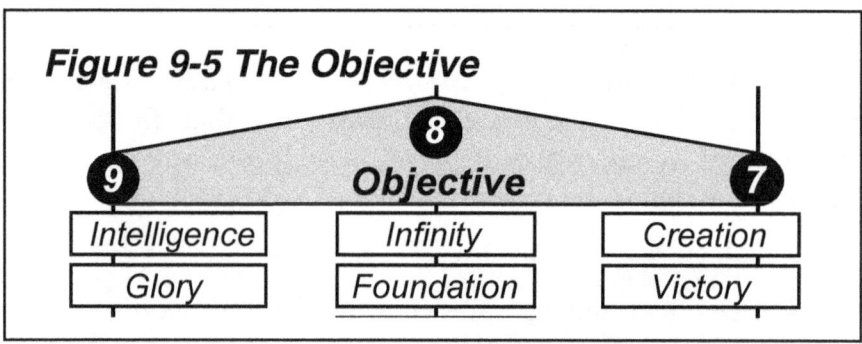

Within Kabbalah writings there are various interpretations from different authors and traditions. The following are the meanings I have gleaned in summary of many variations. The attempt here is to avoid mysticism that is often found in the objective level. The Jews called this the level of creation. This objective or creative level has three generally accepted words.

> **7. Victory**...an attribute of goodness upon *creation* and *infinite* victory over death, Confidence with willingness to sacrifice. "Thou shalt not fear."
>
> **8. Foundation**...the power to *create*. This is the grounding of our beginnings with God. "Thou shalt verify convictions."
>
> **9. Glory**....an attribute over *creation*. Power to *infinitely*

advance with supreme purpose. "Thou shalt increase in the light of truth."

It seams that these attributes, unlike those of the mind and those of the heart, are goal orientated. For example: reason and intuition are internal subjective processes, justice and mercy are the actions we apply to others, and glory and victory are what we hope to obtain for ourselves.

The basic harmonic derived from physics is mass as it corresponds to space and time. The Jews had foundation but often referred to it as creation. In the objective world, mass represents a good foundation for objective existence. The essence of creation is gravitational mass. Without it, nothing would exist. If creation is number seven or one of the objective terms, it should incorporate all of the previous six axioms. Creation is governed by equilibrium—the essence of equality. Creation has a distinction between inertial and gravitational matter. The law of proportion was fundamental in determining the elements. All of the elements were determined because the elements came in certain proportions. The law of conservation in its distinct form governs creation. Creation has symmetry if not purpose or meaning. Creation can be measured in that it has dimension and mass. The essence or intuitive aspects of creation can be found in infinity. This would mean than infinity generalizes creation and creation particularizes infinity. This would suggest that creation is number seven and infinity conveniently the next number eight. Creation would naturally be a feminine term, but this would place it on the right side with infinity a harmonic.

Eight is a perfect harmonic to one. The Jews of antiquity put creation at the lower center often referring to procreation as a human concept. Creation is essentially objective reality, but here discussed it becomes the feminine aspect of sustenance rather than a harmonic.

If seven is on the right and nine is on the left, this can become acceptable. It would not be unlike the left-brain controlling the right side of the objective body and the right brain respectively controlling the left side. The brain wants to read from left to right and the body wants to respond from right to left. Perhaps there is some reason the Hebrew reads from right to left other than tradition. Some people are left-handed when they are more artistic than logical. This is just something to think about. I have just let terms fall where they must and creation would naturally be feminine.

The Hebrew word *victory* is an attribute of goodness upon creation—an infinite victory over death. The confidence and willingness to sacrifice is the work of creation. Victory has been placed on the right but often the Kabbalah would also switch the masculine and feminine sides leaving victory on the left. This could certainly cause confusion from generation to generation. None the less the Kabbalah referred to *glory* as an attribute above creation. Glory was the power to infinitely advance with supreme purpose. Its origins implied intelligence as in the Glory of God is intelligence.[2] Antiquity did not have a word for intelligence and thus glory was used as if light was the radiation of this greatness. Light and intelligence are often associated allegorically as similar.

Intelligence could be used as a masculine aspect while creation the feminine. In physics, light demonstrates both the reflection of mass and the particle of its creation. On the masculine side we are viewing light in its ability to reflect and give us understanding. On the feminine side we understand light as a component of all mass. On one side we have insight and the other we have organization. However, in looking at both the masculine and feminine objective aspects we need to consider that both sides are physical. Just as creation is objective building blocks, intelligence must also be objective in its different building units. This is why I introduced the concept of a control particle to correspond to electric particles with the magnetic particle as the harmonizing field. Magnetic particles interact with the electric to produce matter and magnetic particles interact with control particles to produce intelligence. This gives the objective aspects of intelligence without trying to make intelligence something from electric matter as evolution does. Rather intelligence evolves of itself while electric matter entropies—needing creation.

Earlier, intelligence was associated with the subjective because we were not studying the physical composition of intelligence, but rather we were considering the dynamics of intelligence that produce reason. It is like the dynamics of mass—producing the force of gravity. Consider that the way intelligence comprehends position and dimension is through the subjective reality of space, the predicate reality of time, and the objective reality of mass. Just because intelligence is particular in nature does not do away with the dynamic or subjective aspects of intelligence and its ability to reason.

When talking of intelligence and creation, we are talking of two objective universes superimposed. Between reason and objectivity lies the verb, but between objective intelligence and creation lies the objective harmonic of infinity. There is no better harmonic than the magnetic field. It is the magnetic field that organizes or creates mass. This concept is more fully explained in a book following *The Platonic Idiom*. In *The Einstein Illusion* I will explain how the magnetic field is the cause of gravity and that there is no such thing as a graviton. Relativity will also be intelligently explained rather than remain a mystery.

The harmonic of objective reality is the infinity of the magnetic field. There is no space in which there is no magnetic field and where there is a magnetic field there is a potential for intelligence and electric properties to coexist. Just as light fills the universe without direct interaction with matter, intelligent particles may also fill the universe without any interaction to create intelligence. This is the whole of objective reality. Electric properties are not the whole as science so often assumes. Intelligence is that other universe that is mistakenly assumed to be a part of electric matter. The magnetic fields in the brain are interfaced fields communicating with the physical universe.

The magnetic field is probably subordinate in some way to intelligence but it would be the general essence of gravitational creation. In placing mass as a harmonic I am really talking about mass in terms of the dynamics of intelligent creation. Intelligence has its own particular nature, but its dynamic is to choose to create. The magnetic field is the interface in order to do so.

In terms of fields, objectivity can be defined as:

7. Creation (a physical arrangement of an electric and magnetic field)
8. Infinity (a physical nature of a magnetic field)
9. Intelligence (a physical arrangement of a control and magnetic field)

Intelligence is infinite not as creation but as individual evolution. That makes infinity subordinate to intelligence rather than greater than it. The reason that most minds cannot accept a separate objective intelligence is that most think only in distinction and not relation. Even modern physics that strains to foster a fourth dimension does so with a two dimensional analogy because that is the way carnal minds think. The evolutionist does the same thing. They can only think linearly from one distinctive effect to another. Intelligent cause is not considered. **Figure 9-6** adds the three objective particle fields.

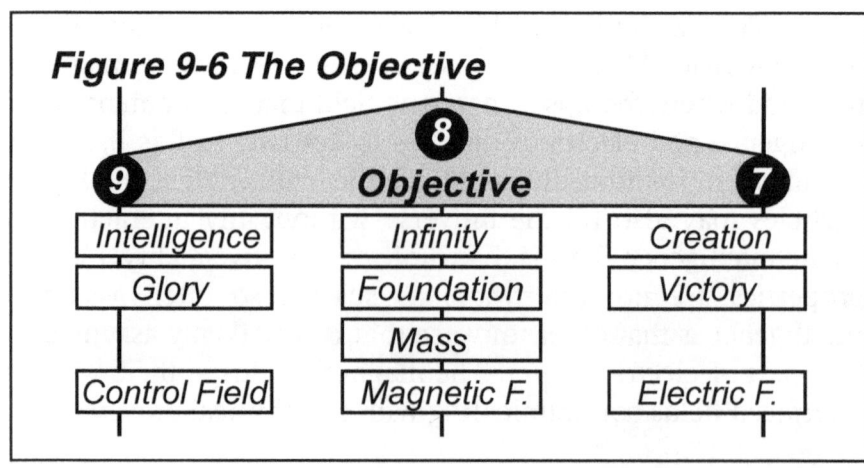

Every dichotomy is Platonic in origin and does not provide variables because those variables imply responsibility. Just as relativity and its defiance of conservation of mass challenges responsibility, so too does evolution. Intelligent creation means we are responsible. Evolution says that responsibility is the figment of man's imagination. Every discipline fosters linear dichotomies to scare away the reality of responsibility. Whether politics, economics, psychology or even religion, the issue of responsibility surfaces as the same. Concoct an idea that will relinquish responsibility and man will fall in love with it. Plato said, leave responsibility to the state and the philosopher king. This same attitude is usually the product of the educated intellectual, because it is their desire to set controls. They are forever learning but never come to the knowledge of the truth.

I was once talking with a fundamentalist thinker who followed certain traditional forms that governed her political, religious, and economic directions. I had frustrated her so much with doubt and taught her to question her own thinking that she cried out, "I just want to be told the truth so I know what to believe." I was shocked to see that minds do not want understanding, because they do not want to question and become responsible. They want to follow blindly what they have been taught to believe. Tradition is stronger than the cords of death. If anyone dismisses an idea without contemplation and questions, he fosters membership in the most irresponsible thought processes of Platonic thinking—it's good because it is forced upon us.

Consider that intelligence has eight components that manifest its ability, as in the ability to see equality, the ability to see distinctly, the ability to see in proportion, the ability to see in conservation, the ability to define, the ability to measure, the ability to create, and, above all, the ability to comprehend infinitely. Intelligence can conceive and it has the capacity to square things such as space and say, "If you come to the end, what is beyond? If existence curves, what lies at right angles to its path?" If you say, "Another curve," I will say, you then have an infinite number of curves. This gives us only eight, so we need a generalizing and intuitive principle to allow intelligence to be a particular of something greater. I will use Pythagoras's word *perfection* as an appropriate number ten. Perfection generalizes intelligence as no other word can. It is what intelligence must strive for or become non-intelligent. Of what value is a lot of gibberish error to a person of intelligent capacity? It is as if he seeks darkness that will eventually make him appear unintelligent. He who is driven by psychological motive is not as intelligent as he thinks.

Consider that every axiom is an attribute of God. Under this condition we have what the Jews called the *Sephiroth*. Sephiroth is a Hebrew word meaning *counting*, *number*, or *statistics*. It is also a representation of the ten Divine enumerations, or attributes in the Kabbalah of Judaism. Authorities vary and each has their own configuration. The sides of the Sephiroth or Tree of Life align to the feminine and the masculine. It is interesting to note that the romantic languages have masculine and feminine articles. Why is this? Perhaps this is what is missing in philosophy, science, and especially epistemology.

I have been interested in Pythagorean principles, knowing that there are many hints and suggestions of an ancient connection between numbers, geometry, and the Kabbalah from antiquity and that the teachings of Pythagoras are Middle-Eastern in origin in that Pythagoras went to Egypt and consented to be circumcised by the Jewish priests in order to gain access to the mysteries. This may have been the origin of the Pythagoras expression, "All things are numbers."

Knowing that the original ways of the masters would have been distorted and added to, I set out to create my own numbering system using the corrected terms of physics. Once completed with the rigid demand of making sure a word had the number of components equal to the number assigned and also placing it in the appropriate reality, I created my own epistemology tree. The purpose was to lock the meaning of things, for it is the nature of man to twist, turn upside-down, and to change in order to suit a personal formula. This process not only helped to resolve problems in philosophy but it also resolved modern relativity and other scientific issues.

Before I end this chapter consider one more tree:

2. Preposition   1. Subject   2. Adjective
4. Agreement   5. Verb   6. Adverb
7. Preposition   8. Object   9. Adjective

Whatever the subject, the epistemology tree helps the mind keep relationships to the masculine and feminine and to the proper reality. Perhaps it is more of an art than a science, but the process is how intelligence works toward a greater ability to relate rather than simply distinguish through a linear fashion or only by a dichotomy. It is a greater ability to find knowledge. It must be understood that laying down meaning consistently is the acquisition of knowledge. Collecting facts and data may show one's ability but it does not show knowledge. To know something is to understand it. If only education could see this we might solve the many problems currently inherent in our tendency to think in terms of position rather than relational concepts. Great minds learn to think out of the traditional norm of linear equations and seek understanding by vertical analysis.

Dialectic dialogue does not establish understanding without continuing the meaning of terms. Plato failed in this regard. Discussion with open questions about meaning will remove many contradictions that cause positioning. It takes several minds rather than one to get perspective. All should have equal opportunity to express without fear of reprisal. The typical lecture simply fills the mind with data and the need to agree with the instructor to get gain. A great instructor follows the format of Socrates and involves all to take a stand and commit his or her worldview to the test.

The essence of the epistemology tree is to nail down the meaning of reality in order to foster clear understanding and avoid superstition, magic, mental illness, and a false sense of existence. This whole process makes you a philosopher of the purest kind. This type of mind is clear headed with understanding and will not be filled with dogmatism. If you think this process is too rigid, then consider that truth must be rigid and absolute. If you prefer truth to be relative then you perhaps desire a little magic, more freedom to see what you want, more freedom to foster some personal formula, and more freedom to escape responsibility.

For those with an advanced curiosity, I mentioned at a point that ten was perfection to Pythagoras. I also mentioned that Christian prophecy spoke of the Tree of Life as having *twelve manner of fruit*.[3] This extends the objective into another level I shall refer to as *kingdom*. This level might be like the subjective state or dynamics of a community, kingdom or state. For the Jews, *kingdom* is number ten. But if we extend to twelve, we need two more. This social level represents the level of man in the highest state. This is not personal salvation as commonly thought of in Christianity but social righteousness. I suggest the following:

10 Perfection
11 Brotherhood
12 Priesthood

Ten is from Pythagoras and instead of using kingdom here as did the Jews, I reserve Kingdom for the whole level. If the Tree of Life was given to the Jewish priest of antiquity two points were perhaps held out because man cannot accept community responsibility without legislated force. If ten represents perfection it should be understood that this could only be achieved on the community or kingdom level and not the individual level as commonly misunderstood. This issue will be covered in latter chapters. In this case, *perfection* is a harmonic. It is the next harmonic in the second octave. It is here that ten represents the third harmonic in the second octave. Perfection is the harmonic of true brotherhood and true leadership.

If you like, come up with your own words or see if you have a better numbering of the above three. I use eleven and twelve because the book of Revelation spoke of twelve manner of fruit in the tree of life as if something were added to the Jewish ten. This suggests that the ideal kingdom of heaven may be a part of what John was seeing. Plato tried to initiate the ideal community, but it fostered control rather than responsibility. The predicate reality demands adherence to responsibility. Predicativism requires action and action implies doing something about truth rather than pontificating upon it.

The Tree of Life is an important representation in nearly every culture. To the Jews the branches reached into the sky, and the roots went deep in the earth as if it dwells in three worlds. The three worlds served as an allegory of three concepts or realities. It was these concepts that made it possible to reach heaven or social sightedness. The dynamics of heaven is often misunderstood, but the earth is usually treated as something evil, but it is actually a world of good and evil or things black and white. The Tree of Life was a method of reaching heaven and rising out of a dichotomy of good and evil. In order for man to rise to heaven's understanding, he must learn to fix the meaning of words in the proper reality and gender. In this we learn responsibility. This was the purpose of the Tree of Life. If we do not accept responsibility, we will term-twist that which is handed down into something mystical. The ancient Priests knew the three realities of mind, spirit (right action) and body. They also knew the purpose of the Tree of Life. When they lost the purpose, the Tree of Life became a depiction of the three carnal worlds rather than three realities that will guide us in the ability to reach heaven—the brotherhood and leadership required for all to gain intelligently. If we cannot gain the brotherhood and practice sound leadership, we are sometimes better off without science and technology. If technology falls into the wrong hands, we will certainly feel that we would have been better without it.

The full Epistemology Tree is show in **Figure 9-7.**

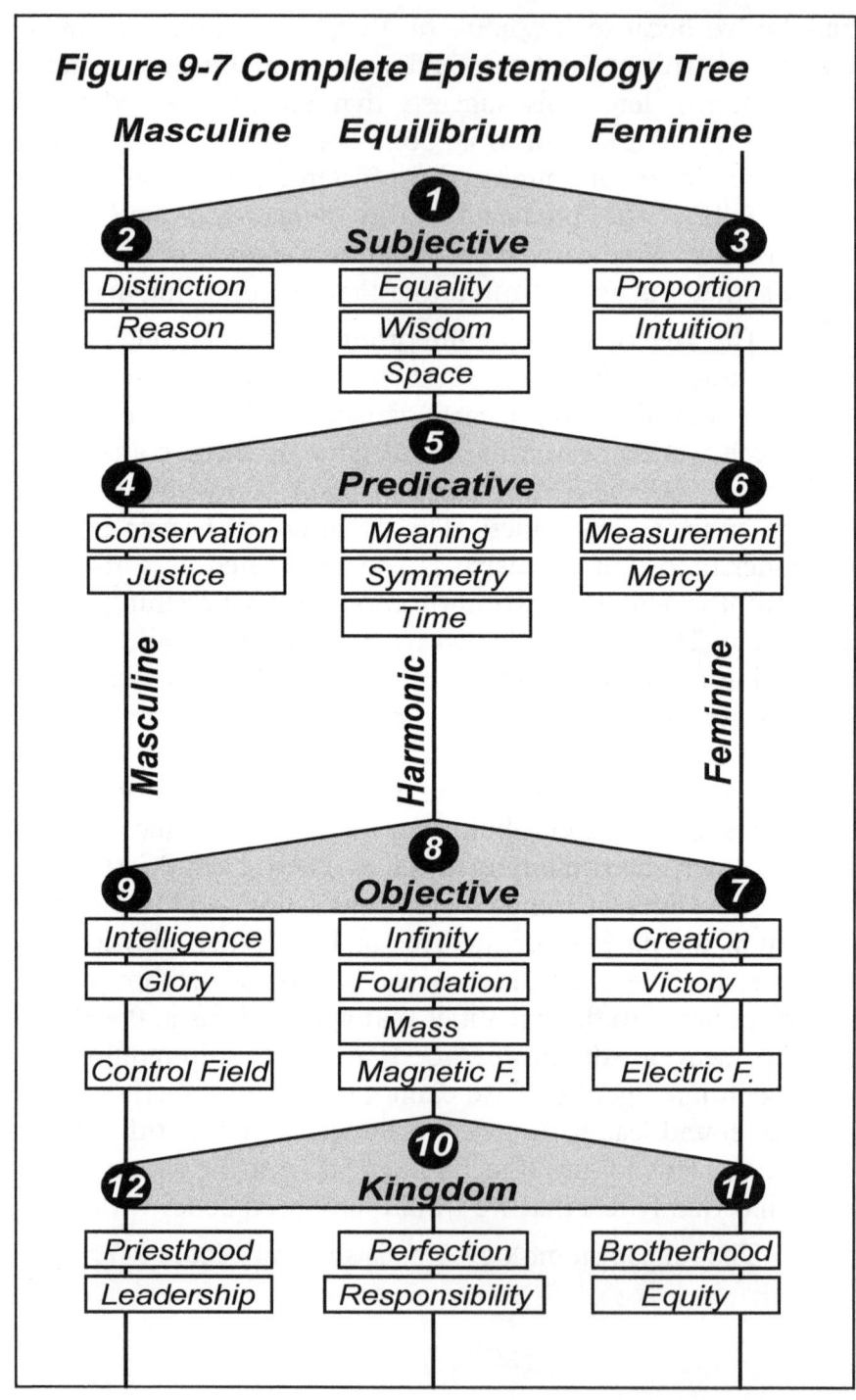

Child insecurity is manifest in both the timid and the bully. As we grow up, we simply cover our weakness by altering the way we position our philosophy and establish our worldview. Our philosophy will become timid or it will bully away our fear. We rarely overcome our insecurity.

Samuel Dael

10. Pushing Reality Around

The meaning of philosophy comes from the Greek meaning "the study or pursuit, or love of wisdom." Wisdom appropriately has a mix of reason and intuition. To have wisdom may suggest one's having or learning some sort of perceptible knowledge. As suggested earlier, wisdom is the harmonic of reason and intuition and thus a complimentary or holistic method of achieving knowledge or the meaning of things. It would be similar to a masculine or feminine methodology of expressing what two see from different points of view. True philosophy must be more than just reasoning. That means that it must include aspects of religion and other intuitive methodologies without resorting to magic and mysticism, which do not support sound philosophy. If a religious concept is mystical it does not aid philosophy unless the concept is allegorical in order to cover the true concept.

From this perspective, we shall study the various forms of philosophy keeping in mind that there is the subjective, the objective, and the newly introduced predicate reality. Instead of finding one's personal preference, we will try to work them all together. This will not be to compromise, but I suggest the possibility that each originator of a particular philosophy is looking from a different psychological perspective rather than from reason and intuition. By psychology I wish to suggest unconscious motive and the desire for eminence. Perhaps some new forms of philosophy are legitimate in pointing out previously accepted errors of one sidedness or narrow-mindedness, but the new philosophy may still be lacking the ultimate truth. We should keep in mind that the holistic process may be more acceptable to all of philosophy than cornering some view into a rigid reality just because something seems odd in the other corner. Plato was the first to overemphasize his corner in order to diminish the other. We should ask: Was Plato looking for eminence? Did he have the love for philosophy that Socrates had?

The need to establish control is often a manifestation of fear and past rejection. Was Plato putting so much control upon his state that it revealed his unconscious fears? Has every mind since been simply a manifestation of the same problem? It is worthy to note that Socrates did not write. This indicates honest intent to instruct rather than satiate the desire to write for eminence. We need to thank Plato for giving us insight into the mind and heart of Socrates and we need to thank the Jewish priests for giving the Greek philosophers the oral knowledge. For without someone writing down the oral we would have nothing to counteract that which is written for aggrandizement.

Nothing ever written is absolutely new. Few consider that a full spectrum of reason and intuition was lost in antiquity. Man does not advance in knowledge as often thought. The assumption that what we have obtained comes from knowledge is erroneous. The knowledge of technology has evolved, but knowledge of it does not foster wisdom. I find that technology often dilutes attention away from that which is fundamental and enlightening. Our minds are filled with such vast amounts of easy things that we no longer see in perspective, as did the ancients.

The perspective of three realities offers the best solution since Plato. If you are bothered by the predicate, consider the mind, heart, and body as representations of three realities. Allegorically, the mind coincides with the subjective, the heart with the predicative, and the body with the objective. We use the three because we intuitively know that there are three realities. I do not wish to suggest that the heart feels something as used in the expression, "I feel in my heart." The heart pertains to the active. By active I would suggest that the statement "It is good to have patience" implies a predicative process where patience is the predicate and the whole statement is a statement of wisdom or intuition depending upon its connotation, source, and contextual application. To better understand the missing predicate, consider first what philosophy studies and how reality is pushed around.

Metaphysics

When we think of physics we think of school day physics and subatomic particles. Philosophy therefore asks if there is anything beyond matter. It also asks: What is the status of the soul or mind and the intelligence it manifests? Is there another form or order of reality other than what science can measure? Also, is there a difference between the way this material world is and the way we perceive it? In other words, does the act of observation see things differently than existence really is? I attempted to answer both these questions in previous chapters. When I suggested the existence of a control particle this was perfectly acceptable as a philosophical form under metaphysics. In addition to this I suggested that the electric field exists as the feminine aspects of objective reality while the control field manifests the masculine aspects of objective reality. The existence of either was dependant upon the interaction of the magnetic field.

It may be legitimate for science not to concern itself with unseen things, but philosophy must always ask such things. Science found its roots in philosophy and to most it has taken control of the truth. This is very sad indeed, for philosophy still adds the questions necessary for science to pursue the unknown. Sometimes a particular philosophy denies the known. In this it has attempted to become an island unto itself. To suggest something additional should not be a problem when that known is not set aside. Science makes the mistake of thinking that all things are electric properties and that the unknown metaphysical cannot be. Some philosophies on the other hand deny the physical altogether. It is one thing to say, "It cannot be," but it is much better to say, "It is not known to be." It is the responsibility of science to tell us what is *known* and what is *not known*. Science should never tell us what is by assuming only an electric reality when a metaphysical answer may make good sense. Keeping questions alive about things beyond the physical should always be a tool of philosophy. To deny the unknown is narrow and assuming. The only concern is to maintain equilibrium and conservation in our thinking.

Epistemology

This brings us to the question, "What is knowledge?" and what is opinion or even what is the relationship between the person who knows and the thing that is known? How do we acquire knowledge and are there limits to what the human mind can know? Is knowledge the accumulation of information or is it the understanding of what we learn? Do we really need to question the aspects of knowledge that science has come to understand? To do so says that knowledge can never be known and that is a contradiction of the very meaning of knowledge. Knowledge is to know otherwise why use such a word that means to comprehend. The pedantic games the philosopher will play often redefine words and meaning to such an extent that there is a tendency to say we really never will know. We do not need to know absolutely. It is sufficient to have a very high probability. And if understanding is based upon conservation, one can bet on that knowledge. If conservation is put asunder, one can bet that what is thought of as knowledge is not as stated.

As said earlier science has the corner on knowledge and thus philosophy has filled its mission for spawning science and the ability to discover truth and thus add to our vast amount of understanding. That does not mean that philosophy needs to neglect the rediscovery of knowledge. I use the term

The Platonic Idiom

rediscovery because the knowledge I am referring to is a further understanding of love, patience, justice, mercy, faith, and many other active concepts we find in reality. The difference between these principles and the knowledge of science is the difference between the predicate and the objective. Science has made very high inroads into objective truths, but philosophy may still be groping with predicate values and axioms. Even though religion has assumed this role for centuries, the Socratic Method most certainly can add greatly to this process—a process that does very well in coming to terms with the meaning of things. Essentially, this is the role of epistemology.

Epistemology has been thought of as some sort of internal ability to know things. Plato's use of the dialectic method assumed that human beings had knowledge stored in their minds at birth, but perhaps at a subconscious level only. Under this view knowledge would have to be brought out through the dialectic process rather than something learned through some logical process. If knowledge is learned, this is no improvement over the assumption that knowledge is within us, for the originator of an idea passes the learned material with various basic assumptions to another. In the whole process we tend to neglect motive to establish oneself. If something within us were already there, it would be in having the ability to distinguish regurgitating information from true understanding. Only when understanding surfaces can we surely say we have knowledge? This inner ability would be to weigh, compare, relate, and question rather than lift some pre-stored knowledge to the surface as Plato suggested. Perhaps this is what he intended to explain and perhaps his use of knowledge misinforms us. I give Plato the benefit of doubt, but we should know that to learn facts is not necessarily the same as to understand those facts. The light bulb that goes on in the mind does not say, "I have added information." It says, "I now understand what I did not understand before about the information I already have learned." First we learn, and then we understand. To learn is to add something. To understand is to see relationships. Intelligence is an ability we already have and knowledge is what we have come to understand after we have learned facts. We should understand the difference between what is learned and true knowledge.

In the military sense, intelligence is to gather but in philosophy it is the ability to understand relationships. Some have the ability and some do not have it sufficiently to understand. More information may help, but some see with little information what the end will be. The mistake we make about intelligence is to think it is quantitative. Over time we may get better in qualifying our understanding as we quantify our information. To know under this definition is to say that knowledge is to qualify while learning is to quantify information. Intelligence may be required for both, but as mentioned earlier, intelligence may come in types. Quality intelligence is like sharpening the image already obtained. It is like giving dimension, depth, and rendition to accumulated information. This is essentially what knowing means. Fundamentally it is clear understanding that gives us meaning and not so called learned information.

The problem we have with epistemology is that one man's rendition is another man's gibberish. Epistemology is like art. Unless one is cultivated in design, a modern art piece is spilt paint. The real difference between cultivated design and accidental swashes is not in the colors but in the arrangement of relationships. Epistemology in this sense clarifies the relationships and arrangement of meaning. Epistemology is like art more than we care to accept. I do no mean that it cannot be a science in some sort of mathematical sense, but I do mean that the clarification in meaning is the beauty of epistemology. Even in music, numbers assigned to particular arrangements reveal the science of harmony in the art of composing. We thus can hope as we clarify the meanings of love, faith, justice and the like that we can eventually come to relationships that help nail our meanings of these terms.

Plato concluded at the end of his first book on the *Republic* that he did not know the meaning of *justice*. Yet, Plato went to great lengths later to suggest that justice was reached when a tradesman remains only in his specified skill. To try another skill was not justice. Perhaps this is the origin of union thinking or maybe a natural propensity of linear thinking. Plato assumed that man could not make a mistake in his own profession. Plato sought for some ideal state and the efficiency of labor rather than considering that the happiness of the individual would make a better state. Too many think that controlling things contrary to individual input actually yields results. This is fallacious. Of what value is a perfect state if the desires of the individuals in the state are not considered? The true State is a compilation of individuals and not an artificial program created by the mind. Plato did not have the wisdom to see that the State quality would diminish because the individual would play second fiddle to the State. Is not justice to allow each individual to discover his or her own skill and the desire to perfect it? Is it not possible for true justice to find adjustment if one chooses the wrong skill and later finds something more enjoyable?

Do we curve fit the meaning of things to our own liking simply to find comfort in our ideas, or perhaps do we change reality in order to deny individual responsibility? Ignorance of the truth is the inability to see the true meaning of justice. Perhaps we have seen so much injustice in the world that we conjure up a system that makes it impossible for injustice to work its evil again. Do we not realize that the new system we have created fosters a new meaning of justice to cover our own inadequacy, fear, and lack of faith in individual responsibility? This lack of faith comes from an intelligence having the inability to relate to broader concepts of conservation such as what goes around comes around. If only we were taught by the wisdom of others, might we avoid the false ideas we create and eventually see justice for the individual as the ultimate meaning applied? It is not much different than when one considers a youthful teenage girl thinking she knows what love is. Peer pressure has taught her a meaning that does not equal the meaning of the wise and she lacks the intuition needed because she lacks the innate ability to see. Her parents never taught her the principle of true love and they rarely came close to demonstrating it for her. Thus the young teenage girl has taken an objective view to the meaning of love as she mixes in the biological drives of nature. She will be blind to the truth until she learns from her mistakes or is perhaps taught by the true love of another. It does not matter how intelligent one is in gathering information. Seeing the true meaning of things is innate or must be demonstrated in order to add to one's intelligence. If this is not done soon, the individual will fall prey to denial and fear and will find it difficult to escape the false meanings of love. Perhaps we were abused as young children and learned to control the lives of others in order to bring equilibrium to the system rather than to learn that true meaning is equilibrium within. Plato had a problem with the meaning of justice as his philosophies manifest. Plato never overcame his childhood ideas about the meaning of things and even Socrates could not help him.

Fear and unconscious motive may drive the meaning of words far more than we realize. The scientist may have a handle on the meaning of physical nomenclature, but have no understanding of words such as compassion. A savvy businessman may have a handle on the meaning of sound investment, but lack the ability to understand the true meaning of justice. A politician may understand the law in every detail but lack the personal ability to love, and a teacher may deliver important information but lack trust in the oral discussion that surfaces questions realized by students. The predicate world is truly an uncharted world as to the meaning of things and in this respect epistemology has only begun its mission. Knowledge of objective things seems clear, but the knowledge of predicate action is so far behind that it behooves us to lay aside our propensities of denial and adopt the Socratic methods in schools, churches, and families in order for proper discussion to bring to the surface true meaning of predicate words and ideals. I have fashioned a way in the previous chapter. The Jews at one time did it for many years and that is perhaps the reason they were able to rise with great intellect. The modern orthodox Jew, however, has come to the level of memorizing the Torah rather than encouraging open discussion. The anti-Socratic mind, if you study closely, is conditioned to mimic what he learns and does not really understand the meaning of things. All the unwise can do is to call the wise evil. Their emotionalism is so wired they cannot see the true meaning of justice or responsibility. Essentially, their epistemology suffers tragically. Every evildoer struggles with a poor epistemology and the meaning of words. To study history as historical data does little for the mind without studying the meaning historical figures applied to words. We have missed the importance of epistemology.

Ethics

Usually thought of as moral principles, can ethics be more? Is ethics related to openness and honesty or does it have some other criteria? How is one justified in doing that which is not ethical? A relational word perhaps may be fairness or the foundation of the word ethics may be rooted in the word equality. Ethics is a branch of philosophy, but writers generally avoid the true meaning of this predicate term in favor of a Godless universal decency. I think this is due to psychologically evasive attitudes that avoid the ultimate responsibility of putting more into the system than you receive or at least being open and honest. Many may think they are ethical as long as they are legal. Ethics in general says that you simply do not mislead or take advantage of weakness. If ethics is a branch of philosophy, it must be shown that hidden motive is unethical. When we hide motive behind justice, morality etc. can we still be ethical? Perhaps we are not ethical with ourselves.

The study of ethics is none other than the study of open honesty, but who is going to be completely open? The more we clarify predicate terms such as justice, love, forgiveness, mercy, patience, and longsuffering, the more we can come to a better form of honesty.

Aesthetics

What is beauty or what is art? Does the judgment of what is aesthetically good differ from the art itself? Does function present an aspect of art or is it the expressiveness of the observer that interprets real beauty? Is beauty in the eye of the beholder or are there rules of design that determine good aesthetics? Should aesthetics be open ended and perhaps be classified as pure opinion rather than a priori knowledge? True opinion suggests that beauty is subjective. The only hope is to find some consensus of aesthetics in order to justify what is good. This also suggests that a better role of epistemology is needed in the meaning of the good as it pertains to subjective connotations. Just as a lack of epistemology gives us poor meaning of predicate terms, so too does the same give us poor meanings for subjective terms such as beauty and good design? Random opinion without some consensus of epistemology satisfies the subconscious more than intelligent understanding. In the predicate this same problem exists as to what is good. Every one has his own view based upon traditional motive and subconscious motive rather than clear epistemology of meaning. As for its meaning, aesthetics poses no different problem than religion does.

Like ethics, aesthetics need a consensus of meaning. Poor aesthetics, like poor ethics, has psychologically based drives. You can study the ethical personalities of several individuals and find that their art appreciation differs in a corresponding manner, as does their motive. Look at the jewelry, hairstyle, and clothing of the typical teen. Does it not suggest a psychological propensity equal to their unconscious motive? Poor aesthetics may indicate poor psychological motive but the same person may still possess good ethics. It could also be said that good choice of aesthetics may actually cover one's poor ethics. Just because the salesman looks nice does not mean that he is honest. Just because one is in rags and does not communicate well does not mean that he is to be mistrusted.

The commonality of ethics and aesthetics is that both have a psychological motive that lies somewhere in the complete spectrum between fear and self-confidence. But this can also be misjudged. Over confidence may be one's denial of fear and one's fear may express concern for the foolish motive of another. The only way out of this dilemma is open discussion and oral speculation. Writing helps, but hearing the responses of others helps us see ourselves as others see us. Too often we wait until someone is socially demented before they receive psychological help. Problems could be avoided if group therapy were constant in education, religion, and family. It would be like having a Socratic discussion regularly in order to avoid being controlled by unconscious motive. Rather we need to manage ourselves according to the true meaning of our actions and the true meaning of words.

Hidden motive is a lack of communication and a lack of understanding. It is caused by social norms and peer pressure and not based upon true meaning, but rather upon traditional control and ill confidence of those who claim to lead us. Even the motive of the movie industry creates a false sense of reality when it attempts to show scenes expressly created to satiate the viewer's own psychology. They call it art. Even though the direction is superb, the script is colorful, and the acting is realistic, nonetheless its design still satisfies a base psychological motive of the viewer. What one would term good art, another would term degradation. It is all due to the meaning of the terms suggested by the art form. Hollywood loves to show mercy for the gay. Their movies suggest that all gays are kind people and deserve acceptance. All gays are not kind anymore than all heterosexuals are kind. Hollywood loves to shoot against the grain in order to satiate hidden motive in all of us. The problem with this inordinate lust of the art is a total lack of meaning for the concepts illustrated in the art form. We are intimidated into believing in the new concepts without any Socratic discussion. Just as the politician, lecturer or preacher controls meaning, the movie does the same. We have lost the opportunity to discuss openly without fear and rejection.

We try to say that the movie depicts reality, but the motive is really to get attention in the same manner as the typical TV newscast. There is rarely honesty in the message on TV or the action in a movie. What we often seek is nothing more than death, sex, destruction, and other spilt paint images because it satiates our poor psychology of denial. There is an apparent search for justice in the movie and the newscast in order to allow the weak to feel good about watching something that just expresses their denial of death. We would rather see how close we could come to death and come out alive than learn to understand the motive that drives us. Those who find the movie artificial might find comfort in other art forms that also show death, contradiction, mystery and uncertainty. We consider ourselves more intellectual because the art is in a museum, but we do not understand that the psychological denial may still be the same.

There is not enough open and honest discussion in schools, communities, families, and churches, and there are more hierarchy and artificial ideals than true values. This pertains to ethics and also art. The consensus changes over time because social denial changes as each generation fails to grasp the meaning of its motive. They attach their own meanings to satiate a psychological propensity that can only be overcome with constant social conversation with the widest variety of people possible. It does not help the child to separate the grandparent from the various adult family figures. Also, when both the mother and father are exhausted from work, the children learn to take care of themselves and have plenty of money to spend. It stands to reason that their meanings about words will be the byproduct of their peers and not a good cross section from the wisdom of age. Eventually these types of youth grow up with surmountable problems finding themselves. What is missing is the epistemology or meaning that they would have received around more adults who took the time to talk.

The Socratic Method constantly asks questions to the group in order for each individual to come to grips with meaning. In this, philosophy has failed miserably. Why do we lecture ethics and aesthetics when our youth cannot get a solid epistemology on the most rudimentary words?

Logic

What is reasoning? Are there rules to follow or is it just dialectic conversation that brings us to the truth? Can rules of thought be developed and systematized as guides to good reasoning? Logic is supposedly the study of good reasoning. This discipline was covered earlier as a subjective process. I only wish to stipulate that any argument has assumptions. It is not unlike an equation that has incorrectly measured data for certain values. The equation is logical, but the conclusion is false because of the measured data. Such is the case of logic and the assumptions we so often insert into our reasoning. These insertions, as in the case of ethics and aesthetics, will definitely cloud the process. Again, the problem is not with logic but with the meaning of the terms used in rational equations. Incorrect meanings foster and support false assumptions.

As one can see, the problem has ballooned in modern times for the neglect of a sound epistemology. For some strange reason we do not test the meaning of the words we use as a scientist would test a theory. It is probably due to psychological factors and the traditional irresponsibility of human nature. Philosophy is no closer to the truth than Plato. In fact, philosophy runs the gamut of man's ability to corner the grand and glorious and extremely various isms in order to demonstrate his eminence upon the philosophical scene. The following represents these basic isms of history. I will attempt to save them in so far as finding the reality in which they belong and thus show that they are one-sided or narrow. In this respect, the authors have pushed reality into a personal corner to satisfy some misplaced meaning about life, God, and philosophy itself.

Monism

Monism is the metaphysical theory that the world is made up of only one kind of stuff or fundamental particle reality. There are still some ether theories that say the magnetic field and the electric field are both made up of ether particles. Reality, as these theories suggest, is simply ripples in the ether. To think of only one physical reality is presumptuous and to think of more than three is perhaps stretching it. Nature lends itself to opposites with a harmonic. Opposing forces in nature are not due to singularity. Even the opposition in things is often created by a third principle. The concept of ripples in a single ether substance leads us to think dissipation. Once quietness is reached as still waters, where does the force come from to gather together without a second element to supply the conditional force?

Materialism

Materialism is only one type of monism. So much of science cannot get into the spirit of a proportional reality. It was Thomas Hobbes who advanced the idea that there is only one reality and that is matter. His expression, "everything matters except nothing, which is nothing, because it doesn't matter" [1] has about as much sense as the meaning of *nothing*. Is not this the denial of responsibility and the excuse and justification of doing what you want to do because everything is predetermined and nothing is by choice? Such a single philosophy has governed the realm of science for generations and suggests that the scientist too has a psychological problem else why does science insist that nothing is real unless it can be measured? It is fine to say that we do not know, but to say it does not exist covers a hidden psychological motive. If we get the attention we so desperately desire, we are like the neglected child who is accepted out of strangeness rather than understanding. Science collects this type of personality and we should consider this scenario before we accept broad based conclusions that deny the possibility of two or even three realities.

Idealism

Idealism is another kind of monism. Idealists believe that the one fundamental reality is made up of minds or spirits and their ideas, a theory widely believed in Eastern cultures. I do not wish to demean idealism. I only wish to conclude that there is more than one reality. The ideas of Plato may have been more precise in definition than physical reality, but that does not say that physical reality does not exist in its various approximating conditions to the ideal. It does not say that just because the mind exists that the body does not. Just as materialism is found in the corner of objectivism, idealism is found in the corner of subjectivism. I think the problem stems from the missing third reality of predicativism that shows agreement between the subjective and the objective. This is what observation does. It is a predicate act and just because every image we see does not precisely equal the ideal definition, we gradually fine-tune our definitions because of what we see over and over again. The subjectivist thinks that what he has come to understand was never introduced to him by any other reality. This is pedantic child's play. Observation introduces to the subjective some sort of objective existence and meaning introduces to the objective what the mind can extrapolate. If philosophy had put observation in a third reality from the beginning rather than place it in the objective, a holistic approach would have surfaced naturally. Also, if philosophy had placed meaning in the predicate rather than the subjective, objective existence would have received the action extrapolated by the subjective.

Dualism

Dualism is a metaphysical theory that there are two and only two types of fundamental reality. Descartes defends a familiar version as mind and matter. This sort of conclusion resides in most Christian religions, but if you look closer to the master you will see the missing responsibility found in the predicate action of faith, love, and sacrifice. People want to believe in things but do not want to leave the dichotomy they so love. They continue to avoid the needed harmonic. Take an example in science that has preserved the dichotomy of the particle and wave theory of light for about one hundred years and has yet to be resolved. It is not that one needs to accept one or the other as one would accept the subjective or the objective. Science needs to come up with a model of light that will satisfy both theories. The spiral helix path of a particle of light does just this. No matter what the dichotomy, there is a third principle that will resolve it, but philosophy and science just do not want to suggest such a thing because it guides them away from their personal formulas that keep them away from the responsibility of clear meaning.

Pluralism

Aristotle was the defender of pluralism. It suggests that the world is made up of a plurality of types, classifications and divisions of fundamental particles. It is called a metaphysical theory, but it rather fits into the scheme of things as to objective reality. It just depends upon how deep you want to go. From Aristotle's four fundamental realities of air, earth, fire, and water to the science of the electron, proton, and neutron, it is not difficult to come up with more than one reality. The problem begins when we divide and further classify any of the physical realities. The only danger in pluralism is in the meaning of the term. Plurality means three or more, up to infinity. Once you go over three, opinion pervades the mind without any sense of harmony. Like Aristotle, we classify and divide into minutia. Infinity can be a form of escape just as making all things left handed or right handed. In some cases a trinity is difficult to accept whether in religion or science. Most prefer a sense of singleness while a trinity makes one feel the inability to put one's finger on things. Most follow a dichotomy of a dual track debating particle or wave, good or evil, and even prejudicial white and black. Monism is not unlike the expression "all three are one" taking all the definitive debate out of it.

The story of Adam and Eve favoring a dichotomy of good and evil rather than the responsibility of right action that looks for harmony in a dichotomy is an allegory for man's failure to assume responsibility under the Tree of Life. If one can think of three realities with three points of view in each, does this not develop better perception, wisdom, and understanding? The knowledge of good and evil is a wilderness of darkness. It is what all men choose and with it they choose death to understanding and meaning.

Rationalism

Rationalists are by and large mistrustful of experience; most particularly sense experience, which, they think, misleads us. This is not unlike Plato's idealism other than that it is based upon rules of reason rather than the dialectic process. Plato, however, was a true rationalist. The argument begins by showing how observation distorts things such as a pencil in a glass of water and other observed criteria. The assumption begins with the treatment of observation as objective. This begins the confusion and the adamant view of rationalists. If the act of observation were accepted as a distinct reality where an almost infinite number of observations of an almost infinite number of four-legged animals that bark and occasionally show their teeth with various sizes, fur renditions, and other somewhat similar conditions at a particular moment in time, a blink of the mind's eye comes to the understanding of the meaning of dogness. The mind's eye could never have come to the conclusion without the act of observation. According to Plato, sensory experience is not the source of our concept of dogness. He believed the concept was already in the mind and that observation only helped bring it to the surface. Such a view is coincidental. Rationalism has still yet to prove that observation, however irregular, does not participate in determining the meaning of objective things. The problem of sensory experience rises when it is used to give meaning to predicate and subjective things without discussing motive and various actions. When we see a young couple making it passionately, we have a hard time putting aside the physical action and considering motive, concern, patience, and charity—the real words that drive love. Likewise, every one has a different opinion as to what reason is. It is even more difficult to observe than love. Try to describe logic without an equation of three components. Rationalism may be principally a subjective process, but that does not deny the existence of the predicate and the objective as variables of any rational equation.

Empiricism

Aristotle attacked the rationalism of Plato and contended that our ideas are formed as a result of sense experience. Objects impress the senses much as a king's signet ring makes an actual physical impression after being dipped in hot wax and pressed onto parchment. Hume extended this empirical realm to a more holistic approach. He gave ability to the mind in what he called combining, analyzing, and transposing. He also gave sense experience the aspects of little experiential atoms of color, taste, sound, touch, and smell. Although reason leads the way, the senses have something to add and that addition is not objective. It is predicative. Empiricists seem more trusting when they think experience is the source of ideas. Could it not equally be that ideas are a source of experience? Experience is far more predicative than objective. This is why it seems to work both ways.

Empiricism does not deny reason. As Hume put it, Empiricism utilizes reason, observation, memory, and induction. He called them four methods of acquiring knowledge, but the expressions memory, reason, and induction are all subjective unless as a materialist you consider memory the motion of atoms. Hume also conceded to the rationalists that analytic truths are known a priori and unaided by sensory experience. Pure reason gives us knowledge of such truths. As I said it before I will say it again: reason is a logical analytic process, but it has assumptions and presuppositions gained by various observations and experiences built in. For example, take the statement, "All bachelors are unmarried." This synthetic statement is logical because the terms bachelor and unmarried carry complimentary meanings. Keep in mind that each person has various memories of experiences that demonstrate both being unmarried and being a bachelor. Simply hearing the description of a word justifies experience. If an individual never saw or heard of what it is to be married in order to relate to the term unmarried, would he still have a concept of being unmarried? We play too much upon the logic of the statement and fail to consider exactly how we come to know the meanings of the words. If our meanings were not correct or agreeable to the logic of the statement, we would consider a statement untrue, making it really not as synthetic as the logician would have us think. Synthetic statements only become synthetic when all meanings are clear and non-contradictory, otherwise we must use analysis to determine the truth of a statement even if that analysis is determining the meaning of the words used in the statement.

Empiricism is the best holistic philosophy we have, but it is dualistic unless you place observation and sense experience in the predicate. Understanding the predicate becomes the focus of truth. Take the traditional *a priori* statement "The shortest distance between two points is a straight line." Are we sure this is *a priori*? If you talk to a relativist you will get a false conclusion. The example usually given is a line on the surface of the earth being curved and thus the shortest distance is not a straight line. The problem with this sample does not inject the third concept of a physical barrier. Here again observation and experience confirm the definition of a straight line even when one understands that the earth is a physical barrier and cannot be traveled within a straight line. The typical relativist assumes foolishly by avoiding the third principle. Keep in mind that the term "straight line" has come to us by definition, and experience vindicates it. It can also be said that definition is a byproduct of repeated experience. Try to define something without showing or demonstrating. This demonstrating and showing is the predicate vindication of the *a priori* statement. Thus all truths originate in the predicate. Because the predicate is avoided, philosophy simply assumes that meaning just simply is and had no origin from experience.

Absolutism

Absolutism is an ethical theory about our morals and standards. It takes the view that there are no exceptions to a literally written law. Since this is more of a religious issue than a philosophical one, I will only state that any law is written to protect others as well as, in the religious sense, to improve our behavior. Law is an equation that needs to be in equilibrium at a moment in time and also over time, thus true justice has merciful eyes that see beyond the literal statement of law. This sort of wisdom comes by experience and a strong sense of balance. Taking law literally can be just as destructive as breaking a law. Harmony is the road to understanding law and wisdom is the art of its application.

Relativism

Relativism is an anti ethical issue that denies any absolute moral code. It says that no act is right or wrong and no human life absolutely good or bad. Cultural relativism is the theory that whether actions are right or wrong depends on cultural mores, which differ from culture to culture, and are merely social inventions intrinsic to the societies that invent them. Societies have reasons for inventing certain morals. They are usually intended to maintain control by those in authority and prevent relativism. If there is a rebellion, the current authority is usually replaced by another with different mores. Constitutional laws are designed in order to establish order and hopefully freedom from absolutism as well as extreme relativism. But when relativism fosters freedom from responsibility it ceases to have value. Relativism is actually the antitheses of absolutism. The extremes do handle responsibility differently. With relativism responsibility is to one's self, but with absolutism responsibility is to authority and tradition. Responsibility should be to others as one would be responsible to his neighbor. This requires absolute principles, but not absolute authority or tradition. True responsibility is relative to need and not relative to cultural code. Too often this distinction is not made. Absolute principles say that relativism eventually destroys responsibility to true principles. As to absolutism you cannot force the good and as to relativism the good is related to responsibility towards others as well as to self.

Relativism can be the enemy to responsibility and if carried to extreme, the pendulum of absolutism will eventually swing. This in turn will bring a pendulum fostering relativism. These two philosophies never seem to settle on the principle of true responsibility. One person may say that responsibility is just a form of absolutism and thus relativism is true freedom. How can you have true freedom without absolute responsibility to your neighbor? Each philosophy fosters one to destroy the other as if good and evil are at stake. Where is the harmony and true absolute wisdom?

Existentialism

The belief that human beings are different from any other form of beings, whether inanimate or animate is the basis of existentialism. This difference resides in freedom. We are born into the world without an essence or nature that predetermines what we are or what we will become. Likewise, God does not exist, so no divine purpose exists to guide our way. "Our life is what we choose to make it." The French philosopher Sartre coined this concept and it was used in the last scene in the movie "*Back to the Future III.*" Sartre recommended being true to oneself as the life worth living.

Idealistically, existentialism sounds good, but being true to one's self does not suggest responsibility to others. The problem with existentialism is that it neglects the law of conservation embedded in physical existence that has an effect on one's choice. In some descriptions, existentialism denies objectivity all together in that free choice is paramount over anything physical. One only has free choice within the bounds of a subjective existence and the conservation laws imbedded in all matter cannot be altered by free choice. On one hand, Sartre says that there is no God, and on the other hand the elements do not predict human behavior. This is an apparent contradiction. If Sartre believed in intelligent substance and avoided physical substance, then he was just positioning himself to the subjective. If there were this eternal intelligent substance, then why not attribute to intelligence the ability for some to eventually evolve to the point of becoming more intelligent than others until you come to the most intelligent of all in a galaxy or universe. You can now attribute to that intelligence some abilities that we attribute to God. You can dismiss the magic and mysticism of a God, but you cannot dismiss the wisdom of a great intelligence. To be honest, what destroys this concept is the motive of the big bang that appears to limit the evolutional timeline of intelligence. It must be said that the atheistic big bangers have a motive to kill God and they use the distortion of relativity to do so.

If there is no intelligent substance to establish free agency, and if physical matter cannot establish the same agency, from whence does it come? Sartre was pushing reality around in order to avoid the absolutism of the time. He missed the mark as so many have done in the past. If freedom is innate and not a prediction by the elements of individual intelligence, where did it come from or who gave it to us? Most existentialists want the freedom from responsibility and also the freedom from the requirements of a God. They fail to realize that the freedom to choose has a built in form of responsibility otherwise you take from another his freedom to establish your own. You cannot avoid the law of conservation. To keep the law of conservation, one must sacrifice for another in order to establish freedom for himself. Either we face the conservation laws in nature (unalienable rights) or we face manmade laws (inalienable rights) and attempt to conserve the same, or we cheat in any way we can, hoping we can truly make our lives as we choose. The latter takes freedom from others and eventually suppresses our own freedom making us more susceptible to the agency of others.

Existentialism is a contradiction for it is absolute in the denial of God and the elements, and extremely relative in its own making. Philosophy changes labels, but the same motive of absolutism or relativism still resides. Existentialism is another form of irresponsible relativism.

If one worshiped a God who must obey the laws of conservation embedded in the universe, it might give the existentialist a more acceptable concept for God. Sartre's God of his tradition was an all-powerful controlling God. This would explain his frustration. For God truly to exist he must obey the laws of conservation just as we must. Miracles are an extraction of energy from elsewhere to accomplish the good in a new place. God does not grant miracles without the willingness of sacrifice. Within the boundaries of conservation we have free choice as God does. This means responsibility is at the forefront and cannot be escaped. The main reason for rejecting God is to deny this responsibility. An existentialist is on the edge of a cliff. One more step into responsibility he might become a predicavist. All he needs to do is experience the law of gravity and recognize the law of physical reality. If free choice is able to deny the law of gravity, then God is a God of magic. The existentialist avoids this magic, but does not acquire responsibility. One cannot have it both ways.

Egoism

The most modern form of this philosophy comes from Ayn Rand. It is a capitalistic philosophy based on selfishness as the prime and necessary part of reality. Without it nothing would be achieved. Egoism has no absolute principles and all things are relative to one's self and the free will to do as one pleases. No one can truly say that selfishness brings a better way of life, for if it were not for the law that protects the innocent where would the Egoist be today? Look at the irresponsible management of big corporations and the failure of law to protect. Does not this selfishness bring misery to many? Even the egoist will eventually suffer. Egoism is an extension of existentialism with more of an emphasis on the objective reality and less on the gift of subjective freedom.

The modern Federal Reserve System is governed upon the principle that the Ego capitalist runs free and the only way to counteract his poor behavior is to adjust the interest rates according to his excess greed. This encourages irresponsibility and suggests that the responsibility needed was neglected. If we could find a more natural way to allow responsibility to be by choice, we would not only have a better economy, but a better world.

Predicativism

Predicativism does not support only the middle ground nor does it shift from side to side. It is a holistic reality that understands that meaning comes from the predicate over time, is solidified in the subjective, rationally deduced or induced and proven again by observation, and the real world receives the action predicted. This cycle is eternal and the predicate reality serves as the pathway to true understanding between the subjective and the objective. Most importantly, predicativism teaches responsibility because its three main components are justice, mercy, and harmony. Subjective reality also has three main components. They are wisdom, intuition, and reason. Objective reality must also have three components as intelligent matter, infinite magnetic matter, and organized or created electric matter. Nothing is denied by pushing reality around and all reality serves its destiny well.

I hope I have shown that human nature walks a tightrope. Philosophy has pushed reality around and falls to the subjective or it tumbles to the objective in order to avoid responsibility. Human motive is the cause and psychology the culprit. We need a better understanding rather than avoiding responsibility. There may be many more isms that position to one side of the spectrum or the other, but the psychology that drives them is usually the same. Everyone wants a piece of eminence without doing anything good. This has been the sickness of philosophy since Plato made the first step to fix reality into a controlling objective state while stating that reality was only subjective. Strange as it seems, Plato was a subjectivist and yet depended upon the objective state control. If we cannot see the psychological propensity in this then we too are defenders of the sinister Platonic Idiom. Why is it that the defenders of the subjective want to control the objective for which they deny?

There is a war going on and it is not a war of freedom verses tyranny. It is a war between worldviews. It is a war of ideals verses the real. It is subjectivism verses objectivism. It is a war of differences that cannot be reconciled by one winning over the other. It is a war that can only be overcome by clear meaning and continual Socratic discussion.

                                                              Samuel Dael

11. The Way of Socrates

When Plato introduced his idealism in the Republic, he was trying to authenticate his argument by using the name of Socrates. Plato was well versed in the way Socrates would question the meaning of terms, but in the Republic there was only one term discussed. It was justice. At the end of the first book the meaning was still elusive when Plato had Socrates saying, "And the result of the whole discussion has been that I know nothing at all. For I know not what Justice is." This was Socrates' style. He did not try to push his own meaning but would rather pull it from others. Socrates would not give up. Plato's style may appear the same as Socrates', but Plato eventually pushed his own meaning of justice in the name of Socrates as something only the state could provide. This was not Socrates' style and suggests that *The Republic* is Plato's doing and had nothing to do with the philosophy of Socrates.

The way of Socrates is expressed well in the first book of *The Republic*. Plato did understand the method and expressed it using a dialogue between Socrates in the company of six. I give a much shorter version with the characters indicated for clarification.

> Several times in the course of the discussion *(on Justice)* Thrasymachus had made an attempt to get the argument into his own hands, and had been put down by the rest of the company...there was a pause, he could no longer hold his peace...
>
> **Thrasymachus:** ...roared out to the whole company: "What folly, Socrates, has taken possession of you all...I say that if you want really to know what justice is, you should not

only ask but answer…for there is many a one who can ask and cannot answer. *(a slam to Socrates style)* …I must have clearness and accuracy."

Socrates: …"Don't be hard on us. Polemarchus and I may have been guilty of a little mistake in the argument, but I can assure you that the error was not intentional. …And why, when we are seeking for justice, a thing more precious than many pieces of gold, do you say that we are weakly yielding to one another and not doing our utmost to get at the truth?…"

Thrasymachus: …with a bitter laugh, "That's your ironical style! …have I not already told you *(to Polemarchus and the others)*, that whatever he was asked he would refuse to answer, and try irony or any other shuffle, in order that he might avoid answering?"

Socrates: "You are a clever Man, Thrasymachus, *(after a comparison using a sum of 12 and discussing the alternative add ends)*…ought he not to say what he thinks, whether you and I forbid him or not? …I dare say that I may, notwithstanding the danger, if upon reflection *(of differing comments thus far made about justice)* I would approve of any of them."

Note: *Socrates' fundamental rule was to not forbid free expression regardless of the agreement. All should have an equal right to "say what he thinks." This was also a pattern of the prophets of antiquity and the defining attribute of the oral traditions.*

Thrasymachus: "But what if I give you an answer about justice other and better than any of these *(offered)*? What do you deserve to have done to you?"

Socrates: "…I must learn from the wise—that is what I deserve to have done to me."

Thrasymachus: "…and no payment! A pleasant notion!"

Glaucon: Thrasymachus, need be under no anxiety about money, for we will all make a contribution for Socrates.

Thrasymachus: "…and then Socrates will do as he always does—refuse to answer himself, but take and pull to pieces the answer of someone else."

Socrates: "The natural thing is, that the speaker should be someone like yourself who professes to know and can tell what he knows. Will you then kindly answer, for the edification of the company and of myself?"

Note: *Edification was a very strong point with Socrates. If one's comments indicated the pride or selfishness of one's statement, it* *did not edify. When Socrates sensed pride he did not argue, but rather asked further questions in order for the opponent to reveal to himself any contradiction due to pride. This was also a pattern of the prophets of antiquity and the defining attribute of the oral traditions.*

Thrasymachus: "…the wisdom of Socrates; he refuses to teach himself, and goes about learning of others, to whom he never even says, Thank you."

Socrates: "That I learn of others is quite true; but that I am ungrateful I wholly deny. …I am to praise anyone who appears to me to speak well…I expect that you will answer well."

Thrasymachus: "…I proclaim that justice is nothing else than the interest of the stronger. And now why do you not praise me? But of course you won't."

Socrates: "…I wish that you would be a little clearer."

Thrasymachus: "Well have you never heard that forms of government differ—there are tyrannies, and there are democracies, and there are aristocracies? …And the different forms of government make laws democratical, aristocratical, tyrannical, with a view to their several interests; and these laws, which are made by them for their own interests, are the justice which they deliver to their subjects…. And that is what I mean when I say that in all States there is the same principle of justice, which is the interest of the government…, which is the interest of the stronger.

Socrates: "…Then you must also have acknowledged justice not to be for the interest of the stronger, when the rulers unintentionally command things to be done, which are to their own injury…not what is for the interest, but what is for the injury of the stronger? …[D]id you mean by justice what the stronger thought to be his interest, whether really so or not?

Thrasymachus: "…But to be perfectly accurate, since you are such a lover of accuracy, we should say that the ruler, in so far as he is a ruler, is unerring, and, being unerring, always commands that which is for his own interest; and the subject is required to execute his commands; and therefore, as I said at first and now repeat, justice is the interest of the stronger.

Socrates: "…no physician, in so far as he is a physician, considers his own good in what he prescribes, but the good of his patient; for the true physician is also a ruler having the human body as a subject, and is not a mere money-maker; ...And the pilot likewise, in the strict sense of the term, is a ruler of sailors, and not a mere sailor? ...And such a pilot and ruler will provide and prescribe for the interest of the sailor who is under him, and not for his own or the ruler's interest? ...there is no one in any rule who, in so far as he is a ruler, considers or enjoins what is for his own interest, but always what is for the interest of his subject or suitable to his art; to that he looks, and that alone he considers in everything which he says and does."[1]

Note: Socrates began to introduce concepts that compared justice with wisdom and virtue. He even slightly suggested that punishment would prevail to the wise if they did not take up leadership positions in the state voluntarily. To do it for money or honor was not just, but the fear of penalty would drive the wise to lead. The wise would say that if they did not take upon them the responsibility of looking after the interests of the people, then one would get into the position with less wisdom and those who are wise would become subject to an unwise leader. This is the penalty Socrates referred to for not serving. The essence of this process is responsibility and sacrifice. This was also a pattern of the prophets of antiquity and the defining attribute of the oral traditions. .

Up to this point Thrasymachus was lengthy in his determination to label justice as the interest of the stronger. After Socrates' alternative was presented, Thrasymachus seemed uninterested and less determined. All of his comments were obliging rather than contradictory. According to Plato, he wanted to take his leave, but Socrates was polite and encouraged that he should remain. Because Socrates was led away from his original inquiry of the nature of justice, he suggests at the end of Book I that he does not really know what justice is. I think this is Plato's conclusion more than Socrates because Plato had a different view of what is in the interest of the members of the state. Perhaps Plato was actually Thrasymachus in the dialogue. Thrasymachus' view was tuned more to the concepts of Plato in later books. It is not rational to suppose that Plato would remember every expression of Socrates without making some comment of his own. Plato could not have been a bystander. I feel he had a keen memory and later compiled his dialogues with the express intent to add his own propensities using Socrates. Plato's dialogues would become more of himself through the way of Socrates than what Socrates would have said explicitly.

Because of Socrates' popularity, it is believed by most authorities that Plato took liberties with his name. I cannot help but suppose that after Socrates' death, Plato would use the character of Socrates to continue his own view in the extensive *Republic*. In the shorter dialogues the way of Socrates is revealed more clearly. The most famous of these were the *Apology, the Crito, and the Phaedo*. The wise need only to look for the freedom to speak openly, the importance of edification when one speaks, and the responsibility required serving the lesser. If these principles cannot be achieved, death is sweeter than life.

According to Plato, Socrates conversed with Euthyphro on the nature of piety before his trial. After a long discourse of questioning, he asked again in confidence, "I am sure, therefore, that you know the nature of piety and impiety. Speak out then, my dear Euthyphro, and do not hide your knowledge.

> **Euthypro:** Another time, Socrates, for I am in a hurry, and must go now.
>
> **Socrates:** Alas! My companion, and will you leave me in despair? I was hoping that you would instruct me in the nature of piety and impiety, so that I might have cleared myself of Meletus and his indictment. Then I might have proved to him that I had been converted by Euthyphro, and had done with rash innovations and speculations, in which I had indulged through ignorance, and was about to lead a better life.[2]

These were concluding words spoken to Euthyphro and it seemed that Socrates respected his opponent's ability to give him knowledge, as he needed it. For the most part every time Socrates would ask a question Euthyphro would simply say yes or I agree or something of the sort. When Euthyphro would say more, Socrates was quick to add, "Rare friend! I think that I cannot do better than be your disciple." In one case Euthyphro answered at length, but said something that Socrates was not so thrilled with. Euthyphro implied that he being a prosecutor was pious for bringing his own murdering father to justice. He also said—"and not prosecuting them is impiety." He justified himself by saying:

> **Euthyphro:** For do not men regard Zeus as the best and most righteous of the gods?—and even they admit that he bound his father (Cronos) because he wickedly devoured his sons, and that he too had punished his own father (Uranus) for a similar reason, in a nameless manner. And yet when I proceed against my father, they (the people) are angry with me. This is their inconsistent way of talking when the gods are concerned, and when I am concerned.
>
> **Socrates:** May not this be the reason, Euthyphro, why I am charged with impiety—that I can not away with these stories about the gods?

Socrates was challenging the stories often given by the poets about the gods, for this is why he was brought to trial. Socrates went on to say:

> And therefore I suppose that people think me wrong. But as you who are well informed about them approve of them, I cannot do better than assent to your superior wisdom. For what else can I say, confessing as I do? That I know nothing of them, I wish you would tell me whether you really believe that they are true?[3]

Euthyphro was missing the point, but did say he believed in these gods that seemed to fight with one another. He said, "Yes, Socrates; and things more wonderful still, of which the world is in ignorance."

> **Socrates:** And do you really believe that the gods fought with one another, and had dire quarrels, battles, and the like, as the poets say, and as you may see represented in the works of great artists? ...Are all these tales of the gods true, Euthyphro?

Euthyphro again agreed and said, "I can tell you, if you would like to hear them, many other things about the gods which would quite amaze you."

At this point Socrates was evasive when he said, "...at some other time." Socrates was not about to let the discussion depart from his inquiry as to what was piety. Socrates continued:

> **Socrates**: But just at present I would rather hear from you a more precise answer, which you have not as yet given, my friend, to the question, what is piety? In reply, you only say that piety is, doing as you do, charging your father with murder?

Euthyphro again says, "And that is true" without any hint as to any understanding where Socrates was going. Eventually Socrates finalized his argument:

> **Socrates**: And further, Euthyphro, the gods were admitted to have enmities and hatreds and differences—that was also said.
>
> They have differences of opinion, as you say, about good and evil, just and unjust, honorable and dishonorable: there would have been no quarrels among them if there had been no such differences—
>
> ...And therefore, Euthyphro, in thus chastising your father you may very likely be doing what is agreeable to Zeus but disagreeable to Cronos or Uranus, and what is acceptable to Hephaestus but unacceptable to Hera, and there may be other gods who have similar differences of opinion.
>
> But they join issue about particulars; and this applies not only to men but to the gods; if they dispute at all they dispute about some act which is called in question, and which some affirm to be just, others to be unjust.
>
> That, my good friend, we shall know better in a little while. The point which I should first wish to understand is whether the pious or holy is beloved by the gods because it is holy, or holy because it is beloved of the gods.[4]

Euthyphro said to this last comment, "I don't understand your meaning, Socrates."

A bit later Socrates continued with:

> **Socrates:** And now I think, Euthyphro, that my meaning will be intelligible; and my meaning is, that any state of action or passion implies previous action or passion. It does not become because it is becoming, but it is becoming because it becomes; neither does it suffer because it is in a state of suffering, but it is in a state of suffering because it suffers.

At an earlier point Socrates described the need for "the essence" of piety as being the true meaning needed and not an attribute only. "...tell me once more what piety or holiness really is, whether dear to the gods or..." *dear to the essence of piety embedded in the universe*? I added the italics to emphasize what Socrates was trying to say. He used love in the same manner when he said, "For one is a kind to be loved because it is loved, and the other is loved because it is a kind to be loved." One meaning is the essence and the other describes a particular situation. It is the same as asking, "Is piety loved by the gods or do the gods love piety?" In more common terms: is money the root of evil or is the love of money the root of evil? It is saying that one man's love is another man's lust. When you are looking for the essence of piety you cannot say a man is pious because the gods love him. That does not give us the meaning. But if we say that the gods love him because he is pious, then that suggests that piety can be achieved independent of the gods and thus the reason the gods love him. The meaning of piety or holiness in essence precedes the decision that one is pious.

The mind in its clever ways will slightly twist the meaning of lust into the meaning of love in order to justify their actions. This is what Euthyphro was doing in order to justify his prosecuting his father for murder. He was giving the punishment the qualities of holiness. It was Socrates' intent to work gradually to where Euthyphro would understand, because if Socrates came right out and said what piety was, Euthyphro would never have grasped the meaning. Such was the way of Socrates. When Socrates was getting close and Euthyphro getting squeamish, it makes perfectly good sense why Euthyphro said, "I am in a hurry, and must go now."

Getting the essence of meaning was fundamental with Socrates and unless the opponent through his own statement achieved it, Socrates was not about to give the answer. The essence of meaning is hard to come by primarily because of psychological motive. That was evident with Euthyphro and, as we shall see. It is evident with others.

I have had my own experiences in trying to find someone with great wisdom to understand my meaning of relativity and overlook any psychological motive. I remember attending the University of California Santa Barbara and in a particular lecture on relativity, given by a renowned writer on the subject, I attempted to ask a question. I had already read some of his books and I had read everything I could get my hands on and had written my own book *The Einstein Illusion*. During the lecture the traditional mention of the shortening of rods at a high velocity was certainly covered in order to explain the Special Theory of Relativity, but when it came time for the General Theory, for which I was more inclined to express myself, I listened intently. The instructor was about to explain the nature of a rod falling into a black hole at near the speed of light. He used his arms as if stretching taffy to explain that under the General Theory a rod would expand. I immediately saw a contradiction and a paradox with relativity.

After the class was over, many students hovered around the well-known instructor with sustaining compliments. I waited to the end when all had left and asked, "If a rod moving at the speed of light into a black hole would stretch significantly, would this not be counteracted by the shortening effect of the Special Theory of Relativity?" The instructor recognized the paradox instantly, but refused to answer. Like Euthyphro he wanted to take his leave and make a way for his escape. He simply mumbled his need to do calculations while shuffling papers upon departure. I said, "Thank you for the lecture" and took my leave knowing that I did not find anyone as wise as I had hoped. I felt like Socrates when he said, "I do not suppose that either of us know anything really beautiful...."

Socrates had the very same problem in explaining the "first class" of his accusers. Socrates said in his defense, "Accordingly, I went to one who had the reputation of wisdom, and observed him—his name I need not mention; he was a politician whom I selected for examination"—and the result was as follows:

> **Socrates:** When I began to talk with him, I could not help thinking that he was not really wise, although he was thought wise by many, and wiser still by himself, and I went

and tried to explain to him that he thought himself wise, but was not really wise; and the consequence was that he hated me, and his enmity was shared by several who were present and heard me. So I left him, saying to myself, as I went away: Well, although I do not suppose that either of us knows anything really beautiful and good, I am better off than he is, -- for he knows nothing, and thinks that he knows. I neither know nor think that I know. In this latter particular, then, I seem to have slightly the advantage of him. Then I went to another who had still higher philosophical pretensions, and my conclusion was exactly the same. I made another enemy of him, and of many others besides him.

After this I went to one man after another, being not unconscious of the enmity which I provoked, and I lamented and feared this: but necessity was laid upon me—the word of God, I thought, ought to be considered first. And I said to myself, go I must to all who appear to know, and find out the meaning of the oracle. And I swear to you, Athenians, by the dog I swear!—for I must tell you the truth—the result of my mission was just this: I found that the men most in repute were all but the most foolish; and that some inferior men were really wiser and better. I will tell you the tale of my wanderings and of the "Herculean" labors, as I may call them, which I endured only to find at last the oracle irrefutable. When I left the politicians, I went to the poets; tragic, dithyrambic, and all sorts. And there, I said to myself, you will be detected; now you will find out that you are more ignorant than they are. Accordingly, I took them some of the most elaborate passages in their own writings, and asked what was the meaning of them—thinking that they would teach me something. Will you believe me? I am almost ashamed to speak of this, but still I must say that there is hardly a person present who would not have talked better about their poetry than they did themselves. That showed me in an instant that not by wisdom do poets write poetry, but by a sort of genius and inspiration; they are like diviners or soothsayers who also say many fine things, but do not understand the meaning of them. And the poets appeared to me to be much in the same case; and I further observed that upon the strength of their poetry they believed themselves to be the wisest of men in other things in which they were not wise. So I departed, conceiving myself to be superior to them for the same reason that I was superior to the politicians.[5]

Socrates recognized that many artisans knew more than he about their skill, but as he observed that they were good workman "they thought that they knew all sorts of high matter, and this defect in them overshadowed their wisdom."

It was the meaning of things that Socrates wanted and he wanted all to find agreement. If it could be done there might not be the disagreements due to political motive. Socrates had a great deal of insight into the psychology of the learned and the proud and desperately tried to stimulate a quest for meaning. This he felt would truly educate one with the ability to move on to higher principles. Socrates would rather die a horrible death than not be able to raise man to the essence of meaning.

Socrates recognized the psychological motive in Meletus as he recklessly and impudently had written an indictment against Socrates "in a spirit of mere wantonness and youthful bravado." Socrates indicated that he must have "said to himself:—I shall see whether this wise Socrates will discover my ingenious contradiction, or whether I shall be able to deceive him and the rest of them." For Meletus certainly did appear to Socrates to contradict himself in the indictment when he said, "Socrates is guilty of not believing in the gods, and yet of believing in them...." Socrates suggested that Meletus did none other than to suggest, "This is a piece of fun."[6]

Removing contradiction was Socrates' way and it was the very method of reaching the essence of meaning. I remember another event in my life when I was able to approach another well-known Doctor of Physics at UCLA. He was pleasant and agreeable in a personal way to talk with me. I made a general statement about relativity and asked him a question suggesting some contradictions. At that point, he went to the black board with a piece of chalk in his hand and, with an enthusiastic attempt to explain the theory of General Relativity, he scribbled various explanations with a culmination of a large oval explaining that space was curved and what was the beginning of light would eventually hit someone in the back of the head. I could not get one word in edgewise. I simply listened to what I had already known making him think he was teaching me something. I was kind as was Socrates, but I could not help but eventually inject a question revealing the contradictory conclusion: "If light follows a circular path, thus explaining the curvature of space, what happens at right angels to this path? Is there no space there too?" I never thought he would change the subject, but like a broken record he repeated over what he had said. I went away learning nothing about the meaning of relativity and I knew in my heart that I might be able to see the meaning of things better than the wisest of all men so I continued to read and to write on my own.

When you have the nature of Socrates, you do not make friends easily. It is as if anyone in a group listens to your question they peg you immediately as one going against the grain. They do not talk with you for fear of being found out. You are treated as foolish and not ready for their advanced mode of communication. If you are slow and methodical you are considered to be unintelligent and of a lower class. When you are able to confront the greatest and recognize a lack of wisdom, then you know the world is running the wrong direction and there is nothing you can do but do what Socrates tried. I am concerned deeply about the things I know that if spoken openly I would gather some who would want to kill me. Socrates was not the first nor will he be the last to seek grander concepts of meaning than the typical demigod in high places.

Socrates had a unique sense of justice when he said:

> ...there seems to be something wrong in petitioning a judge, and thus procuring an acquittal instead of informing and convincing him. For his duty is, not to make a present of justice, but to give judgment; and he has sworn that he will judge according to the laws and not according to his own good pleasure; and neither he nor we should get into the habit of perjuring ourselves—there can be no piety in that. Do not then require me to do what I consider dishonorable and impious and wrong, especially now, when I am being tried for impiety on the indictment of Meletus...for I do believe that there are gods, and in a far higher sense than that in which any of my accusers believe in them. And to

> you and to God I commit my cause, to be determined by you as is best for you and me.[7]

Not only did Socrates tell us what true justice is, he also included the essential meaning of piety in addition to his higher belief in God. The liberty to teach was more important to Socrates than most anything, and if he could not teach he would only accept death as an alternative. Did Patrick Henry (March 23, 1775) read the *Apology* when he said, "Give Me Liberty or Give Me Death"? Socrates condemned paying a fine suggested of him for he had no money. He condemned imprisonment for he would be the slave of the magistrates of the year. He condemned exile, as also suggested when he said; "I must indeed be blinded by the love of life, if I do not consider that when you, who are my own citizens, can not endure my discourses and words, and have found them so grievous and odious that you would fain have done with them, others are likely to endure me."

On law Socrates said this to Crito while in prison:

> But if you go away from well governed states to Crito's friends in Thessaly, where there is a great disorder and license, they will be charmed to have the tale of your escape from prison, set off with ludicrous particulars of the manner in which you were wrapped in a goatskin or some other disguise, and metamorphosed as the fashion of runaways is—that is very likely; but will there be no one to remind you that in your old age you violated the most sacred laws from a miserable desire of a little more life?

Socrates certainly had the highest values that could only be dwarfed by the master himself. What man will not argue his case before the judge, parade his family for sympathy, and importune his defense for accommodation and the judge for mercy? What man will not be pleased with a lawyer that negates the facts and challenges the honesty of the simple minded—all for his eventful acquittal so he can have a few more years of life at the expense of deception? Who would rise to the level of pure honesty as Socrates and accept his fate after all that he could do in honesty? It is far better that God judge the wicked than succumb to wickedness so your sons and daughters can learn from you the ways of the world in order that they too might be corrupted. As Socrates would say, "Is it not better to die than to live a lie of deceit? Is it better for a soldier to leave his post that he might raise his young son to a better life or can he do more for his son if he dies a hero in the defense of freedom?"

Everyone colors the meaning of things to fit their life and dreams. Unfortunately most fall short of the highest values continually justifying their life style. I was reading an interview of a megastar actor justifying his behavior. A certain quote stood out as, "Who's to say what's normal?" As Socrates would ask, to myself I asked, what was the meaning of such a statement? What was the meaning of normal in this context and should have there been a more appropriate word? What if he would have said, "Who is to say what equals good behavior?" This would most certainly show his true intent. For the word normal would not offend, but the word "good" for which he probably meant would definitely show his selfishness. The psychologist may have a norm for normal, but that is a clinical terminology based upon averages. Socrates would ask, "Is normal good?" The smile of the actor seemed beguiling and for the most part justifying of his life style. In the interview he was described as contradictory in the first paragraphs. Surely Socrates would have obtained the same truth.

I enjoy most of this actor's movies, but I also understand that movie actors generally are not wise in their personal affairs. It is the screenwriters that have all the wisdom if there be any in a movie. Wise actors generally cannot act themselves. They have to act contrary to their personality and hopefully in agreement to their looks. Many villains, who look the part, are really not villains in real life. On the other hand, one who has the beautiful looks will often be unwise in personal life. This issue has nothing to do with looks. It is more an issue with the type of intelligence as mentioned in a former chapter. Socrates was not like the typical actor. He was conceptual, inquiring, but not linguistic. If Socrates were to write a word of which he spoke, it would be profoundly different than what Plato would have him say. Plato was a far more eloquent person and gifted with a keen memory for details, as any actor would be. He was able to script Socrates as a very wise man and a gifted person with the innate ability to see through the psychology of the human mind. But when Plato followed his own mind and his own wisdom, he made Socrates out to be a villainous control freak in the *Republic*. Plato was not wise. He sought after recognition and had a motive in writing the *Republic*. The real Socrates would not dwell on particulars suggested in the *Republic*. Socrates wanted to define the essence of things and was not concerned about political control. I thank God for Plato, for without him we would never know Socrates. I also thank many of the priests for preserving the Hebrew means of learning revealed through Socrates.

Euthyphro wanted to call the bringing of a murder to justice a form of piety. Plato wanted to call justice the legislated control of everyday life, and most modern day politicians call for a vote of freedom, but freedom is really covering up a vote for selfishness. There is something sinister about these motives and he who thinks Socrates fosters any of the same does not know the wisdom of the ages, is probably atheistic, and follows a form of rhetoric rather than principle. Socrates sponsored predicate values in the true sense. He sought to remove conflict by searching for the highest meaning and the true essence of the predicate reality, and Plato knew it not for he fostered his own subjectivism that would exist for all time. This was destructive to philosophy yet it was the nature of man to avoid responsibility, love, patience, faith, and longsuffering. Man prefers the idealism of denial. Will we ever look to the true predicate of Socrates and perhaps also of Jesus the Christ?

Once understanding is manifest one cannot help but conclude that even the greatest minds avoid the predicate reality of responsibility toward meaning. Philosophy and science will often go to great lengths to avoid the need to define clearly. Argument will prevail for many generations rather than accept that we first consider sound meaning.

                   Samuel Dael

12. The Platonic State

In this chapter we will discuss what Plato means by justice and the good of the state rather than the interest of the people. We will gain insight into to why Plato's idiom spoke the same turn-of-phrase as communism, fascism, many false Christian religions, and fundamentally how he expresses our typical democratic idiom. I do not suggest that all systems are patterned after Plato as much as it has become the human tendency to philosophize under the same psychology as Plato. In other words, what drove Plato drives every idealistic thinker since the beginning of time.

Plato was a student of Socrates and therefore used a similar question and answer dialogue. The difference was that Socrates was seeking for the responsible meaning of things while Plato was expressing his own controlling idioms. When Plato wrote about the experiences of Socrates he was fluid and clear. Perhaps he wrote many dialogues during Socrates' life and was praised for it. Once this acceptance had come into play and after the death of Socrates, Plato could easily continue to write from memory and gradually implement his own ideas rather than ask questions to obtain meaning, as did Socrates. Plato called it dialectic, but there was nothing in his later dialogues in the *Republic* that would suggest the digging for meaning. Plato would start by asking questions, but would eventually inject his own ideas without giving the meaning of fundamental words. Every one of Plato's later arguments had so many traditional assumptions that it was impossible to consider any rational process in the *Republic*. It was Plato's elegance of expression and rhetoric that attracted his readers for centuries. But just as the minds of the future cared little about meaning, they related more to the Republic to justify their tendencies.

It is generally believed that Plato wrote in dialogue much of what Socrates implied or said, but authorities also believe that Plato took liberties and used Socrates as the main character in many dialogues such as the *Republic* in order to put across his own views.

> According to this interpretation, Republic is categorized among the "middle" dialogues because, among other things, it contains one of the most detailed expositions of the theory of the ideas, which Plato almost certainly derived independently of Socrates.[1]

Plato had the same questioning views as we do today about the state, and even though the democratic process was not part of Plato's *Republic,* the intent of many democracies is to follow the same psychology. I use psychology to describe the human need to look to the state for cures and solutions to ills rather than the community of old. The state represented power and the ability to control, and those who psychologically think in terms of control, will gravitate to this philosophical form. This argument starts with the state's ability to conduct war better than the community. Plato followed this psychology after he first established, with incompletion, the meaning of justice in the first book of the *Republic.* The nature of justice was covered pretty well, but Plato had Socrates say that it had not been covered in order to introduce his concept later that justice will be in the best interest of the people through control by the state. Plato called his argument a dialectic process. Plato's conclusions, however, lacked the essentials of virtue and wisdom, the essentials of freedom and edification, and above all the importance of voluntary sacrifice.

I call Plato's form "unrighteous dominion." This method is psychological and is derived from the overall fear that one experiences with injustice. They prefer to make things right rather than sacrifice for the needs of others, as did Socrates. The best way to test a potential leader is to give him a command that does not edify but will satiate his desires and propensities and see what he does. If he follows the command blindly, he is not wise. If he challenges the command and wants to determine the meaning of it, he is wise. In antiquity, God proved the prophets through this method, but those who question this method disbelieve in God for doing such a thing.

The mind seems attracted to solutions that will wipe away with assurance by law the inequities. We look to the state because it has the muscle to make law. Thus if one lives among great injustices the same will naturally create an ideal plan to allow the state to bring the desired change. Certain types of intelligence accentuate this process, and force in the name of freedom becomes the mainstay of such methods. Either we use the state to make things happen or we use capitalistic leverage to control the people. The first is the Platonic view and the latter supports the Aristotelian view, which I have not discussed. Neither understood Socratic responsibility to meaning or, as I have introduced, the predicate view of reality.

Plato himself described a certain type of intelligence as the most important aspect required for the good of the state. But Plato's meaning corresponded to the eloquence and modern photographic memory of a politician. Plato did not consider understanding or meaning. Plato felt that the philosopher must simply have a good memory:

> Then a soul, which forgets, cannot be ranked among genuine philosophic natures; we must insist that the philosopher should have a good memory?[2]

In another place Plato added "quickness of memory." In another place he called it "quick intelligence."[3] It is this same type of intelligence that seeks state solutions today. Those who are careful, less quick, but have wise insight do not seek for government control. Plato does not use the word force, but every Platonic ideal had the label of legislative force behind it. In a modern democracy this same type of thinking always seeks for government to enslave us with more ill. In general, politicians are of the linguistic mold. Their intelligence is quick with high memory, but they are also clever, as Plato would assign. The conceptual mind is not so quick, but sees the necessity of free will, patience, and individual responsibility. The linguistic mind will be found in most abundance among the devout liberal but does also exist among fundamentalists, politicians, educators and most individuals who gain more by political moves than honest relationships. Conservatives desiring economic leverage over others may also accept Plato, if they are in control. The conceptual mind is usually outcast in his or her youth for being too slow. They tend to be Socratic like and also conservative and perhaps liberals of honest responsibility. This would depend on how one is raised.

Tradition will have a great impact on anyone's direction, but consider that the use of force of some kind is a psychological one contingent upon the type of intelligence. Generally speaking, fear plagues the higher I.Q. more than the lower; therefore they are driven to find solutions that can only be achieved by legislative force or capitalistic leverage. If they are conceptual, they eventually add value whether they are of the hard working poor or hard working rich. Rarely do you find the conceptual mind in Hollywood, straight-A students, or even philosophy. I would consider that there are few conceptual thinkers and when they have something of value they usually speak orally, but not eloquently. Their concepts are far more interesting than their rhetoric. Their writing is not fluid or easy to understand, but they are responsible. I consider Socrates a conceptual thinker and Plato having a linguistic mind. With this understanding, the idiom of using state force is understood. The conceptual mind in antiquity did not write or speak well. Their oral delivery was slow and suffered the need for much open discussion. Their success was due to their ability to see the psychological motive of their opponent. The linguistic mind could speak fluently and also write fluently as did Plato.

The Platonic Idiom

This control idiom using the state to force the good is prevalent in Plato's Republic. The state was to control the lives of its members. This was justice according to Plato.

> Then the first thing will be to establish a censorship of the writers of fiction, and let the censors receive any tale of fiction which is good, and reject the bad; and we will desire mothers and nurses to tell their children the authorized ones only.[4]

Plato called censorship good. This is much the same as religiously controlled societies and dictators. I do not think this method used in various governments was particularly gleaned from Plato. It is a direct reaction to the need to control the people in the name of the good of the people. It is a direct response to the type of intelligence that most have that gain power. The more intelligent the linguistic mind, the more the need to control. A dictator whether political or religious may have been justified by reading Plato but the idiom of censorship begins with the desire to control for the so-called good and not because the idea was read somewhere. It comes from a mind that does not apply faith and individual responsibility. This same mind has a fear of loosing control. Censorship is not justice in the strict sense of the word, but this method says that individuals cannot be taught individual responsibility so we must control what the people read whether it be by force, legislation, or religious guilt. Honest and open Socratic discussion is not acceptable because the people will discuss things unacceptable.

Being a reader does not guarantee wisdom. Mao, Stalin, and Hitler were voracious readers of Plato and similar mind sets, yet still they were oral dictators demanding censorship to control and produce what they thought was the ideal.

Censorship may be acceptable within families and communities and even cultures of learning children, but it must also be made clear that teaching correct principles through discussion among youth is better than saying don't read this. A child must learn through conversation the nature of their actions and personal responsibility to others. When one does

The Platonic State | 252

not learn responsibility and comes to recognize conservation laws, the mind will want to force the outcome knowing that neither they nor anyone else will volunteer right action. When the mind sees too much injustice in growing up, that mind will try to figure out a way to control and prevent that injustice. We seem to eventually learn what justice and conservation are but few are taught true meaning during their formative years and how to apply it.

It becomes an eternal problem from one generation to another until the community of old offers the long needed social security and faith promoting principles. We learn languages, mathematics, history and science, but we do not learn the meaning of things soon enough. A child will never say, "What goes around comes around." An adult, however, knows very well what it means from the experience of making mistakes. Why should we make mistakes in order to learn? In most cases early mistakes are not allowed in order that we may learn. We learn unwritten rules taking a political rout rather than exercise faith in a solid principle. We will curve-fit proven principles into our own liking rather than do the responsible thing.

Essentially, it is not the state that teaches values. Rather it is the community that must democratically offer the personal security needed and encourage free expression upon the meaning of various predicate principles. Traditionally the family and the religious culture have a tendency to allow no other expression than the controlled idiom of morality without understanding. Parents and teachers have too many "because-I-told-you-so" demands rather the patience to listen or teach understanding. There is too much status quo in order to get gain and protect one's position in the economic strata. There is too much prejudice against the weak and neglect of the unfortunate.

During a summit on high school slayings, President Bush urged violence prevention by saying:

> Hopefully, out of these tragedies will come the sense of communal obligation all throughout our country, for people to take an extra effort to comfort the lonely?

The writer of the associated press article said that there was "no new policies nor money announced" by President Bush to solve the problem. Obviously the reporter is expecting the national government to solve the problem in the same manner Plato would attempt to solve it by using the state power. Bush was calling attention to a Socratic or Christian method, perhaps without knowing, while most think that government money will solve every ill. The ills are a lack of values being taught. These values are learned only by open Socratic discussion in formative years of learning. It is very much like group therapy. Philosophy should be required for every student—not a history of philosophy but a philosophy of concepts, principles, and values should be injected into the classroom. Every student should be willing and able to speak and express his or her meaning of things. You would be amazed how a wise teacher could spot trouble. It is also amazing how unwise teachers do not allow the discussion of meaning in class lectures and quickly steer the class back to being "on task" when issues of meaning surface. One of my sons experienced this many times over in college and graduate school and was told when he would ask questions about what things mean, "This is not the time or the place for that." When it came time for his chance to teach at a local college, he created the first ever Epistemology Club designed to let students talk about how we know what we know is true. Over forty students attended the first meeting and the club grew in popularity on campus. The same freedom should exist in families and church discussion groups. But every one wants to control the outcome or they are so busy getting ahead socially, economically, and politically that the youthful mind is neglected and becomes prey to becoming the fear-denying bully.

Discipline has been the hallmark of conservative schooling and it has also been the way of the military. In the same newspaper on the same day the following Associated Press quoted the Pentagon head of personnel:

> In today's Army, shouting is out and a calmer approach to molding young minds is in.

Hollywood may have to tone down its portrayal of the military's screaming, in-your-face boot camp drill sergeant. That means, "less shouting at everyone, in essence, which some of you may remember from an earlier generation as being the modus operandi," said the Pentagon. It was found that today's generation responded better to instructors who took "a more counseling" type role, said Lt. Col. Mike Jones, head of Army National Guard recruiting.[5]

Platonic theory suggested a theory of soldier training that was based upon misappropriated human psychology. Plato assumed that a high-spirited person made a better soldier and that this was inbred as high-strung horses or dogs are bred. A soldier, according to Plato, should seek for honor and glory and would learn best about warfare if taken as a young lad to observe real battles at a safe distance. The psychology that Plato did not understand was the psychology underlying the denial of death. One's lust for blood and power over life and death is not the true nature of a hero. It is the nature of one who is actually afraid of death but denies that he is so. He thus runs to face the enemy as if a hero camouflaging his fear in order to prove he is not afraid. It is the masculine macho personality that is really covering ineptness and the inability to honestly and consciously accept death if it becomes necessary. This tuff bully attitude covers fear in a death-defying soldier as does the Olympic competitor, the hunter for sport, and even the modern daredevil performer. The trophy and the metal of valor fill what is really a vacuum of values.

Even the modern terrorist follows the same psychology of denial. The exhilaration of coming close to death and living or commanding the death of another makes one feel immortal. The trophy and the metals seem to prove it. These minds are controlled by their passion in the denial of fear and not by wisdom. Wisdom accepts death while inordinate passion denies it by facing it blindly without principle. Placing young boys into this mode prematurely only invigorates the psychosis of denial.

What feeds this natural psychology even more is to reward the soldier with honor and the best of women. Honor is a false aphrodisiac for making one feel alive. Having the best women, as Plato suggested in the *Republic*, actually accomplishes the same.

The true hero has a passion for purpose and a mission to bring peace and safety to his friends and even his countrymen. He will sacrifice his life for others because he loves humanity. He does not do it for reward. The true hero is born out of understanding values. The current trend in military training seems to suggest that mentorship not only keeps recruits in the program, but they respond to training better. I would speculate that the bully type macho personality would not advance as well as those with meaning in what they do.

The Platonic idiom is to see things as one would see the dog in man rather than rise above the animal with insight of a higher intelligence. In this respect, Plato had a natural philosophy based upon human propensity and not insight. It is usually the way the linear mind works. It intimidates its followers rather than motivates. What is so tragic is that the intimidator arises to the challenge far too soon and captures every position of leadership having little faith to see through the psychological phony muck of denial. We thus have false heroes and idols to worship rather than the worshiping of values and attributes of Godliness.

This same psychology can be found in a modern television series where the sadistic fear in us denies death by constantly viewing carnage and mutilated bodies. Murder crime solving is only there to justify our unconscious yearning to look death in the eye. If we do not see death and come out alive, we are not interested in watching and we do not feel immune to our own sense of entropy and decay. This would certainly explain the captivation by so many similar programs. For some strange, psychological reason, death, murder, carnage and rape must be the subject of study, whether in the movie or in the news. If this does not satisfy the human psyche we have the sporting event to satisfy the daring spirit within us. In short, it is not news and entertainment. It is human insanity at its best.

The denial of death lies at the foundation of religious doctrines as one seeks for the magic of salvation and the promise of immortality. In this our God is a master magician. Socrates had distaste for the antics of the traditional Gods and was the political reason he was placed before the court. Socrates did not deny the existence of God, but he felt that a true God would be more rational. Plato also believed in God, but insisted there be a state religion that imposed the correct view of God.

> God is always to be represented, as he truly is, whatever be the sort of poetry, epic, lyric, or tragic, in which the representation is given.[6]
>
> ...Shall I ask you whether God is a magician, and of a nature to appear insidiously now in one shape, and now in another—sometimes himself changing and passing into many forms, sometimes deceiving us with the semblance of such transformations: or is he one and the same immutably fixed in his own proper image?[7]

It is certainly an ideal conclusion to say that one must teach the nature of God as he really is and also to suggest that he is not a God of magic, but who is going to decide what God is like and does that mean God cannot perform miracles? Even if the philosopher legislator is right and forces certain religious ideologies upon the people, it does not mean that they will become free from psychological idioms of fear anymore than the philosopher can scare away the fear he harbors through the control of others. The people may need a personal religion to keep the reality of death at bay with the same unconscious intent the philosopher wants to force his philosophy upon others. Each has his own way of dealing with the inevitable in the world and each must come to an understanding of the truth by being raised in a caring community that teaches principles and lets everyone govern his own life. A caring person will project the same attribute upon God and thus conclude that if we care for others, God will care for us. This is the only way to avoid the psychological pitfalls of denial, for it is faith that overcomes this unconscious propensity to stare death in the face just to feel alive.

Psychologically the philosopher has his way and the people theirs. That does not mean that one can control the other just because the one is more intelligent. Being right does not justify forcing one to believe certain descriptions about God. Sooner or later the individual will bolt and rebel. It is fine to teach that God is not a God of magic, but it must be done while teaching principles and values such as the idea that God must obey the law of conservation in the universe and live or act according to that law. In this context we are free to make God as powerful as we like, but he cannot waste energy on a people who do not conserve for one another. God could create His own miracles as He sees fit but that would be a waste of energy upon those who do not care. Most important, you cannot force ideas upon the mind. Teaching is one thing and legislating a belief is quite another. The need to control is a fear-based doctrine. The need to believe in magic is also of the same. Perhaps we should have the people force their beliefs upon the philosopher?

We must see the psychology behind all things and never think that forced legislation is good. Legislation should be to protect the people in the individual sense from forced good or forced evil. We should make the people free, but legislate only for responsibility.

Plato believed in censorship of the printed word. This is something the typical democracy would abhor. The American democracy had this pretty much worked out until Aristotelian capitalism usurped that same idiom of control but from a different approach and for a different aim. Individual religious cultures as well as multinational corporations and large media giants have not come to understand that forcing particular dogmas upon the people promotes bigotry and self-righteousness. As with churches, when big government legislators create laws that force the good upon the people you build costly bureaucracies with many hands taking a share of the tax burden. If a community or township were to do such a thing, it is done so in a pure democratic process and can be undone quickly if the results are not working. But with the state, control becomes more and more the status quo and the direction of control cannot be undone.

Plato called his state the *Republic*. This was a serious error, for when the philosopher dictates a certain way things should be he stands in direct opposition to the meaning of the word.

> Republic: A commonwealth; a state in which the exercise of the sovereign power is lodged in representatives elected by the people. In modern usage, it differs from a democracy or democratic state, in which the people exercise the powers of sovereignty in person.

It is usually suggested that the modern concept of a republic differed from that of ancient Greece. Cleisthenes (about 570-507 BC) introduced democratic government to ancient Greece. It was basically equal representation of ten tribes with 50 members from each tribe to sit on the council of 500 members. This is a representative form of government and a true republic yet it was called democratic.

Ancient Greek city-states were often run as direct democracies in which all voting citizens (commoners, women, and slaves were excluded) had a voice in what occurred. This was usually done at a gathering or public forum. The confusion enters the scene in not defining the difference between the city-state and the nation-state. If the city was small enough, a true democracy could be apparent, but if the city was massive or geographically extensive, a true republic was manifest where representatives were sent to make laws.

If a philosopher king were to make all the rules, as suggested by Plato, this is neither a true republic nor a democracy. Plato certainly used the word loosely. A democracy is generally understood, but a republic is often used to justify a more controlling state. Mixing democracy and republic is also a misuse of the words democratic and republican. Russia was called a republic during the cold war but did not deserve the name honestly. A republic is often used to draw a distinction away from a democracy, but this should not be the case. If the representatives are voted upon in a democratic process, the republic fulfills the demands of a democracy. A republic is simply a more efficient democracy of the people. Plato defied this concept and failed as many to define the difference.

Consider a forced democracy not unlike Plato where the atheist's philosophy continually seeks to force a definition of good upon the people by constantly appealing that a constitutional national government should force cultural change upon the individual and the community by doing away with all vestiges of God. Even though the atheistic image of God is not that of Plato, the methodology and psychology reeks of the same idiom. The atheist adores Plato, but just thinks Plato was not up to date in negating God. There is a psychology behind every need to force others into a particular idiom. Believe it or not, it comes from the same fear that all harbor that lack faith in principles and in the people to choose for themselves. If a community chooses democratically, why complain just because you do not agree? If the state forces upon the people and upon the community certain religious proprieties and limitations because of some twisted personal view, it takes away the democracy of the community for which the constitution was created.

While the atheist wants to raise his child in a Platonic state free of encumbering beliefs about God, the truth is he cares little about their children. Rather he wants to vent his idiom upon others and upon the children through control. I would suggest that these types do little to teach correct principles to their children any more than the religious zealot. We can teach our children to look for the good in people regardless of what they believe. It is the heart that shows true motive while belief syndromes are only scarecrows to help us scare away reality. Once we see the good in man we can tolerate various beliefs and imaginations.

Plato wanted to remove all vestiges of imagination from teaching. He said that the imitations one might use such as "the neighing of horses, the bellowing of bull, the murmur of rivers and roll of the ocean, thunder, and all that sort of thing" were that of mad men."[8] The teacher was to use narrative only and restrict the use of imitations. This is truly Platonic in nature and a boring way to teach children. The mature adult may not seek excessive laughter and may be somber most of the time, but to destroy the imagination within the growing child is a travesty. Humor and smiles of laughter make good medicine to a troubled mind. When we no longer fear, let us become solemn, but as a child we need to do childish things. Often times the adult needs to replay the imagination in order to deal with reality and life.

We must allow free expression among children as well as among adults. The adult cannot intimidate the child nor should the child intimidate the adult. There is a huge issue of adults pandering in child rearing to such an extent that the child controls the parent. The parent wants to feel accepted of the child and thus indulges their needs. Essentially we have a dichotomy of need. The parent has learned that control is not good, but is still insecure about their choices. The child is also insecure, but denies it through the auspices of control. If the parent had learned principles and values rather than simply how to raise a child, they would be more confident and not pander to the child. The child would then learn the same principles and overcome the need to control. When the child never learns, he or she will grow up with a need to constantly control his or her life and the lives of others. No matter how intelligent, such a mind will have rigid maintenance program for all concerned, whether a child, employee, parishioner or citizen.

Plato also wished to control the type of music, as do many conservative philosophies of today. I cannot say that I like the modern trend any more than the next serious minded person. I certainly do not like the majority of the movies and most parents would like to control what their children hear and see. If we would look into the psychology of the trends and not into the so-called morality, we would see the motive and intent. A young teen's attraction to strange music and the love of the horror movie satisfies the same unconscious anxiety as the adult's passion for competitive sports, the lust for money, or even the dogmatism of religion. No one is free of motive and fear. We all need something to deal with anxiety caused by a community that does not care and a state that regiments the good. If the community truly cared we would not have the problems of strange music, excessive need of sports, nor would we have as much greed and corruption. We have created our own demise and the state will never be able to rectify the problem that stems from the failure of the community and not the failure of the state.

Prove me wrong and tell me that it is not the community that created the environment and the circumstances that prompted a youth to walk into a school with a gun and claim the lives of the innocent? Some have no outlet for their fear of rejection so they do the unthinkable. We should never try to circumvent tendencies to strange music or literature. We should see that our own families and communities are the cause of it. Force will never do. Free Socratic expression and open discussion in family, church, and community will do more to overcome than all the laws the state can make, all the moral control the church imposes, and all the money that either can spend.

Another concept of state force is communism. It did not start with Marx. It was Plato who first recorded the concept of all living in common.

> For indeed any city, however small, is in fact divided into two, one the city of the poor, the other of the rich; these are at war with one another; and in either there are many smaller divisions, and you would be altogether beside the mark if you treated them all as a single State. But if you deal with them as many, and give the wealth or power or persons of the one to the others, you will always have a great many friends and not many enemies. And your State, while the wise order, which has now been prescribed, continues to prevail in her, will be the greatest of States...[9]

Plato was wise on one account. It was to clarify that the state was to not be too large or too small. It should be just the right size to create economic unity. Plato suggested that the size should be "not more than 1,000 defenders."[10] It is not clear what he meant by defenders. Was this the size of the state or the number defending the state?

The democracy of the community could decide among themselves to create a common community in order to remove poverty, which is the cause of untold social problems. This is by community choice and not by State legislation. Plato did not recommend this, but should have clarified that the community must elect to live in common and not the state. The size of the state becomes paramount, for when the majority have a say on every point, the remaining are free to leave or participate if the state is small. If the vote is not for the good of the people, they will soon realize a need for an adjustment that can be easily amended at the next vote provided the state is small enough. In a large republic or state, the represented vote to the general assembly cannot insist that the nation or excessively large state live according to what a small community elects to do. This was the downfall of national communism. If each small state or province was autonomous in living in common and had the ability to tax accordingly, communism might have prevailed. When a large country-state attempts to instigate communal life, it is often done by intimidating control and not by democratic vote. This is the error of communism, the error of Plato, and the error of global one-world government designs. If Plato would have allowed a vote in a limited size state there is no telling what could have been achieved. A united country of several states could then tax the various states a percentage of their collection in order to defend the nation. But no nation would impose ideologies of one intellectual upon the individual city-states without their approval. Plato was not clear on this manner nor has any republic or democracy since attempted to liberalize law for the smaller entities and conserve or limit law for the larger. It is generally the opposite. We want to liberalize law on the larger scale through national government, which in turn burdens the smaller communities from achieving anything in a communal and economic or equitable manner.

Modern America has followed the Platonic idiom and the Marxist doctrine to its limits on the national scale and our communities are beginning to suffer. They now reach out for assistance from the national and state governments, yet the communities raised the funds in the first place in order to feed a monster that claims to do some social good for which the community is ultimately prevented from doing. Rarely do small communities attempt social reform. They prefer out of necessity that the State take care of such matters. This is the Platonic Idiom in its most destructive form. Plato may have been right in suggesting a limit to the size of an autonomous community living in common, but if any larger than that point, failure is eminent. If the efforts to make the State the doer of good were to be done on the community level, every social problem would be solved. The believer in the Platonic method does not do this. He never campaigns in the community and mostly never in the existing State. It is the Federal or national level that the Platonic method seeks fulfillment. If one can get a high court or congress to agree, he has controlled a nation. Sometimes this is necessary when it comes to freedom and rights that do not feed massive bureaucracies; but to force good on the national level is devastating when so much bureaucratic overload is needed.

You cannot create a war on poverty on the national level. Eventually you will be spending decades trying to reform it. In time the beast will become so powerful that nothing can be undone or corrected. Such is the case with Social Security. When the time comes when there will be more taking Social Security than those earning wages, hell will break loose. Congress constantly avoids the problem because the beast sustains them while the common worker slaves in poverty, crime, and social chaos in order to someday be among the economic elite. In the mean time greed encompasses every community more and more until we spend more on protection and less and less on education of principle. The community could change this but it prefers to spend more on sports and extra curricular activities than the learning of principle and values. Modern government has truly become the Platonic State at a cost, which is astronomical. For every dollar spent less and less is actually achieved due to bureaucratic friction. We no longer seek to acquire individual values and especially little personal responsibility to one's neighbor.

Plato did not stop with the forcing of the good through a so-called economic equality. He wanted wives and children to be shared in common. He compared the breeding of humans to the breeding of animals and put women on a path of second-degree citizenship. Plato suggested controlled marriage and the artificial raising of children.

> ...in the matter of women and children "friends have all things in common.[11]
>
> The management of pancakes and preserves, in which womankind does really appear to be great, and in which for her to be beaten by a man is of all things the most absurd?[12]
>
> ...but the gifts of nature are alike diffused in both; all the pursuits of men are the pursuits of women also, but in all of them a woman is inferior to a man.[13]
>
> And those women who have such qualities are to be selected as the companions and colleagues of men who have similar qualities and whom they resemble in capacity and in character?[14]
>
> Having selected the men, will now select the women and give them to them; they must be as far as possible of like natures with them; and they must live in common houses and meet at common meals. None of them will have anything specially his or her own; they will be together, and will be brought up together, and will associate at gymnastic exercises. And so they will be drawn by a necessity of their natures to have intercourse with each other—necessity is not too strong a word. I think?[15]
>
> And do you breed from them all indifferently, or do you take care to breed from the best only?[16]

...either sex should be united with the best as often, and the inferior with the inferior as seldom, as possible;[17]

Now these goings on must be a secret which the rulers only know, or there will be a further danger of our (human) herd, as the guardians may be termed, breaking out into rebellion.[18]

The proper officers will take the offspring of the good parents to the pen or fold, and there they will deposit them with certain nurses who dwell in a separate quarter; but the offspring of the inferior, or of the better when they chance to be deformed, will be put away in some mysterious, unknown place, as they should be.[19]

...taking the greatest possible care that no mother recognizes her own child; and other wet-nurses may be engaged if more are required.[20]

But how will they know who are fathers and daughters, and so on?

They will never know. ...the bridegroom who was then married will call all the male children...his sons.[21]

Then the community of wives and children among our citizens is clearly the source of the greatest good to the State?[22]

That the brave man is to have more wives than others...and he is to have first choices in such matters more than others, in order that he may have as many children as possible?[23]

The idiom of having wives and children in common without anyone knowing their own and without personal attachment does not know the nature of animals. You have to go to great lengths to convince a mother ewe to receive a rejected lamb of another. It is not an easy process and for Plato to suggest such tactics shows he never has been on a domestic farm. Wild animals might claim other species as their own. Even the canine that wishes to always please may adopt even a kitten, but specifically bred animals, such as sheep, do not tend to be affectionate or are aware of the flock's needs. Until the mother's own milk passes through, the newborn is often rejected. Humans are not much different in this regard. It is only by nurturing and caring that fosters the will to adopt. Forcing wives and children in common will destroy the progress of caring. A platonic attitude is cold and unconcerned about others, because the state makes all the decisions and the individual eventually becomes irresponsible and not more responsible as Plato hoped.

Artificial procreation was an idiom of Nazi Germany as was also a cultural process among some economic and religious cultures. Proper intermarriage among the social elite is paramount and interbreeding among different nationalities has long been man's objectionable idiom. The nature to control what comes out of the womb has been around for generations. It is the same fear of insignificance manifest in every culture at differing points in time. If we can raise the perfect seed we will be accepted and honored above the common man. We will arise to significance. The problem is a psychological one and is not a matter of platonic or intellectual choice. In the case of cultures that have advanced to great heights as socioeconomic entities, they become perverse when they try to control cross breeding. It is none other than social, religious, and economic pride. It is destructive. You cannot make love and the spirit of caring a deterministic idiom. This is what I find most contradictory about Plato. On the one hand he is idealistic, but on the other he has demonstrated the most deterministic social philosophy ever. Perhaps this is where we can come to grips with the problem of one having the need to control.

> Inasmuch as philosophers only are able to grasp the eternal and unchangeable, and those who wander in the region of the many and variable are not philosophers.[24]

The eternal represents the values and principles that have survived the centuries. If a religion maintains these virtues so much the better will be society. Too many wander into the region of the many, which want control and have not risen above it. When a religion mimics this, the culture turns toward hypocrisy and irresponsibility. Only a semblance of good is manifest, but the poor are still downtrodden. Crime becomes rampant and greed rises to great heights. Where is the meaning of things, and where are the principles we once taught? They have been carried away in a whirlwind of Platonic idioms of state and national control.

The Platonic Idiom

Aristotelean Considerations

Something should be said about the philosophy postulated by Aristotle. The reason is that even though Socratic discussion can pull apart false ideals, it must also pierce through capitalistic Aristotelian-like methods.

Like Plato, Aristotle made regular use of the dialogue in his earliest years, but lacked Plato's imaginative gifts; he probably never found the form easy. Eloquence is a gift and when you do not have it, one should consider that expression does not mean ability for conceptual meaning, but rather the ability to sell an illogical idea just as easily as a logical one. Aristotle did write down his philosophic terms into a dictionary and summarized the doctrines of Pythagoras. A dictionary and interest in Pythagoras would indicate that Aristotle sought firm meaning. Of these, only a few brief excerpts have survived. Aristotle's lecture notes outlining courses treating almost every branch of knowledge and art were collected and arranged by later editors. I would generally say that this author is much like Aristotle in this regard.

In Aristotle's logic, he distinguished between dialectic and analytic. Dialectic, he held, only tests opinions for their logical consistency; analytic works to deduce from principles resting on experience and precise observation. This was clearly intended to diverge from Plato's view where dialectic was supposed to be the only proper method for philosophy. The notion that observation and experience are analytical can be somewhat misleading. Analysis is the process of deduction from observation *as it agrees with prior self-evident principles.* The message of Predicativism would ad the italics to the usual Aristotelian analysis. If principles are derived from or receive the action of observation, what then does the observation agree with? We need some *a priori* knowledge to start with. To be analytical means than prior self-evident terms in conjunction with observation can produce objective fact. If Aristotle developed his principles from observation without any self-evident principles, then

Aristotle would miss the mark, as has modern physics. Analysis is broader than simply deducing from observation. I am inclined to feel that Science does not understand this and perhaps there has been a misinterpretation of Aristotle who might agree with this thesis. Perhaps philosophy and modern science has misread Aristotle as an objectivist epistemologist.

As to meaning, Aristotle disagreed with Plato about the location of universals (the real world). As Plato spoke of the world of forms as a location where all universal forms subsist, Aristotle, on the other hand, maintained that universals exist within each thing on which each universal is predicated. So, according to Aristotle, the form of apple exists within each apple, rather than in the world of the forms or ideas as Plato so linguistically concluded. Forms perhaps came from intelligence as if we are born with meaning. Plato did not differentiate between intelligences as ability and intelligence as something learned. Aristotle suggested the universal idea of apple came from the subject of study or the objective apple. This is agreeable with the predicate view.

Aristotle taught that economics is concerned with the use of things required for the good life. As a pragmatic or practical science as Aristotle called it, economics is aimed at the good and is fundamentally moral. Because Aristotle saw that economics was embedded in politics, an argument has been made that the study of political economy began with him. Aristotle viewed labor as a commodity that has value but does not add value. Labor was not the source of wealth but the goods they command in the market given the value of labor skills. Aristotle explains that labor skills are pertinent to the determination of exchange values.

He also understood how diverse products could have an exchange value or price. Aristotle's objective was to prove that every exchange of goods has to be an exchange of equivalents. Aristotle says goods must be equalized somehow by some common measure. Money to Aristotle served this purpose. A standard of exchange makes the equalization of goods possible.

He realized that what was a standard value at one time would be different at another. The solution was to understand need or demand. If the need or demand changed, so also would the value of the commodity. In the end, the basic requirement of value relates to a person's desires. Value is the ability to satisfy wants. Demand is governed by desirability. Aristotle gave a reasonable representation of supply and demand, but somewhat negated labor as adding to this value.

Aristotle considered a difference between universal justice and particular justice. Particular justice was like an equitable trade and general justice meant more qualitative social and moral codes. This justified the merchant for his exchanges even though the demand inflated the exchange value. According to Aristotle, value is assigned by man and is not intrinsic to the goods themselves. He says that exchange occurs because what the participants want is different from what they have to offer. The moment when one asks more for something because of its demand rather than its intrinsic value before the demand, it is basically capitalistic—taking advantage of demand.

Aristotle did criticize wealth getting in the sense of moneymaking but did not consider that unlimited wealth existed even before money came into existence. Aristotle did not see that when you treat labor as a commodity you are a capitalist. When you ask more for a commodity than the intrinsic value, you must admit that labor put into the commodity what was made from its sale. Aristotle's disrespect for labor suggested what was in human nature. Did Aristotle see what was coming or did man justify capitalism from Aristotle?

The point being made is that just as ideals are legislated in any republic in order to dictate and control the populace, capitalism should be shown to be just as error-ridden with just as much control as any dictatorship. This is even more paramount with modern tendencies for legislatures to use corporations to administer social needs. It is difficult enough for a republic to assume responsibility for social need rather than the community, but to give that responsibility to corporations means that our republic is truly vanishing.

Freedom and justice are at the core of every republic, but there are contrasting views claiming solutions. We continue to shackle our republic with rhetorical differences rather than seek understanding. We solve these differences by removing responsibility from every community and giving it to a single bureaucracy. The high-minded will then say, "Look at the great work I have done." The people of the community will then no longer learn to love one another, and the bureaucracy gradually learns to love itself. We have lost justice, freedom and community responsibility.

Samuel Dael

13. A Vanishing Republic

> Statesmanship can never rise again if we do not work toward a form of government that leverages freedom with responsibility and demands economic democracy within the community.
>
> Mica R. Thomas

The United States Constitution has historically fostered freedom and defended the human desire for the pursuit of happiness, but these principles have been vanishing. If liberal ideals or conservative realities are legislated without regard to human responsibility, freedom is eventually diminished. This is the Platonic way and likewise the path America has taken over the last two hundred years. When power falls into the hands of idealists, we suffer the loss of community responsibility. And when power falls into the hands of capitalists, we suffer the loss of individual freedom. This is essentially the pattern over the years. It is as if freedom and responsibility are placed at odds in our vanishing republic with idealism and capitalism fighting for control.

When we teach freedom from generation to generation without balancing it with community responsibility and asking individuals to question in small groups, liberty eventually becomes a hiss and a byword. Responsibility is both individual and community in nature. It is also truly democratic in character and cannot be resolved through any form of voting for someone else to think for us. Responsibility means that we should gather together in our respective forums and discuss important issues rather than let an individual or committee think for us. If we give up our responsibility to discuss the meaning of things around us, we give up our responsibility to understand and to direct the future of our social environment. Voting without this local forum discussion is irresponsibility. It is none other than a reaction to hearsay judgment of a polarized society that allows national bureaucracies and political dichotomies to think for us. When we select a representative we must first participate in an open forum before we vote. We talk about the responsibility to vote, but without Socratic dialogue and debate among ourselves with the ability to argue back and forth as a jury would about innocence or guilt, we truly are not responsible. Simply casting a vote is not responsibility. It is a vote for darkness. Political caucuses are not forums—rather they are preformatted with political limitations that prevent one from asking questions and making comments. No matter what the gathering, everyone in power plots to avoid debate, questions, and comments if there is an opportunity to vote. If there is no public vote, it is usually controlled by a few behind close doors. Socratic meaning is essentially avoided.

A local discussion forum was the way in ancient Grease and what we know of as the beginning of the democratic forum. If Socrates did not begin this process, he learned the process from the traditions of the prophetic priests of antiquity. We have forgotten the process in that we vote for a president who thinks for us, and we vote for a city mayor who thinks for us. In both extremes we do not participate in open forums before we vote. We do not understand and thus we fall sway to a polarized and political society. We even vote for representatives without a forum. By forum it is meant a long discussion of questions and answers equal to the dialogues taught by Socrates through the hand of Plato. Most important, each of us should be asked questions in order to reveal our lust for eminence and no one should limit others from asking questions or expressing ideas.

This sounds impractical to most, but consider how much time and money we spend to listen to polarized views and vote for presidents, senators, and congressmen but never give a

The Platonic Idiom

moment of time to personal questions or to questions directed to us in a community forum? One is apt to wonder if things are turned upside down. Parties caucus for candidates, but why do we not caucus on local needs, principles, and issues? We talk of democracy rather than a republic, but when it comes to local and national politics we vote for someone to think for us rather than participate in a democratic forum that is truly Socratic in nature. Most of our time is spent against the backdrop of a national stage without any participation in a discussion. Local discussion is the backbone of a democracy and when we do not ask questions or serve ourselves up to be questioned, we do not practice democratic principles. We would rather watch television with its artificial political spin about candidates that can do very little to change our lives. Why are national elections more interesting than local issues? Why do we watch the nightly news about local accidents and crime far more than political issues of local importance? It seems that we care little about Socratic discussion. We prefer to be pounded with artificially generated news that we cannot participate in. We are forever looking for our view but find that it does not exist in a polarized media. We must learn the left and the right, but never know the intelligence within us.

National political news is easier to package and pass on to each local media at a small fee rather than the local media spending large sums of money to investigate local politics. We are forced through syndicated channels. Because of this cheap news, what we learn is polarized national propaganda. Even then it comes in the form of sensationalism in order to compete for our attention. Sensationalism is like gossip that never passes things of true value. The national stage does exactly what like-minded gossip is in respect to our community. If it is not sensational, it is not discussed. In addition to this, we do not become involved in local discussion because we would rather become immune to the process of revealing ourselves. This is due to the way we are taught from childhood. When we are taught to think a certain way and perform according to established culture without an avenue of expression, we learn to think one way but speak another. Speaking out among neighbors reveals this duplicity in us and therefore we avoid forum contact. We vote secretly rather than in a forum discussion for the same reason. When we do vote openly it is to agree with the accepted norm rather than object and give one's reasons.

There is no democratic forum that each person has an equal right to speak and an equal right to vote openly unless it is in a polarized or conditioned forum where only a certain mindset is expected to attend. There is so much controlled and polarized structure that there is no chance to edify or be edified with fresh ideas. Whether it is in a political caucus, a town council, a commission meeting, or a lecture hall, visitors are intimidated by rules of non-commitment and executive distance on the part of those in charge. Secretly they will be open with those like them but not in a public forum. Why? It is because of their political duplicity. This political duplicity is found in education, business, organized unions and large lobbying groups, and it is found in religious organizations. Open forums are prevented and few say what they really think. Some are expected to cry out illogically, but there is none to challenge them or ask further questions that will reveal real intent. Challengers are simply dismissed without question and the vote is usually closed to a few. This is the way of duplicity and not the way of democracy.

Pretty much every decision is predetermined and structured by those in power and those with the money that control those in power. Local politics is not democratic and inherently can never be for lack of communication through forum dialogue. People know that they can do little unless they have leverage with wealth, power or honor. Candidates seeking for position seek for these things. Support does not come without pleasing those who have what one desires. Essentially we are beholden to the election process based upon things of selfishness and not true values. We talk of virtue, freedom and high ideals, but we fail to define them articulately. We use them as clichés to cover our duplicity. We are void of understanding and void of what Socrates would have us know.

The Platonic Idiom

The human sociological problem is that every one has a traditional box around them that is full of undefined values. What makes them undefined is that they are used as scarecrows to cover one's real intent to find power, honor, and wealth. Ideals are not the real driving force, but rather sheep's clothing that covers that which one refuses to admit openly. Our box is none other than one's undefined values and principles mixed with the unconscious need for wealth, honor, and power. When one enters our box to get gain, they patronize our personally boxed values. Even when we understand those values we are susceptible to those who gain our attention by flatteries. When we really come to realize that someone is trying to get leverage over us, it is too late. Our mistake is due to our lust for honor and acceptance. Even when we enter another box or worldview, we tend to flatter their belief in values in order to get gain for ourselves. Eventually a box is created which holds a number of people all climbing for power, honor, and wealth in the name of some accepted value. We are all guilty of this political game whether in our community, our profession, our church, or our political party. Values are our cover; principles our fleece and our desires are seditious. Even if one's box is full of values without pride or selfishness, those entering from outside the box learn to adapt the same view because the same person is seeking for something subversive. Some do like the principles and will thus seek and identify with them, but most do not. Eventually the box becomes enlarged as more and more enter therein. This box then becomes the traditional watered down view. Anything outside the box is intimidated, pushed aside, and the gathering is structured just to keep anyone outside the box from expressing anything contrary to accepted tradition.

Even if the one with power, honor, and money does not seek after these things, those coming into the box do want such things and therefore become flatterous in order to obtain position and honor in the box. The one with power and honor often cannot see the political opportunist unless he or she watches closely within the structure of a Socratic method. The wise will structure every entry with a discussion and the express intent to weed out the phony optimist. The wise do this by setting an example. The wise give up power by asking all to have an equal opportunity to speak. The wise look for edification of each who speaks. If they suggest pride, the wise asks questions in order to make the one entering the box clarify his intent and reveal his pride. Last, the wise look for eagerness to sacrifice without reward. These three points were mentioned in *The Way of Socrates* as essential to overcoming the need for wealth, honor, and power. The following are the three disciplines of a forum and what each can overcome.

- Equal opportunity to speak—Checks Power
- Edifying remarks that avoid pride—Checks Honor
- Willing to sacrifice without reward—Checks lust of Wealth

This is the Socratic Method at its core. One must give up power to a discussion, question remarks that are not edifying, and encourage members to sacrifice in behalf of the lesser. It is the nature of almost all men that as soon as they get the power desired they begin to nullify the three disciplines. They do it in different ways, but here is a list of practices.

To avoid loosing Power
- Lecture to avoid comments and questions.
- Limit the time and items of discussion
- Do not allow a vote
- Do not allow injected remarks outside the accepted box

To avoid loosing Honor
- Limit who speaks
- Do not acknowledge new attendees specifically
- Do not ask for volunteers
- Do not question out-of-the-box remarks. Ignore them

To avoid Sacrifice of Wealth
- Maintain a status quo
- Follow a strict process
- Discuss trivial things
- Dismiss an issue before resolution because of time rather than bring it up at the next discussion

The Platonic Idiom

There are certainly many ways of covering over our fear of loosing power, honor, and avoiding sacrifice. In most cases the three run together but usually advance from the desire for wealth to the eventual lust for power. Those who have gained wealth and honor and still need to obtain power often talk of the need of others to sacrifice suggesting that they gained their position through sacrifice. The truth is they did not. It was done through duplicity of saying one thing and thinking another, but others are expected to sacrifice agreeable to the traditions.

When one watches local or community government it is easy to see what those in charge do in order to keep the political box fitting to their traditional form. The same is done in church gatherings, business, education, and most obviously in political parties. At all costs it is imperative that no one be allowed to speak outside the box. Every organization has a certain box generated by the traditions set by the one in power, the one of honor, and the one of wealth. If that person has great values, those values will probably be in the same box but will gradually diminish or their meaning will be turned upside down over time. Any one speaking outside the box is never questioned in order that the rest can understand, as Socrates would question his opposition. Instead, those speaking outside the box are ignored or dismissed with clichéd remarks.

It has become the tradition for those in authority to ask members of a business group to think outside the box in order to appear current in their approach, yet they still have a catchall opinion that keeps the discussion from diverting from the traditional box. It is not unlike the controlling manager asking all supervisors to practice the *One Minute Manager* technique without even attempting it with their supervisors. It does not matter how many books are sold illustrating better practices; power, honor, and wealth are the driving forces rather than equality, edification, and sacrifice. For this reason, all valued boxes eventually vanish, as any good republic will do. Even if something of value is generated out of a lust for freedom, some will eventually obtain the box by flatteries and begin to change it over time. There is a tendency to hold onto a semblance of values inherent in the original box, but those values are eventually hypercriticized into watered down rhetoric. Such is also the case of every religious institution. Even the use of freedom in every democracy or republic is nothing other than rhetoric to appease the masses.

If we were raised on open discussion, community life would be more democratic. Since every church, educational system, corporate hierarchy, political party and government process collects individuals that want honor, power or money, there is a tendency to maintain status quo or follow in obedience for reward. The unwritten rule is not to rock the boat. Those who want to serve as best they can may speak out occasionally, but the established political norm will stifle any independent thought. This is the politics of life and people do not get involved for fear of reprisal. Because of this vacuum, political life fosters two polarizing views in order to avoid meaning and understanding.

This political process is not a conspiracy, but rather the duplicity in the nature of man. Men do not gather to secretly control things around them. They gather because of like-mindedness and the desire to avoid differing opinions. The reason few will admit to this process is because individuals on a particular step to money, honor, and power sense the duplicity of those above and honor them in reference to their values, but secretly they seek a reward for themselves. They will not counter those above for fear of losing their position on the latter. Many will follow a command to do something not right just to keep the position. In this way the highest level of duplicity is protected without so much as a single plan to get subjects to obey. It is as if there is an unwritten rule that each learns to follow without actual instruction or conspiratorial command. The two guiltiest of this process are political parties and religious institutions. Both do not allow anything contrary to their norm. Those in power are not afraid of loosing values as much as their power, honor, and their wealth. They refer to protecting the values, but they are really protecting the duplicity of themselves and those positioned above.

The Platonic Idiom

Changing Our Republic

When the founding fathers gathered together to discuss and deliberate the Declaration of Independence, the U.S. Constitution, and a Bill of Rights, they did it under the principles of a Socratic method. It took much dialogue and debate. It was as if no box had been established and every representative was invited to speak. The discussions lasted years in preparation and over a month in actual face-to-face dialogue, and there was much correspondence between the already developing Federalists and the Anti-Federalists. The Anti-Federalists were an early precursor of the Democratic-Republican Party, lead by Thomas Jefferson. They opposed the ratification of the federal constitution advocating states' rights. To some degree this debate still exists between liberals and conservatives. It seems that polarized party politics have been at play since the beginning. This suggested that issues were not settled and the constitution would have inherent errors because of these differences. The errors referred to would be due to a lack of clarification and differing judgments. The most classic of these were that in lacking the Thirteenth Amendment, the original Constitution permitted slavery to continue; deficient of the Nineteenth Amendment, it did not secure the right of women to vote; and, absent the First Amendment, it provided no protection for religious freedom, not to mention other rights.

Imperfection was a lack of precision and meaning through discussion. Dialogue sometimes needs to go to infinite lengths to reach perfection. When one considers that the southern colonies would resist clarification on slavery and most men of the time would resist clarification on woman's rights, neglect is often a condition of maintaining power and wealth. Resistance to clarification is a political duplicity rather than a true search for values. Only after much deliberation can man come to the true meaning and the knowledge of the truth. Sometimes that takes over two hundred years to complete a ratification of clarity as in the Equal Rights Amendment. On the other hand, change can be detrimental as well as constructive. Congress was never immune to the need of power, honor, and wealth and thus much needed change would be avoided and improper change would be a byproduct of these drives rather than following a sense of values.

Congress was very much a politically polarized body where the two sides constantly sought for power. When an individual seeks for power, others can basically check it, but when a whole body seeks for power, destruction is inevitable through associated duplicity. By associated duplicity it is meant the networking of wealth, honor, and power through a political party. All congress needed was an excuse to give complete power over to their respective political parties in the name of democracy in order to foster more of this associated duplicity. That excuse came in 1800.

> The electoral system was devised by the drafters of the U.S. Constitution, who hoped thereby to entrust the responsibility to people whose choice would be unaffected by partisan politics. In Article II, Section 1, of the Constitution, the method of selecting electors is delegated to the separate state legislatures, and the voting procedure to be followed by the electors is carefully defined. According to the electoral procedure originally specified in the Constitution, the electors were to vote for the two most qualified persons without specifying which was preferred for president and which for vice president. The candidate receiving the greatest number of electoral votes, provided the votes of a majority of the electors were received, would be president, and the candidate winning the second largest number of votes would be vice president. A serious flaw in this procedure was revealed in the election of 1800, when Thomas Jefferson was the presidential candidate of the Republican (later the Democratic) party and Aaron Burr was the candidate for vice president. The electors, by voting strictly for candidates of their party, gave Burr and Jefferson the same number of votes. As the Constitution provided, the election was referred to the House of Representatives, where a protracted struggle took place, requiring 36 ballots before Jefferson was chosen president and Burr vice president. Therefore, in 1804 Congress enacted and the

states ratified the 12th Amendment, providing for separate electoral votes for president and for vice president.[1]

As said, the founders of the constitution *"hoped thereby to entrust the responsibility to people whose choice would be unaffected by partisan politics."* The 12th amendment complicated the process even more by requiring separate candidates for president and vice president. The change gave parties more power and not less. That is what congress wanted because every member wanted his party to have more power. This actually magnified partisan politics. The 12th amendment was not designed to solve a tie in the presidency. It was designed to take away power from the people and give it to party politics—all in the name of democracy. Just because there was a tie does not mean that the original concept needed to be completely overhauled.

The problem with the party system is that eventually only two parties will survive due to the idealistic and realistic natures of man. This political positioning keeps us from finding a true harmonic. Freedom of choice is diminished if the public must choose between two polarized parties. Originally if fewer legislatures chose a certain candidate at least their view would be represented in the office of vice president. The all or nothing program forces every citizen to work within a party rather than simply vote for the best character. There is nothing wrong with party politics as long as the party stands behind the candidate who has his own view rather than the party actually having the power to determine a candidate, thus causing candidates to position themselves to a party rather than to a personal philosophy based upon experience, judgment, and wisdom. This is the networking of associated duplicity where the group says one thing such as freedom and prosperity, but thinks another such as raising more money, obtaining more honor, and gaining more power. Party duplicity does this under the fleece of freedom or some other value. Political parties destroy the individuality in every man and every woman.

If we had a situation where religious organizations determined a selection of candidates, we would cry foul. What is the difference? Polarized religions are little different than polarized parties. If we cannot get it right through individual thinking and dialogue then the diversity of many parties is better than one or two.

> Electoral procedure is unchanged, but the significance of the presidential electors has changed. As political parties developed and vied for power, party interests became the dominant influences on the votes of the electors. Another development was of even greater importance. Before 1820, most of the state legislatures applied their constitutionally granted power of selecting presidential electors by appointing them. But as suffrage in the U.S. was broadened after 1800 and the electorate began to exercise greater political influence, the states instituted the direct, popular election of presidential electors. By 1828 this practice had been adopted in all the states except South Carolina, where it was not instituted until 1868. To attend this change, political parties began to present lists of presidential electors who were tacitly pledged to vote for the candidates of their party. Thus originated the practice of the electors of a state voting as a unit, a procedure that was subsequently made mandatory in most of the states and that has aroused serious criticism.[2]

It was not so much the electorate that wanted change. It was the political parties that inspired each state to change the political process. To think that each state was simultaneously thinking in the early 1800's of choosing the electors based upon a popular vote is a little far fetched. The idea had to be sold to the respective state legislators from national party propaganda for the states to even think of it simultaneously. It was an easy sale because a popular vote always appears as a democratic pretense, but it will never be what the traditional mind imagines it to be. The real reason for pushing a popular vote was to give political parties great wealth and popular acceptance. No one would consider that the popular vote would become so polarized in party competitiveness for power that the democratic process would become nothing but slogans and a one liner. The public seeking wisdom and understanding generally reach a consensus through discussion and do not move to a polarized political philosophy that the popular vote will foster void of extensive discussion. We forget that polarization is caused by one political party seeking power and honor and contributions from the people by positioning their ideologies opposite to some extent of the other party. If a difference is not demonstrated, the people will not shift. Political philosophies differ and eventually become extreme, and sometimes changing completely like a pendulum. There is no harmony in the political party system and the more the people have to vote without discussion the more power the party system will gain.

The term populist comes from the ability of the peasant masses to vote socialist ideas onto their government, thus providing the control they think will benefit them. What is popular is not a good representation of wisdom. This is due primarily to a lack of Socratic discussion over the meaning of the terms espoused by the masses and the political parties. Subliminal forces and hearsay information govern the popular vote more than true knowledge. The evidence of this is demonstrated by the power of advertising and also by the power of gossip. One little negative image will destroy a candidate and a sound bite of magic will elect one into office. What is most interesting about that which is popular is that the masses follow a majority and the wise often follow a minority. The pollsters feed the party system by helping the party change their directions in order to appease the populace. Anything the party seeks after is not necessarily good for the people. Essentially, how can you desire power for a party and not abuse it when it is obtained? Even if a party is founded on sound principles, each candidate will move according to a popular vote rather than a vote of wisdom. Party politics brings out the worst in everyone. That most horrible result is the lust for money, honor and power. The Socratic Method, on the other hand, brings out the best in people by fostering the ability to come to a consensus. Party politics is anti Socratic while the Socratic Method fosters wisdom. Party politics magnifies differences while the Socratic Method leads to understanding. The only good thing about a two-party system is that it stimulates competition, but keep in mind that if one party tries to elucidate true values through responsibility and another party speaks of gain on the part of the populous, the latter will always win because the latter capitalizes on subliminal motive among the voters.

It takes a lot of educated voters to counteract an unwise popular vote. For this reason time moves in the direction of a socialist ideology specifically to the method of Plato. This is due to the greed and lack of a responsible populace. They want something for nothing and they do not want to learn wisdom through Socratic discussion. The masses want it to come easy. Few understand that it is far better to have a man of integrity appointed by a democratic consensus to make a decision as to who would be the best president than turn it into a subliminal media blitz full of sound bites and issues that the popular voter cannot think clearly about because there is no ongoing discussion where the voter can question and be questioned by a Socratic master. The reason we have no masters is because we have no school teaching the way of Socrates. We have debate clubs and academic competitions, but these are not Socratic. Debate is simply polarizing arguments and academic competition is favored rhetoric—the very same method used by political parties.

When you consider that there are basically two political parties and that both think the other as evil or not very wise and that most decisions are made according to party wishes, good judgment is often buried in party rhetoric rather than surface with wisdom and understanding. Every party wants a popular vote because without it the party would dissipate for lack of subjects. When a candidacy attaches to a political party it will be very difficult for them to admit they are simply positioning themselves for acceptance by the party. When almost every commentator for and in behalf of a party repeats the same words without any insight, as if all met to decide what to say in unison, it behooves us to really question party methods. The idea of party unity is really anti Socratic. The human mind does not follow current party candidates because of convictions. They follow because of party prejudice and acceptance by the party. If a candidate did not have a party attachment there would be twenty different comments for each twenty persons. If the candidate were attached to a party, about half would sound alike in an apposing manner and the other half would sound alike in an agreeable manner.

Political duplicity and the networking of similar views is openly one thing but collectively many motives are hidden. In this respect party politics is the enemy of any democracy. What each party really thinks about is getting more money and more power. The issues are simply secondary. Those issues are what the party will do for the people. Parties are essentially saying, "Give me all the honor and money and I will solve the country's problems." The people give, but the problems become worse at every generation.

Today the republicans and the democrats have control of who runs for president. This should not be the case and a pure representative election (original electoral collage) rather than a popular vote would have prevented this. Once each state forced the Electoral College to vote according to popular vote, freedom was taken from the wise that represented the citizen and given over to the ignorance of mass opinion. This was precisely what the founders wanted to avoid, but those since wanted to control the outcome. You cannot control wise legislators, but you can manipulate the masses through party control. Even though the people get wise to party politics there is always a new generation that thinks a new way will solve the problem. They want change, but the party system does not allow for it, and change will not occur until every individual and every generation learns how to think, ask questions, and be asked questions by a master of Socratic dialogue.

The change in elections in the constitution indicated that the people did not understand the intent of the constitution, which was to avoid partisan politics. Once a party is able to manipulate the outcome it would naturally seek a popular vote and overturn the intended representative vote. Imagine if the framers of the constitution turned over the decisions to the people? Could the people ever realize that giving power to individual states rather than a direct vote by the people broadens the judgment base and prevents power mongers from gaining control? The people simply want what they want regardless of future generations. This is the popular way. But it is not the way of a sound republic. We have a responsibility to all and to every generation after. Selecting what we want for ourselves today always proves to be debilitating to our children's children. You cannot give the people what they want if it affects the next generation. It is like saying parents can do what they want with their own children and never feel responsible for what difficulties they face in the future. This is the fundamental problem with a so-called popular vote under party politics.

Originally each state legislature would select a person of value to decide who should be president of the United States. This would be more Socratic than a popular vote without everyone participating in a dialogue. If the State legislatures wanted to turn over to the people the ability to vote, let them organize small groups that will vote after a lengthy discussion. If the people are not willing to endure a lengthy debate, then their vote will fall prey to partisan politics and have far less wisdom than the voter who participates in a Socratic Method. This method could be preserved at the smallest level and a single vote or vote tabulation could be sent up to the next level of government for determination. Then the total votes could be tabulated from group dialogues rather than from media sound bites. It is paramount that the discussion should not be about party politics; otherwise the debate does not get into the meaning of things. The Socratic Method is a democratic method preserved at the lowest level. The Socratic Method is also a representative method preserved at the highest levels. Popular voting is a democratic farce. Popular voting is like an on-the-spot survey. It changes from day to day—not by wisdom but by what is popular at the moment. A democracy requires

The Platonic Idiom

questions and answers for all those who vote. Popular voting has no questions and has no answers. It only votes according to where the wind of gossip blows.

The problem of party politics was recognized in the beginning, but since a candidate could only climb by identifying with a party, we have lost the vision of this problem that we know intuitively but rationally and openly we will not admit. I am not original to this thesis. It is the undercurrent of modern thinking and yet the wisdom of George Washington.

> I have already intimated to you the danger of parties in the state, with particular reference to the founding of them on geographical discriminations. Let me now take a more comprehensive view, and warn you in the most solemn manner against the baneful effects of the spirit of party, generally.
>
> This spirit, unfortunately, is inseparable from our nature, having its root in the strongest passions of the human mind. It exists under different shapes in all governments, more or less stifled, controlled, or repressed; but, in those of the popular form, it is seen in its greatest rankness, and is truly their worst enemy.
>
> The alternate domination of one faction over another, sharpened by the spirit of revenge, natural to party dissension, which in different ages and countries has perpetrated the most horrid enormities, is itself a frightful despotism. But this leads at length to a more formal and permanent despotism. The disorders and miseries, which result, gradually incline the minds of men to seek security and repose in the absolute power of an individual; and sooner or later the chief of some prevailing faction, more able or more fortunate than his competitors, turns this disposition to the purposes of his own elevation, on the ruins of Public Liberty.
>
> Without looking forward to an extremity of this kind, (which nevertheless ought not to be entirely out of sight,) the common and continual mischiefs of the spirit of party are sufficient to make it the interest and duty of a wise people to discourage and restrain it.
>
> It serves always to distract the Public Councils, and enfeeble the Public Administration. It agitates the Community with ill-founded jealousies and false alarms; kindles the

animosity of one part against another, foments occasionally riot and insurrection. It opens the door to foreign influence and corruption, which find a facilitated access to the government itself through the channels of party passions. Thus the policy and the will of one country are subjected to the policy and will of another.

There is an opinion, that parties in free countries are useful checks upon the administration of the Government, and serve to keep alive the spirit of Liberty. This within certain limits is probably true; and in Governments of a Monarchical cast, Patriotism may look with indulgence, if not with favor, upon the spirit of party. But in those of the popular character, in Governments purely elective, it is a spirit not to be encouraged. From their natural tendency, it is certain there will always be enough of that spirit for every salutary purpose. And, there being constant danger of excess, the effort ought to be, by force of public opinion, to mitigate and assuage it. A fire not to be quenched, it demands a uniform vigilance to prevent its bursting into a flame, lest, instead of warming, it should consume.

> From George Washington's Farewell Address to the American people in 1796.

The above was lifted from the Internet as an argument for change. The argument was thus:

> Wise words from George Washington have come to past. The two party systems in this country have run its course. It's time for true Democracy to come back again to America. It is time to give the people a real choice instead of the moneyed choices we get year after year. Parties do nothing but wear away the Democratic process, and as we have seen right now in America to the point where it is unrecognizable from the original intent. The only way to bring real "change" is to then change the process instead of only changing the players. Real choice is real change. Even our founding fathers knew that. (Comment edited for clarity)

The above is a perfect example of ignorance and the common way of turning the meaning of something upside down to justify one's political motivation. Even though the writer was correct in saying the party system has run is course or better yet never should have had the power given; turning back to a democracy is not what George Washington was suggesting. Presidents were not elected by a popular democratic vote. A representative elected them or as Washington put it when he said that the spirit of parties should not be encouraged in "Governments purely elective." A democratic vote rather than an elective vote fosters party control. As long as you have a democracy, you will have parties. If you limit votes to a representative form of government, you will diminish party power naturally. Originally a republic, the U.S. Constitution had to be changed to a popular vote in order to establish a democracy of control. Giving power to the parties was the way to establish this form of democracy. You cannot take away the party method without taking away the nature of a democracy. Party politics and one man one vote democracy is one and the same thing. Perhaps George Washington should have warned us against creating a popular democracy rather than a two party system. We can see somewhat the dangers of a two-party system, but we often fail to see the dangers of a democracy and the eventual infirmity of the platonic state we have become.

A Change for the Worst

Taxing methods are never discussed in depth and the early founders probably had a lot of conflicts. Plato briefly mentioned the word *tax* once in his Republic without so much as a single argument as to how the state should tax. How can one talk of justice in many things without demonstrating the injustices of taxing methods? Plato, like most of us, simply did not want to discuss this issue. When it comes to taxes no one wants to pay, yet the same want the government to bring justice to the unfortunate. For some strange reason the obligation, in the minds of most, should be that taxes should be delegated to the rich. But what we have in the United States is a taxing system that aids the poor, lets the capitalist find a way of escape, and taxes the middle and upper working class sufficiently to pay the interest on deficit money. This is not justice and the cause of the problem comes from legislators in power who have gained their position by the vote of the poor and unwise masses and through the contributions of the capitalistic rich. The middle and upper middle class could do something about it, but they are aligned with one or the other parties and are not able to see possible change. We are left to the liberal poor complaining to the rich and the conservative rich complaining about the poor with everyone else split between a devotion to a party or simply unknowingly independent. Where is the wisdom in such a constant populace? Most legislators eventually become wealthy through capitalistic involvement and would never vote for a tax that would affect them. We thus have a taxation nightmare with a very high bureaucratic cost.

Salmon Chase first put the American way of income taxation into place during Lincoln's term. It is based upon the assumption that the ideal method of taxation would be for the government to take a piece of the economic action or product of labor. It is the same method of protection racketeering and certainly the purpose of the Federal Reserve System, which is an independent entity of bankers collecting interest on the national debt. Bankers do not want loans to be paid off. If they were paid off, they would cease to collect a percentage of all the economic action. This is the way the government thinks. When there is an economic downturn, the leaders give out money and ask the people to go out and spend it knowing that every time the money changes hands, big brother gets a piece of the action in order to pay the debt while the rich invest in land and other secured investments where there is no sales tax upon purchase.

The income tax is somewhat graduated, a concept endorsed by Karl Marx. The graduated income tax is a socialistic concept, but those of wealth have always popularized any income tax based on labor. In both Europe and the United States, the income tax had to be repealed and changes in the constitution had to be made to justify it. Keep in mind that the wealthy capitalist and those desiring possessions have controlled the legislatures from the beginning and they have gone to great lengths to condemn the property tax and favor the income tax. This change in the constitution, which was greed based, was not equitable and would eventually foster an albatross of bureaucracies. When you add the income tax to political party power, the United States Constitution has literally vanished.

One would argue that taxation is needed and that an income tax is the only fair method. This argument is one of the most twisted concepts that political power has propagated. It might be well to give a brief history and the origins of modern taxation. Very few will wish to agree with what follows:

We know that the income tax never had its origin in the constitution nor did it have any origin in classic government. It began to surface after the reformation in opposition to the property tax corrupted by the Catholic Church. The origin of the income tax came from affluent businessmen. Its justification came from an incorrect comparison to the tithes of the Old Testament. Religious parishioners were gradually indoctrinated to think that tithes of income originated with God. The motive for this was because the Catholic Church had corrupted the tithe—not by collecting a property tithe but by making a central treasury where everything went to Rome. Tithes originated with Abraham who paid a tenth of all that he possessed to King Melchizedek. Abraham was a lower level of government and the king was the higher. What Abraham possessed was property and thus his tithe was a property tithe. Tithing has been thought to originate with the Mosaic Law. This is incorrect when Abraham is considered. The law under Moses was not as difficult. In some cases it was every three years and not annually. In other cases it was a tithe only of increase. Some interpret this to be income. The Old Testament is not clear and the word increase was used only once. The Mosaic variations were not as demanding as Abraham practiced it. Christ, however, restored the law as Abraham and Enoch practiced it. The concept of living in common in the New Testament is a misunderstood concept and perhaps a misuse of the word because of the great sacrifices the saints made in supporting the poor. The tithe was basically for the poor. When one had more than needful when they came into the church, it was imparted willingly, but thereafter each paid a tenth of their possessions annually. The poor would actually receive from the church treasury of the tithes collected from the wealthy. Our current property tithe is a residue of early Christianity. The Christian Tithe most certainly differed from the Mosaic tithe. The new wine of early Christianity would naturally encourage the saints to consider their neighbor as themselves. They would share much more in common with a property tithe than an income tithe on labor.

Since the early days of the church, some have tried to re establish the law in various forms of communism. In this they have misunderstood. When one paid a tenth value of their possessions annually, their total tithe over ten years would be equal to all of their possession. One would have to work very hard to add to their possessions each year and if the poor had no possessions, they would pay no tithe. This would prophetically raise the valleys of the poor and lower the mountains of the rich over time. Communism does not tax according to possession, but puts all in a treasury and redistributes according to need—usually in a corrupted form. Communism is an enemy to free enterprise but a tithing of possession is not. Tithing of possessions requires free enterprise to replace what is paid annually. This difference is not known, as it should be.

The Catholic Church practiced the tithe according to property, but corrupted it by making a general church treasury. Instead of each bishop collecting the property tithe and using it for education and for the welfare of the poor, he was asked to send it all to Rome and Rome would return very little. This is much like the Federal Government today in its corrupt form of an income tax. Each Bishop should only have been required to give one- tenth of his collection to the Pope rather than all. Because of the undue stress required by the Church, the Priests and Bishops had to learn new ways of obtaining funds such as allowing the purchase of indulgences. That turned into the most controversial issue propagandized by the Protestants. The largest push in the Protestant reformation came when more distant kingdoms refused to send the requested tithe to Rome. Instead they reformed Christianity so they could keep the funds more local—all in the name of some doctrinal value such as baptism, grace or some other issue. Because the Protestants were motivated politically by the wealthy, it became customary to redefine the tithe contrary to the way the Church of Rome maintained it. To be local would not satisfy those of wealth so it became customary to associate a tithe to income rather than property. This was a total misunderstanding of the Biblical word. Even though no government practiced a tax by income it was nonetheless a change in religious thinking of the time. The concept was of bourgeois in nature, but Karl Max wanted to make in graduated because he knew that any percent was not just between the bourgeois and the worker. Thus the income tax originated from corrupted Protestant thinking and was eventually tried in America and Europe but was repealed in both cases only to be reinstated later. The rest is known history. Thus gradually man has distorted a biblical concept and changed it to suit the wealthy.

A property tax is the hallmark of free nations and a measure of free enterprise and community development. Property tax gathers more from the rich than does the income tax while at the same time it liberates the enterprising spirit. Since the 1950's, property tax has not kept up with inflation. It has actually diminished in total collection relative to what a dollar will buy. This is the primary reason why so many businesses are boarded up in malls and main streets. Commercial building has been overextended because low property taxes do not inhibit the construction process. It is also why the small business has a harder time surviving the newer competition. Small businesses have to hire less people to survive because of the excessive competition developed through low property taxes. It is too easy to build a new building down the street to make the current, perfectly adequate business, appear old and decaying. If the property taxes were higher, the old business could keep pace against needless construction. The higher volume of business would make the overhead proportionally smaller. There is a sense that we lost something since the 1950's as old nostalgia is weaved into new construction creating a false sense of old prices. Eventually the nostalgia is seen for what it is—high priced merchants with few employees. There is always a new building gimmick to draw younger crowds. If construction were not so rampant, the older business could survive and the prices would be lower. Simply raise the property taxes to a more equitable level. There would be less competition, more basic jobs, and lower prices. Lower prices are due to the fact that too much competition eventually rises prices because of the excessive required overhead that does not diminish with competition. There would also be more local money for education and local health care as it was prior to 1955.

The typical capitalist, Republican and especially a Brigham Young Mormon type, would argue against the above conclusion and also against a rise in property taxes by claiming they have allodial rights without any local responsibility, but consider that the capitalist earns wealth often without adding value. Many do not create jobs or add anything to the property they buy and sell at inflated prices. They do not want to pay taxes on their property wealth because it inhibits their ability to speculate. Actually, higher property taxes reduce speculation and also create more public services. Once you reduce speculation, you also reduce inflation. With a low property tax, the rich get richer and the poor get poorer. Understanding the difference between an income tax and a property tax helps in understanding the difference between capitalism and free enterprise. An entrepreneur knows too well the difference, whereas the typical investor refuses to think there is a difference.

A direct income tax was the only way to tax the working class without affecting the wave of capitalism. It was obvious to the capitalist that the income tax was a tax on labor and not possessions. For this reason a property tax was understood to naturally affect the rich in greater proportion than the poor. A capitalist's excess possessions indicates that he has taken more out of the system than he has put in so why not tax those possessions as a basis of tax to equalize the playing field? The wealthy capitalist should be able to earn as much as he wants without taxation, but as soon as he purchases a possession, that property should be taxed annually as an asset owned. Most will say that this is not feasible, but when you consider what costly methods we use to collect taxes, it can be done with far less bureaucracy than we have today by abandoning the income tax, slightly adjusting the sales taxing methods, and adding slightly to the property taxing methods. Comparable to income tax collection the savings would be phenomenal. Some, however, would say that savings is a possession and it is difficult to tax. Cash and savings are not possessions as in property. It is a measured accounting of labor performed and until converted to a possession there should be no taxation. The more you encourage people to save, the lower the prices, and the more money available to loan for being enterprising, and the slower the inflation.

Bureaucratic Nightmares

Consider that the larger the government the greater the bureaucratic implementation. This has come directly from the instigation of the income tax. The tax has produced corruption because we put someone in charge too distant from the people. This is not unlike a virus becoming immune to a particular host. No matter what the large system has to offer, there are con artists that will find a way to infiltrate any large system. Each small system is sufficiently independent that a corrupting virus may only work in one or a few small systems but not all. Smaller systems can then implement more efficiently to protect themselves and at lower costs. Above all this, the smaller systems inspire responsibility because the people are in control of their own destiny. If one small system succeeds, then it will encourage others to adopt similar methods. If one large system fails, it takes years to correct and in most cases the bureaucracies are so strong that they are only modified slightly with additional costs. When we take responsibility away from the people we break the law of conservation in a closed system. A rotten apple in a bushel can cause little harm to the whole harvest, but place all of the apples together with no isolation and the whole lot can be destroyed. If they are saved it is due to a more substantial cost greater than keeping the bushels autonomously separate.

Consider that the United States was once no larger than an average single state in population today, and that some cities will dwarf original states. As time moves on it becomes more apparent to move responsibility down to smaller and smaller systems. The Platonic idiom fights this because of the loss of control. The realist likes it because he knows that property taxes diminish in proportion to taxes based upon labor. We do not pass responsibility down as we should and we also loose our freedom to become responsible when more and more responsibility is given over to larger governments. We should understand that freedom moves up the latter through representation and responsibility moves down the latter through forums of democratic votes. You cannot equalize differences across the nation. If it benefits only a few, then the community must decide. That is the essence of responsibility. A rule in one small system may not work as well in another small system. That does not make it a bad rule. If it works then another small system will take up the same and reject things that do not work. Responsibility must move into the hearts and minds of smaller systems in order to be effective. Giving responsibility over to a big system simply develops an albatross of problems.

The endless array of bills created to control the national populace will only produce the need to reform the bureaucratic viruses that breed on national implementation. It is like a mutated virus in a large organism. We are constantly coming up with new vaccines to counteract that which breeds within a large single host. Local ways and means are like natural antibodies of volunteerism and sacrifice. We have chosen to become nationally antiseptic and so Platonic that human choice is at stake. Eventually we become a dictatorship—not because of an individual, but because we give up power to big governmental bureaucracies and corporations.

Another way of looking at our bureaucratic nightmare is to compare it with politics. The larger the system the more difficult it is to change the momentum and also the more difficult it is to change the politics. Political bureaucracies, governments, and corporations react and act just like momentum. They are immovable the larger the system. Smaller systems can adjust more easily just as the energy in a smaller political mass can be redirected more easily than a larger political mass. Even though a new president is elected, the various bureaucracies are almost impossible to alter. The Pentagon and its relationship with business manufactures of military products is a machine that has imbedded itself in albatross proportions since World War II and the very reason the Viet Nam war continued beyond any sensible purpose. We always hope that will not be the case, but it is inevitable in the marriage of big government and military corporations.

Health, education, and welfare in the United States are gross examples of Platonic and bureaucratic thinking. The national state is too large for such a method. In every case from education, health care, social security, and welfare, there are insurmountable problems. The bureaucratic politics is so powerful that it cannot be reversed or changed in direction. The local constituencies have lost the freedom they once had and can no longer deliver the social services of their respective community. Many receive and should not, and many needs go unheeded. We have broken the law of conservation by putting too much responsibility into the hands of big government. The costs will balloon and the money spent will eventually do less and less. What appears to be a benefit is simply barrowed money. He who has to borrow money to feed his family is lower than poverty. Borrowing for a house or any long-term benefit, such as defending freedom, does not cause a problem. In these methods, the future is stronger. But barrowing to eat is destruction. There is no future benefit to justify the credit.

As to social services, we forget the law of supply and demand. As soon as the public gets wind of social benefits, more and more twist and turn the machine to benefit the greedy rather than those in need. The bureaucratic machine is so heavy now it cannot be altered without breaking the bank. We have barrowed too much for short-term things. Education and welfare to individuals and communities, as funded from federal and state governments, defy the law of conservation. Even if our taxes were somehow equitable, why send taxes to the national government only to loose friction in the return? This sort of funding can never become equitable according to need. Corruption is a byproduct and inflation adds fire to the constant borrowing. The only way out is for us to gradually pass responsibility to the local communities and counties as it was during the nation's grandest growth after the depression. Education and health care have become monsters since those days. No matter how much money you put into the system, supply and demand inflates the cost further and further. Only when communities and counties pay for their own needs will waste come under check and new ideas will flourish. Social responsibility has to be reduced to the lowest system possible to check the waste. This is a law of conservation and will never change, regardless of the idealistic jargon postulated by the Platonist, and the Liberal.

Ideally the law of conservation works best in a closed system, but this is not realistic. There must be a proper exchange between smaller and larger systems in physics and in economics. If any system takes in low energy from smaller systems, combines that energy into higher levels, and then emits it at broader beneficial levels, there is value added to the whole system. If we substitute higher government levels in the place of smaller systems, it becomes apparent that equilibrium within the whole system is diminished. Equilibrium between the

The Platonic Idiom

smaller and the larger government must be maintained in order to preserve freedom and the economic conservation needed to sustain a Republic. If the founding fathers could see the future more clearly, perhaps they would have built in a safety net in the constitution to prevent poor conservation amendments in regards to representation and taxation.

In the beginning it was the Federalists and Antifederalists who could not see that there was a way to preserve the equilibrium needed between states and a new nation. Instead, each side wanted to become the primary form of control. It was not unlike the idealists wanting a Federal government and the States-rightists wanting to follow a more realistic level of independence. The problem continues today. The federalist and idealistic concepts can be compared to *The Bee Watcher:*

> Oh, the jobs people work at!
> Out west, near Hawtch-Hawtch,
> there's a Hawtch-Hawtcher Bee Watcher.
> His job is to watch ...
>
> is to keep both his eyes on the lazy town bee.
> A bee that is watched will work harder you see!
>
> Well ... he watched and he watched
> But, in spite of his watch,
> that bee didn't work any harder.   Not mawtch.
>
> So then somebody said,
> "Our bee-watching man
> just isn't bee-watching as hard as he can.
> He ought to be watched by another Hawtch-Hawtcher!!
> The thing that we need
> is a Bee-Watcher-Watcher!"
>
> WELL .....
>
> The Bee Watcher-Watcher watched the Bee Watcher.
> He didn't watch well. So another Hawtch-Hawtcher
> had to come in as a Watch-Watcher-Watcher!

> And today all the Hawtchers who live in Hawtch-Hawtch
> are watching on Watch-Watcher-Watchering-Watch,
> Watch-Watching the Watcher who's watching that bee.
> You're not a Hawtch-Watcher. You're lucky, you see!!!
>
> Dr. Seuss.

There are aspects that need to be watched on a national level, but health, education, and welfare are not appropriate for the federal government. This is to the extent that the federal government collects funds from local communities and returns to them based upon some means of special requirements. We will never solve the problems in education or welfare of any type as long as we continue this process. It will only get worse and the people will be drugged with a desire for more. Each time we increase national control, more and more depend upon it. Bureaucracies are increased and costs are escalated because everyone is looking for a greater return than they put into the system. By everyone we mean a government employee, recipient, corporation, professional, organization and even a smaller government? This is because the bureaucracy is so large.

It is not any different than what the master said, "And whosoever of you will be the chiefest, shall be servant of all" (John 10:44). Rather than becoming servant of all, the government has become a bureaucracy of moneychangers. The higher the level of government, the greater responsibility it is to become servant of all rather than a moneychanger to the lesser. Rarely does a legislator serve. He rather becomes rich from his position—something Socrates abhorred. He campaigns and says what he will do for the people, but when you give the people what they want and at the same time take away the responsibility they once had, you become an idealistic federalist and you defy the conservation of responsibility as the cost multiplies to the people. Essentially you are doing for the people what they should do for themselves. Legislatures serve the people in things they cannot do for themselves.

Our bureaucratic nightmare is a direct result of changing the constitution by giving parties political power and instigating the income tax. We would not have the problems today if other measures were taken. The federal government could have received funding to perform tasks that the smaller governments cannot by simply assessing each state a percentage of their tax collection. The states would have insisted that they do what they can and would gladly pay for services they cannot perform. We need to pass down responsibility and end the nightmare. We would then become *"lucky, you see!!!*

Our problems are inherent in a corrupted constitution. For this reason no founder statesman can ever come up with the perfect constitution that will apply to all future situations unless we understand what we have missed. A Republic based on proper equitable representation and equitable taxation is the only way, *as we shall see.*

Reading things that stress personal responsibility rather than what is traditional or authoritative may cause great frustration to those who prefer to follow the flow giving responsibility to those over them rather than assuming it themselves.

Samuel Dael

14. A Manifest Constitution

> And a thing is not seen because it is visible, but conversely, visible because it is seen.
>
> Socrates

Introducing a clear, unambiguous constitution may seem to be a pedantic scheme because nothing ever laid down can stand the test of time without being changed at some point or set in stone in such a way that it will become impossible to craft needed change. Either way, we can wonder if a workable constitution can even be written. Writing a constitution becomes like hair splitting and the creation of distinctions when there does not seem to be a difference such as in the Socratic statement above. In writing a constitution we need to see the distinctions needed in order to avoid assumptions later. If we cannot see the distinction between what is visible and what is seen, we probably cannot write a good constitution. The reason is that we cannot see the flow and the dynamics clearly. We think in terms of subjective and objective states rather than the active dynamic. Is not the act of seeing more dynamic than that which is visible? This inability to see the proper distinction between seeing and what is visible is similar to the inability of the atheist to distinguish between belief and faith. Belief is what to believe and faith is the dynamic action of a sound principle. We all have ears to hear, but do we hear and do we see the distinctions. Perhaps both Socrates and Christ learned the principle of distinction from the same oral traditions. Plato was able to record the words of Socrates but likely did not understand. Most of us see but do not understand the distinction between equal rights and freedom.

The atheist thinks that since God does not bring about the proper state of things he is obliged to do it for God. The faithful, on the other hand, think that the natural dynamics are at play and in order to bring about anything good man must look for natural equilibrium rather than think to steady the ark for God. The atheistic scheme is having Platonic ideals to believe in and faith's method is Socratic understanding toward responsible action. The action is always greater than stating a principle. We will get a Platonic structure or a Socratic constitution depending on our ability to rely upon natural and predicate dynamics rather than set fourth our hand to control the scheme of things. God does not get involved because man so often refuses to follow predicate methods. This leaves us to eventual destruction in order that we might learn the truth. To understand that God will not correct everything we do in order to make us wise is paramount. We have to see our own mistakes using His general instructions as a compass. It is these general principles that focus on the dynamics of life. This is no different than the parent and child relationship. If the parent controls too much, the child becomes a submissive robot or a rebellious tyrant. We must learn wisdom and God cannot be there at every step. Too often there are power icons that want to make things right without considering the proper parental, natural or God-like dynamics. Seeking for this power is the Platonic way and the reason for the eventual fall of every constitution—we ignore first principles by distorting them. We establish freedom but burden our equal rights.

The difference between Socrates and Plato has been demonstrated but those who will object to the distinction are most likely Platonic in nature and do not see the distinction between states and dynamics, between belief and faith, between equal rights and freedom, and as Socrates put it: "We do not know the difference between seeing and that which is seen."[1] As Christ would say, "We have eyes to see but do not see" the distinction between equal rights and freedom when it comes to establishing a constitution. Plato was so keen on repeating what Socrates taught, but like most of us, he resorted to the state of things in his republic. It is not unlike the Apostle Paul writing about the state of receiving Christ's grace and missing the dynamics of good works. Socrates and Christ show the distinction between a man's act of doing something and the state of simply being. If one asks, "Is it the righteousness of man that God loves or is it God's love that produces righteousness?" In this case man's righteousness precedes God's love, for the meaning is revealed that God loves righteousness. Man is not righteous because God loves him. Man is righteous because of his own choice to do good works. We need to understand what comes first—the state or the dynamic action.

Socrates made several attempts to illustrate the need of a predicate or dynamic process rather than objective and subjective states:

> The point which I should first wish to understand is whether the pious or holy is beloved by the gods because it is holy, or holy because it is beloved of the gods.[2]

The above was the beginning of the argument to establishing Socrates' defense. Socrates knew of political prejudice and hypocrisy and that this was due to emphasizing states rather than the action of responsibility where the gods love those who are holy. People are not holy because they are loved of God. The argument continues:

> ...is that which is carried in this state of carrying because it is carried, or for some other reason
>
> ...And the same is true of that which is led and of that which is seen?
>
> ...And a thing is not seen because it is visible, but conversely, visible because it is seen; nor is a thing led because it is in the state of being led, or carried because it is in the state of being carried, but the converse of this. And now I think, Euthyphro, that my meaning will be intelligible; and my meaning is, that any state of action or passion implies previous action or passion. It does not become because it is becoming, but it is becoming because it becomes; neither does it suffer because it is in a state of suffering, but it is in a state of suffering because it suffers.

In terms of reality, Socrates did not mention the subjective or the objective state that requires predicate dynamics in between. He used one action that preceded another. I think this was a language difficulty or there was no philosophical term that Socrates could use to explain the predicate meaning anteceding the subjective and preceding the objective. Socrates was referring to the action that precedes the objective or agrees with the subjective state. It is not unlike the object receiving the action or the subject showing agreement to the verb. In discussing piety, Socrates tried to illustrate his distinction in the use of attribute, as representing a state, and the essence of meaning, as corresponding to the active. In this I attribute Socrates as a teacher of the predicate reality. The whole problem in expressing this with clarity was perhaps Plato's inability to see the necessity of dynamics over his linguistic ability to remember details. Plato did not stress meaning sufficiently. He wanted to get to the state of things. Even though Socrates could not get a conclusion about the meaning of piety, we get the essence of his meaning as being different from traditional hypocritical forms of self-righteous piety. Socrates was forever trying to find the meaning of things in the active and, for the most part, the words he selected had this unique double meaning of essential action or state. The reason for this distinction comes from the nature of predicate dynamics.

The responsible mind chooses one meaning and the irresponsible mind chooses another. Subjective and objective terms often end in a psychological dichotomy because the action is not seen in the whole as Socrates tried to illustrate in "any state of action or passion implies previous action or passion." Dynamics is the continuity from action to action. We often miss the continuity and simply delve into subjective and objective states. Euthyphro began to see Socrates' attempt to define piety in the predicate. This caused him to feel a sense of responsibility that he did not want to accept. Euthyphro's final response to a pointed question was, "Another time, Socrates, for I am in a hurry, and must go now." We all avoid the action of responsibility and prefer some definitive state of being without responsibility. I do not think Paul twisted the meaning of salvation as much as the generations that followed, but none the less the tendency is to seek the state of salvation rather than act responsibly in order to obtain it. Society must have ears to hear and must also hear to understand the difference between hearing and one who hears and between equal rights and freedom. An equal right is the state of a constitution and freedom is the dynamics. When one claims some right in order to control the behavior of others does not understand the difference. Equal rights do not provide for the freedom to control behavior. Equal rights have limits. Many a judge does not understand the dynamics of freedom when they extend rights into the dynamics of behavior. What you get is less freedom for the many in order to provide more freedom to the few. Small issues are treated in our courts as inherent rights rather than simple acts of freedom. A case in point is school prayer and time will only show that many other issues will arise because we think we have more rights than a constitution can provide.

Now within a good constitution, the predicate action might be freedom and the state might be assumed that all men are created equal. We can question this order by asking which comes first, equality or freedom. If equality is a state, then freedom is the active dynamics that agree with a subjective state or the objective state receives the action of the dynamics. The state is not the action as also equality is not the freedom. Verbs are not subjects nor are they the objects. This would mean that if equality is distorted in any way by trying to become a verb, freedom becomes unclear and equality has been misaligned. In order to be free we must be equal in a limited way, but equality cannot be forced behavior. Behavior must arise out of natural or psychological dynamics and cannot be imbued with pedantic rights. This is the essence of the whole issue of understanding the distinction between equality and freedom. If equality is forced without individual responsibility, we do not have the dynamics of freedom. Equal rights beyond a point will actually destroy freedom.

Defining the limits to equality is essentially the key to every constitution. Talking of freedom is meaningless until equality is defined. The reason being is that freedom is the predicate dynamics and equality is the subjective and objective state of society. In order for the verb to work according to its meaning, the subjective and the objective must provide a clear meaning. This is the nature of a truly predicate dependant constitution or should I say freedom dependant. None the less we need to divide equality into two distinct forms before we can find its limitations. The first equality state could be equal representation. The second equality state would be equal taxation. Anything more or less than this will predict an end to a constitution.

When Lincoln said that all men are created equal, no one can say what he really meant because every man coming into the world does not come with the same amount of equality. God does not give out equally, but he does give us the same equal agency to think, speak, and decide. This is because of our inherent intelligence and the ability to choose. When man endeavors to take away that agency he does so in order to control the state of equality and limit our freedom. If every person has an equal opportunity to think, an equal opportunity to speak, and an equal opportunity to decide, the dynamics of freedom will be manifest without a single law to control the state of equality. When we use equality to control others we miss the point. Equality pertains to representation as an equal opportunity to think, speak and decide. Equality also pertains to taxation as an equal obligation. This obligation also has three sub principles. They are a tax obligation based upon an equal time basis, an equal basis of worth, and an equal percentage basis. The states of the constitution are its rights and obligations manifest. A true manifest constitution requires both to be clearly defined. Freedom is only a preamble between the rights written down and the obligations required. Define the states to be more or less than the above and you destroy or shackle freedom. It is like an injured baseball pitcher trying to throw a fast ball and a catcher trying to catch a foul curve. The action is distorted if either the subject or the object does not perform correctly. That is the nature of freedom.

When we attempt to force legislate equality in any other way than thinking, speaking, and deciding, or tax with different percentages over different times and distort worth, we will more often produce inequality and relinquish our freedom. The right to think differently (freedom of religion), the right to speak differently (freedom of speech), and the right to decide (freedom to vote) is basically the core of a constitution, but we often tend to neglect the obligation to tax equally. Equality of rights is the essence of democratic thinking and equality of taxation is the essence of a long-term existence. Equality of rights without equitable taxation a sign that the end will eventually come—almost always will it happen under a financial crisis and then a revolutionary war. Now a democracy is the hope of a constitution having equal rights and a strong nation is the hope of a constitution maintaining equal taxation. A democracy however is not about the majority any more than a strong nation is about financial might.

The first point to consider is that a democracy is about discussion and debate as first adopted by rational Greek philosophy. Democracy is about arguing freely and equitably in order to arrive at the wisest and most sensible conclusion for the community and even the nation. True democracy must manifest the equal opportunity to think, speak and decide. The majority is simply a means of measuring the outcome, but does not make the result the best direction. Democracy means that all must be on an equal foundation and must enter into a rigorous debate and not simply listen to media sound bites. Every one must participate in a critical thinking process. If the citizenry are not willing to think and are not willing to speak openly, should they have the opportunity to decide? Another question: How can one have an equal opportunity to decide who does not have an equal opportunity to speak or even an equal opportunity to think? Thinking and speaking must be equal with the ability to decide and cannot be separated. Democracy is far more than majority rule and simply the ability to decide. It is critical thinking and voicing your view that makes a real democracy. We too often ignore other essentials and focus only on the right to decide. We forget that the right to speak and to think is centered more on the processes of representation than simply the ability for one to stand up in a park with a picket sign just to voice a personal vendetta. Sensational guts do not measure equitable representation. Also media sensation is not equitable representation. What is thrust in front of us is more subliminal than equitable. Forum discussion of every individual in order to be properly represented is the basis of all equity in the right to think and speak. The proper form of representation is the mainstay of a democracy. Without equal representation a democracy eventually becomes bureaucratic forms of complex dictatorships.

The second point to consider is that when government makes laws that force certain forms of economic equality independent from equal representation, it does this by thinking that its citizens must be made economically equal in order to force the equality necessary for freedom. Controlling this type of equality is the antithesis of freedom or better put: controlling economic equality without equal representation is the destruction of freedom and the strength of a nation. It is no different than the expression: *taxing without representation*.

The concept of equality and freedom have always been politicized and expanded or limited beyond bare essentials. When one talks of economic equality, it sounds more as if someone is attempting to limit our freedom. This is never the case when we have implemented a dynamic form of equal taxation. When one talks of rights, it sounds more like a political maneuver to get what one desires. This is never the case if the equal ability to think, speak, and decide is maintained. When we establish equal taxation and equal representation we need no other form of equality. If we try to inject more than this we at the same time limit our freedom. Plato pushed equality beyond its constitutional purpose. Most follow this same method through party politics. Parties upstage the constitution with rhetoric about economic freedom and economic equality without limiting the meaning laid down by a constitution. Party politics mixes in economics with inherent rights rather than letting the natural flow become a result of proper inherent rights and equitable taxation. Natural dynamics is essential. You cannot force right action by manipulating legislation that subtly diminishes the right to think, speak or decide, nor can you tax with various degrees or allow special deductions suited only to get votes and satisfy some idealistic or platonic way of thinking. It is like mixing equality and freedom into one state rather than letting the equal right to think, speak and decide and the equal right to be taxed as a precursor to freedom. Politics would rather think that equality and freedom are constantly reestablished by some continual legislative means. If this is the case we do not have an equitable constitution and our freedom has become a hiss and a byword.

Equality must be limited to inherent rights in the constitution and should not be debilitated by constant legislation that forces behavior. Equality in taxation should also be explained in the constitution and should not be incapacitated by constant changes in the tax code. More important than the above is that the constitution should place the responsibility of the sub categories of equal rights and taxation in charge of a lower form of government—a level that can administer tax collection as well as determine the percent basis of tax collection according to the constitution. This same level should provide an equal opportunity to think, speak and vote. The lower forms are better suited for the basic essentials leaving the larger governments with the responsibility to maintain rights, defend liberty and set the percentage of the tax collected for national needs. The lower forms set the percentage collected from individuals and the national government sets the percentage collected by the lower government. If taxation cannot be determined by the same level that has an equal opportunity to speak, but becomes collection determined by national government, then we have taxation without representation. In order to illustrate the stupidity of national tax collection suppose we had a United Nations that decided to tax every citizen in the world individually rather than tax each country on the basis of their gross national product. Everyone would agree that this would be an improper taxation. Should not the same case be to national and state governments having the ability to tax individuals without an equal opportunity to voice their choices? By representation is meant an equal opportunity to speak and vote within a forum discussion.

It is generally a problem when big government tries to do it all. In doing so the bureaucratic system bogs down the essence of equality and inhibits the expressive dynamics of freedom in the process. Traditionally, the county government has performed this service better than both state and national governments. At the county level people have more of an equal opportunity to participate and decide on a tax basis. If the national government decides the tax basis, it is really taxation without representation because the opportunity to speak is taken away from the individual and placed in the hands of the state and representatives paid by the government rather than the people. National systems cannot provide equal representation as easily as a smaller system, so the same system that starts the representation process should establish the taxing basis according to the national constitution. In this, taxes are also collected locally and a percentage is sent to the state and national governments according to the constitution. The dynamics of freedom are only preserved at community and county levels. Anything larger does not preserve freedom.

Plato made the fundamental mistake against democracy in his *Republic*. He thought of how things should be and did not consider any form of natural propensity for the good and the just. Instead, the state must force it at the expense of freedom. Socrates asked, "Does God love a pious man or is a man pious because God loves him." If God loves a pious man, then the acts of man determine the outcome, but if a man is pious because God loves him, then we assume that the man has become what God determines and not what is determined according to free choice. A constitution works the same way. It does not determine the good. It only allows man to fulfill the ultimate good he has the capacity to reach. A constitution does not make a man good any more than God can make a man pious. Yet God and a good constitution will love and agree with a good man. A constitution is like a conscious will. The people must be free to do good rather than be forced to do it. The only way the people can achieve this is through equal representation on the smallest and most reasonable level of government.

A constitution works on the highest levels of government for inherent individual rights and community or county governments work on economic freedom and economic equality. This is a fundamental law in economics and should be sustained by every constitution. The more particular a principle the more particular should be the representation. The dynamics of national government is maintained by inherent rights and the dynamics of local government is maintained by equal representation. Equal representation is almost impossible on the national level so we should limit national government to inherent rights, security, and defense of those rights. Any government in between is but a mix of the two.

In general, if a constitution does not lay down an equitable taxing system and an equitable method of representation for each level of government, the constitution will be left to others to do, as they will. Even the best of intentions will break in and destroy the original constitutional design. Taxation and representation are the predicate dynamics of every constitution. Equitable taxation without equitable representation or equitable representation without equitable taxation produces a controlling constitution designed for those in power. The dynamics of representation and taxation will determine the success or failure of any constitution. A manifest constitution must have the equity of representation in thinking, speaking, and deciding and the equity of taxation must also be according to the same time, the same basis of wealth and the same percentage. A constitution without equity in every aspect does not manifest clarity. A manifest constitution is a clear unencumbered constitution.

Representation

Constitutions are usually written by representatives of the people to protect certain inalienable rights. Even though a representative forum historically determines the articles of a constitution, the process is far more political and sometimes more dictatorial by certain powers than the people would like. This is the reason for eventual failure—the cause of which is inequitable representation in the first place. There is always an illusionary democratic process that does not truly represent the people equitably. If a constitution survives over time, it is not the democratic values the public thinks to be the cause of a good constitution—it is the representative principles of equity that determine the life of any constitution. Every democracy will eventually end with various bureaucratic dictatorships entrenched within a state that does not have the dynamics of equity in their representation. Few take the time to clarify, but there is a difference between a democracy and a republic. The U.S. Constitution was started as almost a pure form of republic representation and has gradually evolved into a popular democracy. The reason so many complain about Washington in modern times is not that our democracy has changed, but because our republic has become a democracy. We toss the word democracy around, exalting it and even being patriotic about it, but it has become Washington's demise. We defend the constitution thinking that we are defending a democracy. What we should really be defending is the freedom to be represented equitably. To be represented in congress has been far more enduring than the right to vote for president. Every four or eight years we look for change with a new president, but we only come to realize that change will never happen because congress has given power to the presidency in order to dictate the state of things without proper representation. We need to look to congress as a form of representation and not the presidency as a form of democracy for the change we seek.

Most of the time, a democratic process will elect a dictator promising solutions. The people will give power to someone else to change the laws and even seize property on some basis. The promise to us is life will be better for the poor or the majority, but corruption multiplies within every bureaucracy that does not have equitable representation. When we look for a king to rule over us, we sell our freedom to be represented equitably. Even a president fills the demands of his party and power structures rather than the people. One man cannot represent the entire nation except in issues appointed him by a represented body. A democratic candidate always says, "Vote for me and I will bring change." The problem is the people loose the ability to discuss in some represented forum the particular changes being made. The people eventually realize they voted wrong, but they make the same mistake by voting in someone different who will dictate new particulars. The problem is never resolved because the vote is democratic, where there is no checks and balances in open discourse, rather than representative, where there is. There is no freedom of expression in a popular democracy.

Constitutions created under any form of dictatorship have limiting benefits. Sooner or later future dictators change the constitution, whether through a single leader or various bureaucratic agencies. If a body politic gives power to any person or entity to rule over them, the people have created a dictatorship through a democratic process. Even if the power ends at a specified period of time, each and every dictator manipulates the constitution into a more changeable form for the next in power. Over time, every constitution is eroded through this illusionary democratic process. We should understand that it is eventually the democratic process that erodes every constitution. Even though a republic of representatives may form a constitution, every democracy eventually becomes a dictatorship and the cause of every failing constitution. Wherever the people give up power or stand by a certain king, they create their own dictatorship. A dictatorship may not seem so bad, such as during times of total ignorance of the people and during invading countries, but dictatorships and democracies do not uphold constitutions in the long run.

There is no such thing as an ideal democracy, for if there were, it would require every adult to vote on every line item issue after he or she has had time to think and speak openly. To vote democratically for a leader to think for us transfers our government from a pure democracy to a democratically born dictatorship. The only way to prevent any form of dictatorship is to form a republic. But before we can classify the ideal republic and how a constitution can be created and preserved within, we need to understand a very important aspect of corporate-like dictatorships. Political parties do mimic a wholesale corporate dictatorship. The nature of this process is to purchase a dictatorship from an established or rising political power. Thus the political party becomes the dictatorship rather than an individual. Using the term dictator loosely in this context is not changing the meaning of the term. The attempt here is to classify the process of giving up power. Just because a democracy can change dictatorships at constitutionally specified intervals does not change the meaning of dictatorship. It only limits the new power, but not the trend. Even though a democracy can change powers or dictatorship assignments at any interval, makes it no less a dictatorship operating within the confines of a constitution. In most cases, we give power over to dictatorships born of some committee or government agency without regard to a continued represented vote. The IRS is a perfect example. Even though there is no constitutional law authorizing the IRS to collect income taxes, and even though we voted for representatives to represent us in congress, we allowed congress to vote democratically to create a dictatorship in the form of an agency. The fault of this lies squarely in the hands of the founders of the constitution for not establishing a clear method of equitable taxation. As clearly manifest, if there is no equitable form of taxation there will be an inequitable change in representation.

The Platonic Idiom

How do we avoid democracies that give power to individuals, parties, commissions and agencies? First, the constitution has to bar any form of democracy unless every issue is voted upon in an equitable fashion. The people cannot vote for an individual, party or agency to rule over them. The people can only vote for representatives that in turn think, speak, and decide with critical thinking in mind. Voting for someone directly to think for us is insanity. Representatives can tackle every issue that we cannot and avoid the pitfalls of a democracy. Voting for a leader to think for us takes the representative power away from us.

A constitution must state the lowest level of a democratic process that would include equity in speaking and debate by each and every individual. Beyond that the people must vote for a representative rather than an individual because the representative thinks, speaks, and decides in the next forum above. If a mayor, governor or president decides the decision is not an equitably representative decision, these positions are better filled by a representative forum than by a popular vote directly because leaders are intended to administer what the representative body decides rather than what the majority want without individual expression. Popular votes are fundamentally depreciating over time because line item decisions made by a leader are not represented equitably. Popular voting is destructive to equitable representation because the populace at large does not have an equal opportunity to speak and decide on a thought provoking level. Judgment is removed in the popular movements and thus with it democratic dictatorships are formed without equitable representation. Constitutions should limit popular movements to a properly represented forum where each has an equal opportunity to speak and decide. Popular votes do not think and they do not voice a decision. They voice only a choice of dictators to think and decide about individual issues for us.

A constitution should provide that no legislative body should have the power to appoint a committee, commission or agency that will make decisions. Committees, commissions and agencies are fact-gathering bodies only. The legislative body should make all decisions. Individuals and commissions could only administer what the legislative body decides. When any administrator is elected by a popular vote there is a tendency for the legislative body to give up too much decisive power to that administrator. Such is the case with the President of the United States who has advisors to help or make decisions without legislative debate.

When individuals and commissions become permanent bureaucracies, they will eventually usurp power and make decisions for the legislated body, and from that time onward the people are no longer represented. A dictatorship is then born. Just because the legislative body of representatives can change things is not a solution. Bureaucracies lobby information that will propagate their power rather than rescind it. Eventually, the people will loose representative power to a political dictatorship. Our problem with senators and congressmen is that they do not represent lower bodies, but rather ideals created by their respective dictatorial parties. Over time every one not chosen by a representative body and also paid by that body will fall prey to political and economic powers. What has happened since we have given up our voice to parties and killed the representative process is that state and national candidates cannot rise without these political party dictatorships.

Upon true inspection, we find that the lower the government the more democratic it becomes and the less representative. This eventually moves all local government into bureaucratic, mayoral and commission dictatorships. Changing a commissioner or mayor from time to time does nothing to change the political forces in play because all we change is the democratic dictatorship. We call it a democracy, but we do not have a voice on issues. We have only a vote on which dictatorship will rule. Actually the people choose what is best far less than they think, because it is the party, the media, and corporate or financial power that choose who should run for office and the people only select out of that choice. When someone comes along and attempts to rock the boat based upon some particular issue that affects them, it only indicates that they are speaking for themselves in order to get gain and not for the people. Very few governments get to the essence of true representation. Every politician rises saying, "Give me all the honor and the power and also the funds and I will make things right." This is satanic because it takes responsibility away from equitable representation.

Consider that a community, city or a small body could choose democratically a representative to attend the next highest legislative body such as a county, which in turn could vote democratically on issues of that level and also choose a representative among them to attend the state legislature. Likewise, the state legislature would select for the national legislature. In this scenario, there would be no political party in control, there would be no corporate or financial power that could control the outcome, and the media would be unable to choose for the people by simply popularizing one candidate over another. Most important, all representatives would be paid by the body that elected them and in return would report to them and answer back. If they do not please the legislative body they represent, a new representative would be selected for the next forum. Who knows a representative better? Is it the people, the media or the legislative body that the representative voices his or her daily views to? We learn more about an individual in a forum than through media hearsay or party politics. This is because of the duplicity present in every man. It is harder to hide in a forum than it is in the media or a party that protects its own. A true republic has a democratic forum of representatives on each level. If a constitution were written with this in mind, there would be no need for the election of individuals other than for them to fulfill the requests of the respective legislatures. Popular voting can never work because the people can never be informed sufficiently to make a valued choice. Most of all they have no voice.

Representative power cannot be corrupted if kept equitable and proportional at every level. On the other hand, democratic choice, outside of the lowest level of government, is eventually corruptible. If one wants power, the first thing they foster is a democratic vote in order to obtain it. One knows that you cannot sway a forum dedicated to represent the various constituencies. Those who argue against a representative form of government think the people really can choose better. Give the people the power and you eventually give all power to media, party powers, lobbyists and personal selfishness. Every power monger will argue that the people have a right to choose an individual or party. This is not unlike allowing a person to build a home on his property any way he chooses. Eventually that home falls into the hands of the next occupant with all of the errors and poor judgment included. Eventually, a future generation will complain about someone's freedom to build the way they did. Freedom to choose should be limited to selecting a representative who will have equal ability to think, equal ability to express and equal ability to vote. Selecting an individual to think for us begins the process of a democratic dictatorship.

The fundamental question is: should a democracy have this power to set up a dictatorship assignment—even for a specified time? Before this question can be answered, we must ask, what is essentially the responsibility of a democracy? No one will question the right of the people to democratically vote for a representative. Such should be the understanding that a democracy can also create a republic of representatives. Now a representative differs from a dictatorship in respect to its constituents. The constituents of a dictator are not limited to a particular part of the whole. They are the majority of the whole. A chosen representative has constituents that are limited geographically and are separated from the whole. A dictator may not have been chosen by all parts of the whole but he usually has the majority of the whole or a particular segment of a large population that votes specifically for its selfish desires.

All of the other differing segments must accept the majority even though their choice may be a better one. Representation breaks this power up into segments in order to have all segments be represented rather than just a heavily populated area controlling the outcome. Thus was the purpose of the Electoral College. A democracy is a representation of the majority of the people without regard for geography with differing natures of people. This begins to tell us that the danger of a democracy is within its quantitative nature we call the uninformed majority. A representative is both qualitative and quantitative. Simply put, the democratic majority does not always make the best choices. This could be due to bias or to the communication at large. Since political parties and political bias control communication, it is practically impossible for the people to make the right choices. Since the individual citizen is perplexed by the need to choose a party rather than a representative, the party becomes the dictator of who shall be among the choices to represent. Political parties are corporate dictators that eventually inhibit the electoral process and make it virtually impossible for a people to be represented.

When a constitution was changed to augment the party system, the political process became a party of a dictatorial process and diminished the value of our republic. When democracies change the constitution, usually through party platforms, it is eminent that corporate dictatorships gradually diminish the constitution. Constitutional change may be good, but when political power dictates change directly or indirectly rather than through democratically selected representatives, we need to question such change. This leads us to the conclusion that democracies should not have the power to vote for dictatorships. Rather this power should be reserved for representatives, provided each representative was not elected by or controlled in any way by financial power or political party. We can easily conclude that a democracy is more easily corrupted the larger the whole and less likely to be corrupted the smaller in relation to the other democracies. A public forum in a community can be a democracy because one-man one vote in a community is less likely to be compromised by big powers. Nations are susceptible to national corporate, national political and national economic powers where a community is only susceptible to its individuals. National powers will find it impractical to change a community. For this reason, it becomes easier to control a nation through popular voting than thousands of independent communities.

In the case of a modern democracy, the smaller the body the more dictatorial it might tend to be. This can best be illustrated in a small town scenario. If each person selects his or her choice for mayor, even if there are no party ramifications, the majority will select a dictator to make decisions for them. If they choose wrongly, this will not affect the rest of the nation. If they choose rightly, others will look at their choices as an example. If a nation chooses wrongly, there is no return or possible correction, the bureaucracy now controls permanently.

A representative process can work with the selection of a town council or even a commission. Simply let each local community be able to select a representative on the council or commission. It will be easy to note that this is not the way it is done because way back in time there was always some rich or religious leader manipulating the community. He would have no part in a representative forum because he knew power would be lost. Every power person, whether religious or commercial, would simply suggest the people elect democratically a person or appoint a committee that he knew he might control more easily. A democracy can be manipulated, but a number of representatives paid by their community constituents cannot be manipulated. The whole reason politics gets a bad name is because of the nature of democratic popular voting.

Each representative should be more cognizant of his particular community rather than party, political contributor, other power centers in the community, or personal political advancement. Anyone who has ever attended a commission or town council senses all too well the interconnectedness of influential people, party politics, and personal status. This is all due to a lack of each panel member representing a particular segment or community as in a representative form. A representative system has always been avoided in community politics. When you think about it, those with economic, religious, and political power would naturally avoid the establishment of such a system. People tend to look at leaders showing success and not leaders as having wisdom. There is always a certain power struggle among icons of a community and in order to gain favor of the people they foster a democratic vote that will give power to an individual or commission that can be manipulated. A group of representatives of various cities and communities that are paid by their constituents cannot be controlled or manipulated in the same way a few commissioners can. Controlling powers know this and thus avoid representative forums. They prefer democratic dictatorships but twist the meaning of democracy from what it really means to instead give someone the power to think for us without regard to geographical representation.

The power icons are always more vocal than others. They will suggest that if there is a conflict that a committee or body of a few should be set up in order to study the issue further. If possible, they will suggest that the panel or commissioners have the power to decide. These same icons will nominate certain candidates that they can control or they will volunteer to serve themselves. The whole intent is to suggest a vote for a panel that can be manipulated more easily than allowing each issue to be put before a representative body. On the other hand, a true leader will stand up and suggest that all those living on the west, east, and south and north of a particular landmark, separate into a corner, select a representative, and return with a panel to do the debating and investigation for the whole. A power icon will naturally be part of the committee or panel, but will usually be checked by natural forces from other areas. This is the dynamics of representation. If each member of a panel or commission is not chosen by a particular segment of society, it is not in true representative form, is not equitable, and is not a way to keep the dynamics of representation afloat. A democracy is not a dynamic process when powers decide for us with the intent to establish a certain state of things.

You can further avoid the democratic mud and mire by letting local legislative bodies select from their own communities' representatives to the state rather than letting the public directly vote for a state representative. If this were the case, a representative would answer to the county legislature who would be more tuned to the issues better than the public. The county would then pay the cost as would the state for federal representatives. This concept was implied in the original constitution in that the original body of representatives never intended the President of the United States to be elected by the people directly. The original process had been corrupted by giving power to the two major political parties and the state following with a democratic concept of making electors vote according to the popular vote and not according to the respective state legislatures.

One of the biggest reasons that the democratic method is inequitable is the cost of maintaining it. An election process in a democracy is far too costly for what the people receive. The information coming from the greatest expenditures is only sound bites of slogans and one liners that aim to criticize, but do not encourage understanding. The party or individual stating the most critical views of the opponent often becomes the front-runner. In other cases, a sound candidate does not get the attention that others may get due to a lack of name recognition and speaking voice. Very good prospects are past over because of general prejudice. One can listen to a candidate for months and never get what he or she is really going to do. In most cases a candidate carries an aura of duplicity by saying one thing and thinking another. Above all, only the rich can run.

Without a proper constitution, there will be a willy-nilly tendency to constantly make laws to fix errors created through the lack of represented processes. These laws will change like a pendulum between political forces and will build bureaucratic dictatorships that can never be removed. Constitutions must provide correct representative processes that prevent dictator takeover. The process of equitable representation must be articulated. Laws then can be created on much lower government levels and can be more easily changed if proved to be ineffective. Piling up national legislation will eventually feed various bureaucracies rather than fill an articulated need. One would argue that laws would be inconsistent across the country if such were the case. Consider that when one area provides for successful legislation it will naturally spread to other areas. Bad legislation in one area will eventually fail and not be accepted by other areas. The people will eventually change it. The more national the legislative control the greater the evolution of bureaucracies. We become so entrenched by self perpetuating bureaucracies that law becomes irrevocable which in turn means the bureaucratic dictatorships evolve into greater and greater control. What is referred to here is legislation regarding health, education, and welfare, which should have never left the county level. State and national legislation should be confined to equity in delivering legislation pertaining to broad needs rather than collect and redistribute funds through a bureaucracy. It all depends upon the flow of money. If funds are collected from local taxation and sent to Washington only to be returned for individual needs, this indicates that Washington legislation was out of line. This process is not economical and was a direct result of democratic tinkering with a representative constitution in addition to adding the destructive income tax.

Taxation

The conservative view of taxation is usually something on this order:

> A rule of law regime would require that we scrap the Internal Revenue Code in its current form. What justification is there for different tax treatment of one American because he has a higher income, minor children or receives his income from capital gains instead of wages? Equal treatment would require Congress to figure out the cost of constitutionally authorized functions of the federal government, divide it

by the adult population, and send us each a bill for our share. You say, "What about the ability-to pay for the cost of government?" That's just a politics of envy concept that would be revealed as utter nonsense if applied to any other cost. Would you apply the ability-to-pay principle to, say, gasoline or food purchases where different prices are charged to different people depending on how many dependents they had, their income, or whether their income was derived from wages, dividends or capital gains?

The fact that Americans have become ruled by orders and special privileges helps explain all the money and graft that we in Washington. We've moved away from a government with limited powers, as our Founders envisioned, to one with awesome powers. Therefore, it pays people to spend huge amounts of money to influence Congress in their favor, that is, get Congress to grant them privileges denied to other Americans.

Walter Williams (June 2007)[3]

The first paragraph suggests that the current system in the United States is not equitable. This inequity is then associated with the second paragraph suggesting a cause of corruption. In the first case, should a poor man pay the same percentage share as a rich man? This sounds equitable in a certain sense, but it is not. It is missing the element of responsibility in equity. The ability to pay must become some aspect of taxation. For this reason, taxing income from labor is the wrong way because it takes so much income just to survive that anything beyond this defines the real difference between the rich and the poor. For example, if we take two household earners of $30,000 income from labor and knowing than one household has two dependants and the other nine; it behooves us to understand that it takes more for the nine to survive than the two. The current tax code does have exemptions, but that only indicates that the wrong taxing method is used even though the survival of a family in one area differs from another. The dynamics is not built into the system and constantly need readjustment and tinkering in order to make it more equitable. This tinkering allows the wealth to lobby for special benefits and through popular voting it allows the poor special favors beyond need.

The Platonic Idiom

Yes, the tax code is totally inequitable, but not for the reasons mentioned by the conservative Walter Williams. Equity and responsibility must work together. The greater the share manifested must also suggest a greater responsibility. Taxing income from labor does not produce the needed responsibility. Once labor is part of the taxing criteria, one must understand that time becomes a limiting factor. If it takes one man 10 hours to survive and another only 10 seconds of labor, there is definitely inequity by taxing income from labor. Everyone first needs their basic needs satisfied and then anything above that might be taxed, but this requires juggling and manipulation by lawmakers if we use income taxation. Manipulation breeds corruption and that sponsors a monstrous tax code. It is not a natural dynamic methodology, but rather a political one.

A theory of taxation might be considered a debate between a positive and normative theory. You might ask, "What is the difference between positive and normative?" Walter Williams would say that positive statements deal with what was, what is, or what actually will be, while normative statements would deal with one's own personal subjectivity of good or bad or what ought to be or should be. Traditionally, we understand the difference between subjective and objective statements and to some degree we think of subjective as just opinion. I prefer objective statements in contrast to subjective statements, but we can get into a lot of mischief if we do not clarify the difference.

In general, one might say that it is good to tax the rich and give to the poor. This would be a subjective or normative approach unless you have some evidence to show your particular theory obeys the law of conservation. The conservative approach says that equity is fulfilled if each person pays the same percentage of his or her income. This sounds objective and positive, but it basically is not a positive statement. It is a normative statement because what we are taxing is labor and not income without labor. If one person makes one thousand dollars a second by applying little labor and another makes one thousand dollars after working sixteen hours with his hands;

it behooves us to ask if taxing income from labor is really a fair method of taxation. Legislators have spent years trying to equalize the taxation process by making it graduated and allowing certain exemptions and various deductions. By the mere fact that doctoring the system indicates that it is not an equitable system to tax income from labor. The mere difference between capitol gains being lower than that from labor income should tell us that something is wrong with the system. Any time you need to make exceptions for certain individual types, you can also corrupt the same system.

It is very strange that legislation has generally given breaks to very low income and in a somewhat same slight of hand, given breaks for the very rich. Man usually learns that if you do not pamper the poor, you will get an uprising and if you do not pamper the kings, you will not get the jobs and you will not get the protection. Essentially, the average laborer pays for the poor and for the rich. It is this twisted tax on labor that has become an insidious method that we mistakenly call objective. It sounds equitable on the surface, but it is really a sinister method. If you make a straight flat tax, as some conservatives would suggest, equity would not result because each individual would require about the same to survive and yet the poor would not even have enough to do that. You have to subtract survival costs before you even begin to tax the people. Doing this with income is too arbitrary, political and prejudicial. It is not a natural dynamic process. It is too dependent on human tinkering.

One should easily see that taxation on labor is not a natural or positive method. Too much is left to human will, greed and improper legislation. If taxing labor was so positive, why do we place so many band-aids upon the system to keep it in check? Equity should be the basis of taxation just as equity should be the basis of representation, but the modern tendency is to twist and turn, calling what is simply normative subjective and giving it the status of positive. This action turns things upside down in the name of the poor, but it really binds them into lassitude. Taxing of labor is a relatively modern method and is certainly a byproduct of control type thinking. Plato would probably like it and Karl Marx would love it, for it was he that considered a graduated income tax. Taxing by income does not obey the law of conservation in economics. Taxing income from labor is similar to the protection rackets—taking a piece of the energy every time money changes hands.

Taxing by labor creates an economic yo-yo effect to the economy. During a recession the government may provide a stimulus package hoping the people will spend—knowing that every time the money changes hands the government gets a percentage. Like the racketeer, we are promised protection with side benefits, but the cost is inequitable. Also taxing by labor creates an albatross in bureaucratic systems from the ever-increasing promises made by politicians voted in by democratic processes.

Political economists talk of various methods of better taxation, but never focus upon the only true form of taxation. In fact, the only two forms of taxation are that of taxing labor and the taxation of possessions. If the tax is an annual process, it is usually a tax on possessions. If the tax is more frequent, it is based on a tax on labor. In this respect a sales tax on food is obviously a tax on labor, but a sales tax on something that lasts years is simply a tax on one's possession. It is important to look at it in this way; otherwise we cannot see the distinction. Another way of looking at it is the difference between a consumption tax and a use tax. A consumption tax is proportional to one's labor and a use tax is related more to the possession used. Is a gas tax a consumption tax? If you consider that the tax is used particularly for highways and that the individual possess a particular portion of that highway that no other can possess at a given time, a gas tax is really a possession tax and not a consumption tax. On the other hand, a tax on heating fuel would be a consumption tax. In this way, it is possible to determine if our labor or what we possess at any given time is being taxed. A possession tax is the only equitable tax as long as the percentage is constant and equal to all. Our labor is taxed in so many ways we do not realize it, for if we performed no labor to tax, the income from such would be zero taxes and we would have no income to purchase and possess anything. An annual possession tax is really based upon what we take out of the system after we satisfy all of our consumption needs. In other words, after we take care of essentials, we then spend what is left over on possessions. This means that possessions represent that beyond necessity to live.

Now a possession tax is only equitable if it is based upon the purchase price and not some audited value. If someone keeps something for a long time and its value goes down, that should be measured in the sales price. Likewise, if the value goes up, the tax is determined by the amount of the sale. Since a possession tax is an annual tax, the item sold can be prorated to obtain a refund or pay what should have been paid each year if the sale price goes up. In the case of a possession sales tax, one could simply pay a sales tax based upon the sales price times the probable lifetime of the possession purchased. Food would have no sales tax while furniture would have a several year tax imposed at the time of purchase. If not, it becomes a tax on labor and not one's possessions. Long lasting personal items can be listed along with real-estate property to be paid annually. To pay sales exempt tax would require the seller to document the purchase with the county the customer resides in just as an automobile purchase; otherwise the purchaser would be required to pay the lifetime tax. If anyone were to think that this would require too much tax collecting paper work, consider how much paperwork could be saved if the income tax was abolished? The trade off would save billions with a very small addition the sales taxing and property taxing methods.

Of course the next argument against abolishing the income tax would be that the states and federal government could not tax property with as much control as they do wages from labor. The solution is: let the states tax a percentage of each county's collection and the Federal government could do the same with the states. The bureaucratic IRS and the bureaucratic state franchise tax departments could be eliminated at a substantial savings. The cost of implementing a graduated sales tax by length of life would be very small compared to what is saved in income tax collection. Sales and possession taxes based upon the purchase and sales price make it virtually impossible for the purchaser to defraud the government.

Every soul and every enterprising speculator would wail if such a possession tax were instituted. This would come mostly from the wealthy and to some degree from the less fortunate who are desirous of many possessions or from those hoping to become a possessor of wealth. Think about it. Those who have much obtained it by the labor of others. Therefore, if they purchase more, let them pay more. No one should care how much a man makes, how much he saves or even if he earns money without labor. What one should care about is if the rich are taxed proportionally to the poor for all their possession purchases on an equal basis. Annually this would curb the lust for possessions naturally just as high prices do. On the other hand, it would drive prices down and could naturally solve every social need imaginable if each county controlled the collection of such a tax.

One can argue that there are better ways, but they will not be equitable. Typically, the higher income tax bracket keeps some from laboring more unless they earn money on investments. Why the rich get a break on capital gains seems inequitable. Perhaps they argue that it stimulates investment. If that is the case, then the income tax is wrong in the first place. Let the capitalist or even the common laborers earn as much as he desires. Let him put it in the bank to be invested. Let him collect interest without limit, but simply let him be taxed annually for all of his possessions he chooses to buy and sell.

A possession tax is a tax paid by all possessors of property. If you buy a commodity outside of your county, the tax would naturally benefit the county in which it was purchased rather than your own. This would stimulate local business substantially.

It has been known that some counties give property tax breaks to entice business to their local area in order to increase jobs and thus the county's tax base. This is foolish for it places a greater burden upon the current taxpayers and can hurt current businesses. There is a much better way. Although personal possessions should be the basis of all taxation, businesses can receive a break based upon their use of local labor. If all profits and payroll remain in the county to residents as laborers or owners, there should be little to no property tax other than that needed for fire, police, and similar public services. Let each pay according to personal possession and let the business save substantially. This would increase pay and the increase profits would simply go into the pool of purchases. If, however, most of the labor comes from out of the county and the profits leave the area, let the business be taxed as any individual proportionally due to the loss to other areas. This would naturally promote local business, encourage local ownership, and make it unprofitable for corporations to snatch up small business and dominate the landscape. Jobs would be far more stable and there would be less outsourcing and more independent ownership. The proper dynamics of taxation solves almost every economic problem naturally and dynamically without patchwork laws.

The key to all taxation is to keep it reasonably local such as a county and let larger governments only take a percentage. Economics is like energy, keep it contained and it benefits the system more. When a local individual casts his bread upon the water, it will return unto him seven fold. If the economic waters are the nation or the world, nothing will return without taking advantage of others. This is a simple law of economic conservation, yet few can see it. Understanding this brings us to the most important principle in economic conservation. No government should have the power to tax the people individually toward any central control far distant from the taxpayer. It produces inequity and corruption. More important, no higher level of government should disperse funds to an individual or government less than itself. This breaks the law of economic conservation. When the states and federal government collect taxes from individuals and then build a bureaucracy for distribution back to individuals and smaller governments, there is a substantial loss in the process. All funds should flow upwards and out at the final level and never return. A national government can build a military, but when they feed the individual poor, the cost of distribution far succeeds what the poor receive. Health and Human Services has become the largest agency of the U.S. Government and the cost to operate it is beyond comprehension. If each local county was able to use the money directly, they could accomplish much more with the funds. The more local things are the more efficient and the more involvement one will find volunteers.

For the federal and state government to take on such tasks as education actually produces less education. The current situation will never be solved as long as the larger governments are involved. Every local board of education spends more time building a bureaucracy to get as much from the states and federal governments as they can. The attention turns to this rather than to the education in the community. Every board of education no longer serves the people. They serve the state and the larger governments because their attention to get these funds surmounts the attention needed for better education. Local governments also turn to the state and to the federal government for assistance. High paying jobs are created just to keep the money flowing back. When you add the bureaucratic skimming of federal, state and now local governments to keep the down flow coming, no wonder education is a farce.

The Platonic idiom runs rampant in every nation thinking that big government, big corporation, and big centralized religion will solve all of the ills. Instead, crime mushrooms, ignorance pervades, and poverty lines our streets. This is all due to the way we tax, how the money moves, and how we allow the rich to pay fewer taxes proportional to their possessions than that of the middle or poor classes.

As a small example of this sinister movement, consider the head tax of antiquity and how unfair it was. In a certain way, we are bringing it back. It's called a fire or perhaps a garbage fee sent to us from a utility company based solely upon a single meter for a single residence. The fire fee, for example, is the same for a large mansion or even a humble abode for the poor. It is not proportional to one's possession or even income. It is a head tax created by the rich in political power. In the old days, these costs were taken care of by the county. At one day, back in the first half of the 1900's, counties even funded hospitals as well as a better education. If the trend continues, perhaps we will some day have a police fee attached to our electric bill, because all our taxes will eventually go to fund do-nothing bureaucracies.

There has got to be a change and soon. Simply consider the uncertainty of Peak Oil or the continued oil cartels that manipulate the price of oil for windfall profits despite abundant supplies, and consider the day when there will be more people on social security than those earning income to pay for it. Consider that the national debt feeds the rich who have insurmountable possessions relatively free of taxation. The real rich do not even pay income taxes relative to their real wealth. Only the laboring rich are caught into the snare through withholding taxes. The poor live for free and often get money back on income taxes when nothing ever was withheld. It is called Earned Income Credit—credit for working and not paying taxes. This is all fine for those in need, but the system reeks of corruption, greed and bureaucratic ballooning. We think all is well because we have curb and gutter, wide streets and shopping malls. It will all come to an end when the oil continues to rise in costs and when we have sprawled out to the point of suffocation, and all this will come to an end when it costs more to feed the poor, the bureaucracies and the retirees than our own needs.

It has often been predicted that 2045 would be the time when there would be more on social security than working to pay for it. It has also been predicted that about the same time the oil reserves will basically be exhausted. Why should a wealthy businessman build a refinery, regardless of the yet obtained oil, if the refinery will not bring a quick return, and by limiting refinery production the price of oil is increased, thus obtaining the same return by adding no value? We have built cities and urban sprawl that give more space for the automobile than for the humans that drive them. We spend more and more transporting goods at long distances than ever before. The average American leaves a two and three car garage, drives on a freeway, and turns on a wide road to a very large parking lot to shop. No one thinks of the fuel cost added to every commodity—including the asphalt and automobile to perform such a feet. When the oil goes or becomes too costly, our system will begin to fail. The earth's labor over millions of years is burnt up in a single century. We are the rich living off the labor of others. It is time to pay our due. We should tax ourselves for all of what we possess in order to find equilibrium.

Understanding that God's method of tithing would suggest a method that would discourage the need of possessions and encourage the reward of labor. The capitalist thinks opposite of this process. Thus capitalism is an enemy to God just as popular government programs are an enemy to God when they take away the responsibility of the individual and the liberty within the community. As can be seen, there is a polarization of evil in party politics that fosters capitalism on the one hand and government control on the other. One party generally fosters leverage by capitalism and the other fosters control by government.

Capitalism And Freedom

There has been an assumption that capitalism and free enterprise is one and the same thing. This has been the most insidious fraud put upon the American people. After 9/11 the association of capitalism with freedom was also politicized fraudulently and inappropriately. Did anyone ever consider that the World Trade Center, the Pentagon, and the White House represent capitalism to many countries and cultures? Communism was not the first to suggest this association. We can easily bring destruction upon ourselves by embracing capitalism as something good for man. Free enterprise adds value, but capitalism does not. Also, free enterprise adds value where communism does not. You could also say that free enterprise adds value where any form of dictatorship does not. If capitalism and free enterprise seem to be married, the distinction above tells us where the two diverge. It all depends upon the value added. Sometimes a better description of capitalism comes with the term speculation. When one speculates on value increased without adding value, they become a pure capitalist. When one speculates by adding value they become an entrepreneur of free enterprise. Another distinction is found in the way capitalism controls value while free enterprise spreads it about. Once these distinctions are made clear, understanding of how capitalism has infected the U.S. Constitution can be more clearly determined. This author will discuss this more intently in a later book.

It was primarily the changes in the constitution that gave power to political parties and the instigation of the income tax that left the American way vulnerable to the impropriety of capitalism. Up until that time free enterprise was the hallmark of the United States with limited inflation. After the income tax, inflation has run rampant with so many speculating without adding value. It does not matter if it was big government or big business, the income tax created an array of vultures ready to take advantage of the new way to inflate and balloon value where value was not to be found.

Because of those in power there will never be a dynamic solution to our ever-increasing infection of capitalism. Capitalism is now the hero rather than the villain. It is similar to a drug addiction that we all become dependent upon. It is also similar to protection racketeering that expects a continual piece of the economy without adding value. It is not necessarily

The Platonic Idiom

found in a large corporation, but it is found in many individuals and especially the elite who control large governments and who also manipulate the marketplace. There are many would be capitalists that climb incessantly to become the elite, but disrupt the economy in order that the elite can take greater advantage. It should be understood that this infection not only affects the market, but it infects big government and many individuals wanting something for nothing—wanting to get gain without adding value. The most elite of capitalism seem to be attempting to play God with the world—thinking they know what is best. The enemy is not Warren Buffet or Bill Gates. The enemy comes from secret infidels unknown to the world with an untold number of copycats following their lead.

Capitalism is congruent with our loss of freedom as was party government and income taxing methods. It is a virus that has infected host governments and world economies. One might be able to argue that some capitalism is good such as the ability for one to increase his or her net worth and to increase one's possessions. These are natural desires, but there is a difference between speculation that does not add value and enterprise that does. There is a difference between manipulation and the opportunity to fill a need. You cannot make a law against this infection; otherwise you affect the good businessperson along with the capitalist. The constitution protects both. A healthy organism can avoid infection, but when we become drugged with false illusions we are hooked. All we can do is attempt to curb the illness naturally. It can be done in only two ways. The first is to reduce big government and abolish the income tax with a replacement on the local level to increase property taxes with deductions relative to income kept local. Property owned by individuals and corporations outside the local taxing area would get little or no benefits. The reason you limit large government is because the capitalist is the beneficiary of the waste, the controller of the national debt, and the manipulator of political power. If you abolish the income tax, the capitalist will find it unprofitable to buy and sell without adding value, because the property taxes would limit the tendency to speculate against inflation. The basic cause of inflation is government waste and the speculation the capitalist demands out of inflation. Every depression and recession is initiated by ballooning speculation—a favorite hobby of every wishful capitalist. They bet on the rise of prices and thus contribute to the rise by removing the supply in demand. It is hidden speculating cartels that drive a Grand Canyon wedge between the rich and the poor. It does it primarily through the anticipation and manipulation against inflation.

What Americans receive in a high standard of living, such as a three car garage, peripheral gadgetry and other high tech solutions is not due to capitalism as some would try to tout, but from free enterprise and technology. The part capitalism plays in the game is the use of credit seduction. Capitalists do eventually buy most of the small companies that prove to be innovative in order to make large profits for stockholders. They do this through cutting services and labor costs. Their worth increases at the expense of labor. Outsourcing also becomes the norm rather than an occasional necessity. And if one thinks that capitalism protects liberty, think again. Capitalism takes the power from community and the individual who adds value and leaves the enterprise in subjection to speculation that adds no value. If anything can be compared to Capitalism it would be big government and big business that prevents individuals and communities from building value. Big government and big business do not add value, but rather they control it. When an enterprise surfaces that produces a great value, the capitalist comes along and seeks to buy the business to control that value and limit the competition. When the government has much to spend, the capitalist is there to spend it with a tendency to add waste and corruption. This is most evident in military spending and will perhaps become evident in medical expenditures. The corporation can do a more efficient job than large government, but there is still too much waste with too much government spending that could be handled on a lower level. The enterprising

The Platonic Idiom

person seeks only for the freedom to be enterprising. The capitalist looks for a guarantee by the government to control the value.

Without the control over the value, enterprise is free to add additional value; instead, liberty is suddenly lost when the capitalist begins to control market value. The enterprising spirit does not have this time advantage because of payroll costs and other expenses. The enterprising spirit eventually looses out to the capitalist who simply buys and sells without adding value. The capitalist would not have the runaway power if it were not for the income tax and low property taxes.

Walter Williams made it a point to say that commodities speculators are not villains. He said, "Instead of condemning commodity speculation, we ought to recognize the vital function it serves." The following is his argument:

> Say that today's price of corn is $6 a bushel. I have a hunch that because of future supply and demand conditions, such as drought, war and increased other uses for corn, that in May 2009 corn will sell for $12 a bushel. I stand to make a lot of money if I buy corn now for $6 a bushel, hold it, and in May 2009 sell it for $12 a bushel. Sure, I've made a bundle of money for myself but is my speculative activity deserving of condemnation? The answer is no; I've served a valuable social function.
>
> Supposing my guess is correct about future supply and demand conditions and corn will be scarcer in the future, what is the socially wise thing to do now so that more will be available in the future? The answer is to use less corn now. How do you get people to voluntarily use less corn now? If you said, "Let the price rise," go to the head of the class.[4]

Mr. Williams tries to justify speculation by saying that it is a natural storage method for future tough times. What he does not say is that when the speculator buys in the market place at a given time it reduces the supply and increases the demand and thus inflates the price above and beyond the rate of production. Naturally the supply will be reduced because the purchase is not consumed. It is held as a possession for future price increases. The speculator eventually sells at a higher price—partially induced by the speculative purchase in the first place. The capitalist does not add value to the commodity. Whether it is land, real estate, stocks, oil or commodities, speculation inflation is a direct result, and if done too excessively, a recession is a byproduct. The ballooning of the housing market and high oil prices are the primary reason that we had an economic meltdown in 2008. It affected the entire world. I do not think that those in power suffered as much as the many would-be capitalists trying to invest for their retirement. When capitalism goes too far, everyone suffers.

I do not suggest that we make a law against speculation or try to control it in any way. This is the Platonic method. Since speculation is due to low possession taxes, simply raise these types of taxes for all. If a speculator has real estate waiting for the price to rise from inflation, a high property tax will reduce this type of speculation by reducing inflation. It will also keep rents down. Most important, local taxation will produce better schools and other social benefits. If government lived off the capitalist and less off of the enterprising person, budgets would not falter because the property and possessions would remain relatively constant throughout each country.

The dynamics of a higher civilization require that man choose a natural course of equality rather than follow the animalistic survival of the fittest. Once intelligence rises above the animal and has the power to control its destiny, social equality is essential to preserve humanity. If man does not learn to volunteer this natural course buy returning a percentage of what he has to the system, his extinction is eminent. Greed runs rampant because the earth bares us plenty. Even though the earth is full with enough to spare, if we do not return in a regular percentage according to what we possess, the earth will no longer be the mother it has thus been. Controlling our destiny is a test that few learn. They make the tragic mistake of forcing the system rather than creating equilibrium. One simple law can bring all to a higher plain. That law is paying to the community a percentage of what you possess annually. Fostering Platonic states full of idealism, force, and control will eventually destroy us. Consider that the environmentalist could make the same mistake as the capitalist elite. It would not be surprising that certain icon capitalists want environmentalism to flurry in the world so that they may control value all the more and tax us all according to our carbon footprint, all in the name of crisis that they manufacture.

Two methods have been illustrated to correct our yo-yo economy. They are more dynamic than simply making Platonic controls. The dynamic way is the predicate way—a way to seek natural dynamics that foster natural solutions. The Platonic way is to police, control, legislate and above all dictate how a democracy should be because the constitution is incorrectly structured. Proper forum representation and equal taxation of possessions will make any state a true republic that will never come to its end. The U.S. Constitution is fast becoming a hiss and a byword because it no longer manifests the essentials of freedom. When it unravels, believe it or not, it will be the community that will survive. This brings us to a final trend that now has come full circle.

Prior to the constitution, the trend was imperialism. Then the rise of the individual through constitutionally recognized rights. This was followed by industrialism, which liberated enterprise, and then corporatism that quickly sought to control the value added by enterprise. Afterwards multi-national corporatism or globalism became the insatiable appetite of corporatism that must consume or die. It is as if we have come full circle back to imperialism, only this time it has joined forces with elite powers and not family royalty. It is not surprising that a constitution founded on the sanctity of the individual would morph into the centralization of greater and greater power often unseen. This is all because inalienable rights were defined without standing in agreement with local responsibility.

What then is the new trend to carry forward in a way that something will liberate the cause of both equality and freedom from our constitutional responsibility? Such a trend will be a community of individuals that use their inherent rights to do well for its people. If they can say that they no longer need the state and the nation for such things, we have a true revolution for our seventh millennium.

References

1. Understanding the Masters

1. Jaroslav Pelikan, Whose Bible Is It?", p.16
2. 1 Corinthians 7:6

2. Philisophical Motive

1. Daniel 2:43
2. Jeremiah 9:15
3. Ernest Becker, "The Denial of Death," p. 47
4. Isaiah 1:18 compare with the Mormon's D&C 50:10
5. Definition concluded from Einstein's Photo Electric Effect for which he received the Nobel Prize.

3. The Socratic Method

1. Christopher Phillips, "Socrates Café", p. 9
2. Ayn Rand, "Introduction to Epistemology", p. 99
3. Christopher Phillips, "Socrates Café", p. 4
4. Christopher Phillips, "Socrates Café", p. 6
5. Edwin A. Butt, "The search of Philosophic Understanding", p. 1
6. Edwin A. Butt, "The search of Philosophic Understanding", p. 1.

4. The Platonic Position

1. Plato's Republic Book 6, 507b
2. Plato's Republic Book 6, 510b
3. Plato's Republic Book 7, 527a
4. Plato's Republic Book 6, 527b

5. The Platonic Position

1. Richard P. Feynman, "Classic Feynman", page 19.
2. "Atomic Clock," *Microsoft® Encarta® Encyclopedia 99*
3. Nigel Calder, "Einstein's Universe," p. 61
4. Letter from Faraday

5. The Platonic Position Cont.

5   Nigel Calder, "Einstein's Universe," p. 94
6   Nigel Calder, "Einstein's Universe," p. 35
7   "The Penguin Dictionary of Physics", p.230
8   Arthur M. Young, "The Geometry of Meaning," p. 16

6. Subjective Reality and Intelligence

1   Current Controversies, "Genetics and Intelligence", Greenhaven Press, p. 12.
2   Current Controversies, Richard J. Herrnstein, "Genetics and Intelligence", Greenhaven Press, p. 38
3   Current Controversies, Richard J. Herrnstein, "Genetics and Intelligence", Greenhaven Press, p. 38
4   Current Controversies, Howard Gardener, "Genetics and Intelligence", Greenhaven Press, p. 116
5   Donald D. Hoffman, "Visual Intelligence", p. 201-203
6   Daniel Goleman, "Emotional Intelligence", p. 297

7. Subjective Reality and Reason

1   See, e.g., "Kant, Immanuel", in The Columbia Encyclopedia, Sixth Edition
2   Immanuel Kant, Critique of Pure Reason [1781], trans. Norman Kemp Smith (N.Y.: St. Martins, 1965), A 51/B 75.

8. The Nature of the Predicate
(Endnotes)

1   Edwin A. Butt, "The search of Philosophic Understanding", p. 20.
2   (Metaphysics, Book VII, Part 17.)
3   Wikipedia The Free Encyclopedia on the subject of the Law of Identity
4   Plato's Republic 438 b
5   American Dictionary of the English Language, Noah Webster 1828
6   American Dictionary of the English Language, Noah Webster 1828
7   Ibid., p. 40 also: Bertrand Russell, "My Philosophical Development"

9. The Epestemology of Meaning

1   Pyramid Its Devine Message by D. Davidson and H. Aldersmith Vol. 1, London, Williams and Norgate, LTD. 1927.
2   A theme of the Bingham Young University and an expression from Mormon modern scripture. Since the word intelligence was not in use during religious antiquity, the word glory might have been used by the Jews to describe the meaning of intelligence.
3   Revelations 22-2

10. Pushing Reality Around

1   Steve Herman, "Everything you need to know about philosophy", p. 35.

11. The Way of Socrates

1   Plato, "The Republic" Book I
2   Plato, "The Trial and Death of Socrates", Dover Thrift Edition, p. 17
3   Ibid, p. 5
4   Ibid, p. 9
5   Ibid, p. 23-24
6   Ibid, p. 28
7   Ibid, p. 37

12. The Platonic State

1   Elizabeth Watson Scharffenberger, "Plato's Republic Introduction", p. li Barns & Nobel Classics.
2   Plato's Republic Book 6, 486d
3   Plato's Republic Book 6, 503c
4   Plato's Republic Book 2, 377c

12. The Platonic State Cont.

5 Associated Press Oct, 11, 2006
6 Plato's Republic Book 2, 379a
7 Plato's Republic Book 2, 380d
8 Plato's Republic Book 3, 296b
9 Plato's Republic Book 4, 423a
10 Plato's Republic Book 3, 296a
11 Plato's Republic Book 5, 449c
12 Plato's Republic Book 5, 455d
13 Plato's Republic Book 5, 455c
14 Plato's Republic Book 5, 456b
15 Plato's Republic Book 5, 458d
16 Plato's Republic Book 5, 458e
17 Plato's Republic Book 5, 459d
18 Plato's Republic Book 5, 459e
19 Plato's Republic Book 5, 460c
20 Plato's Republic Book 5, 459d
21 Plato's Republic Book 5, 461d
22 Plato's Republic Book 5, 464b
23 Plato's Republic Book 5, 468c
24 Plato's Republic Book 6, 484b

13. The Vanishing Republic

1 "Electoral College," *Microsoft® Encarta® Encyclopedia 99.*
2 "Electoral College," *Microsoft® Encarta® Encyclopedia 99.*

14. A Manifest Constitution

1 Plato The Trial and Death of Socrates – *Dialogue with Euthyphro*, Dover Thrift Editions, p.10
2 Preceding the above
3 Walter Williams is a conservative editorialist
4 Walter Williams is a conservative editorialist

Index

A
Abraham 4, 6, 291
absolute principles xiii, 225, 228
absolutism vii, 224-7
acceleration 74, 81-2, 157
aesthetics vii, 134, 214, 217
agreement ix, xvi, xviii, 50-1, 53, 57, 60, 79, 148-50, 152, 157, 166, 168, 181, 184-5, 199
Alexandria 174
Allah 5-9
American Indian 97-8
analog vi, 52, 65, 67, 69, 75, 107
angular momentum 63, 70-1, 188
anthropology 174, 176
antiquity iv, xii, 1, 8, 58, 61, 98, 109, 140, 175, 177, 179, 194-5, 199, 232-4, 249-50
antithesis 166, 225, 310
Aristotle 31, 49, 142-3, 165, 173, 220, 222, 266-9
artificial intelligence 89-91, 101-4, 108, 110-1, 113, 143
assumptions 31-2, 34, 48, 71-2, 77, 102, 112, 131, 133-4, 137-8, 145, 150-1, 156, 162, 206, 217
astronomy 55, 173-4, 176
atheist 7, 8, 21, 30, 32-3, 105, 259, 303-4
atom 64, 68-9, 71-2, 74, 84, 223
atomic clocks 72-4, 79, 343
axioms 43, 60, 152-4, 156-7, 165-7, 182-3, 185, 191, 194, 199, 209
axis xiii, 57, 66, 69, 70, 74, 156, 180, 182

B
Babel 175-6
Babylon 173, 175-6
blacks 94-7
blind 3, 4, 138, 151, 165, 212
Brigham Young xv, 11

D
dimensions 55, 119, 133, 177-8, 186-7, 191, 194, 196-7, 210

direction xvii, 55, 69, 70, 74, 77, 86, 133, 165, 186, 188, 215, 242, 250, 257, 284, 297
disciples 1, 2, 7, 10-2, 14, 39, 173, 235
distinction 45-6, 48, 54-5, 60, 62, 79, 81, 122, 145-6, 148, 151-3, 155-7, 183, 185-8, 303-7, 336
Distinction Equality 192-3, 197
distinction, law of 88, 145
distinctive statement 122
dogmatism 38, 41, 45-7, 200, 260
duplicity, associated 280-1

E
economic conservation, law of 28, 332-3
Egoism vii, 228
Egypt 17, 172-6, 199
Egyptian priests 173-4
Egyptians 173-4
Einstein 11-2, 22, 68, 71, 75-6, 105
Einstein's Universe 343-4
electric fields 64, 66-7, 69-71, 74-7, 79, 82-5, 88-90, 103, 188, 207, 218
electric matter 65-6, 69, 78, 80, 88, 113, 115, 195-6
electron
  flow 69
  recoils 69
Emission of Light vi, 69, 70
Empiricism vii, xvii, 222-3
energy vi, 9, 22, 30-1, 43, 61-5, 67-8, 70-2, 76, 78, 81, 84-5, 115-7, 125-7, 188, 297-8
  angular 63, 70, 81, 188
  gravitational 188
  levels 72
epistemology vi-ix, 35-6, 39, 40, 44, 48, 57-8, 64, 75-8, 134-5, 151, 169-70, 184, 190-2, 198-200, 208-10, 212-4
  tree x, 48, 178, 191, 199, 200, 202
equal taxation 308, 310, 341

equality vi, xviii, 57, 60, 125, 142, 145, 152-3, 155-9, 180, 182-90, 198, 203, 277, 307-11, 340-1
  economic 264, 310-1, 313
Equality of rights 309
equality state 308
ethical 20, 90, 107, 213
ethics vii, 42, 90, 97, 106, 134, 147, 213-4, 216-7
Europe 96, 290, 293
Euthyphro 235-9, 245, 305-6, 346
existence 27, 54, 63, 66, 77-8, 83, 85, 88, 125-6, 137-8, 157, 168-9, 189, 200, 207, 222
existentialism vii, xvii, 225-8
existentialist 227-8
experience, sensory 221-3

F
Faraday 69, 75-6, 343
feminine 35, 41, 178, 180-1, 183-4, 186-7, 192, 195, 199, 200, 207
fields 49, 50, 65-7, 69-72, 76, 80, 83, 85, 88-90, 103, 197
  intelligent 89
  third 82-3, 87-8
five senses 64, 66
formulas, personal reality 57, 159
forum 272, 276, 296, 317, 319-20
  open 272, 274
free choice 106, 226-7, 313
free enterprise 191, 292-4, 335-6, 338
free will 82, 98, 104, 113, 228, 250
freedom ix, xvii, xviii, 12-3, 131-3, 151, 170-1, 200, 225-7, 244-5, 270-1, 277-8, 281, 296-7, 303-4, 307-12, 314-5
  dynamics of 307-8, 312
  economic 311, 313
  essentials of 248, 341
  of religion 18, 309

G
gays 215
genetics 85, 87, 91, 95, 97, 99, 103-4, 344
geometry 55, 60, 174, 199

glory 8, 193-5, 197, 203, 254
God 4, 7-10, 19-21, 28-30, 32-3, 82, 127-9, 169-70, 226-8, 243, 249, 255-7, 259, 304-5, 312-3, 335
  definition of 32-3
  of magic 28, 30, 33, 228, 256-7
gods 236-8, 241-2, 305
gospels 3, 4, 26
government
  big 20, 297, 312, 333, 336-8
  control 12, 249, 335
  federal 292, 299-301, 325, 330, 333
  large 337-8
  larger 296, 299, 311, 332-3
  level of 300, 313
  local 313, 318, 333
grace 21, 105, 127-30, 293
graviton 75, 83-4, 196
gravity 66, 71-2, 74-6, 82-4, 125, 155-7, 188, 196, 227-8
Great Pyramid 4, 172, 175-6
Great Tower 175-6
Greek philosophers viii, 172, 174, 206

H
harmonic 58, 152, 170, 178-81, 183-4, 186, 192-4, 196, 201, 205, 218, 220, 281
harmony 40, 64, 153, 169-70, 177, 182-6, 210, 220-1, 224-5, 229, 283
heaven viii, 4, 5, 8, 173, 176, 183, 201-2
hero 21-2, 244, 254-5, 336
holy 237, 305
honesty 166, 213, 216, 243
Hopi 98
Hume 222-3
hypnosis 90, 106-9

I
i think 87, 183-5
idealism vii, 55, 58, 219, 231, 245, 271, 341
idealists 59, 141, 219, 271
ideals 43, 45, 58, 169, 212, 269, 275, 318

identity 87, 94, 106, 135, 142-3, 344
  intelligence 89, 90, 101-2, 109
  real 95, 109
ideologies 30, 44, 48, 132, 159, 163, 170-1, 262, 283
idiom viii, 14, 50, 59, 87, 247, 250-1, 259, 265
ignorance 8, 13, 16, 98, 167, 178, 189, 211, 235-6, 285, 288
immortality 18, 21-2, 26, 87, 105, 110, 173, 255
income
  tax 290-5, 301, 316, 330-1, 334, 336-7, 339
  taxing 326-9
indeterminism ix, 51-3, 161
inertial mass 125, 154-5
infinite number 74, 198, 221
infinity 78, 80, 193-4, 196-7, 203, 220
inflation 293-5, 298, 336, 338, 340
injustice 59, 211, 248-9, 252, 289
institutions, religious 43, 278
intelligence vi, 36, 38, 40, 82-5, 87-110, 112-4, 121, 144-5, 165-6, 195-8, 209-12, 226, 249-51, 268, 344-5
  definition of 91
  biological 89, 95, 108
  conceptual 99
  emotional 101-2, 344
  native 95-6
  objective 196-7
  preexistent 90, 92, 113
  real 95, 101-3, 108, 143
  tests 100
  types 99, 100
  visual 101-2, 344
Intelligence Infinity 187, 192
intelligent substance 226
interface 101-2, 181, 196
intuition 40-1, 51-3, 58, 78, 80, 134-6, 138, 152-3, 156, 161, 165, 181, 185-7, 189, 192-4, 205-7
intuitive nature 78, 120, 186
invariance vi, 152, 159, 161-2, 166
  law of x, 161-3
inverse square law 74

IQ 90-3, 97, 99, 100, 103, 105
  tests 91, 95, 99-101
Isaiah 2, 3, 343
Islam 6, 7, 9, 10

J
Jesus 2-6, 9, 10, 25-6, 28, 38-9, 245
Jews 4, 8, 10, 14, 17-9, 172, 175, 180-1, 185, 187, 192-4, 199, 201-2, 212, 345
John 9, 25, 27-9, 201, 300
justice xv, xvi, 35-6, 56-8, 131-3, 138-9, 166-7, 172, 178-9, 191-4, 209-13, 231-4, 242-3, 247-8, 250-2, 269-70, 289-90
  Plato 172

K
Kant vi, 133-8, 145, 165, 344
knowledge 29, 30, 32-3, 45, 50-2, 58, 114, 134-6, 153-5, 175-8, 181, 200, 205-6, 208-10, 212, 221-3, 235
  scientific 175
Koran 5-9

L
laws xv, 8, 9, 115, 142-3, 145, 151-2, 170-1, 188-9, 224, 227-8, 249, 257-8, 291-2, 298, 324-5, 340
  liberalize 262
learning 26, 37, 93-4, 97, 100, 103-4, 139, 174, 198, 205, 210, 233, 245, 253, 263
life style 244
light vi, 15, 22, 29, 31, 38, 52, 62-4, 67-72, 74-7, 79-81, 84-5, 188, 195-6, 239, 241-2
  smallest particle of 70
  spirals 77, 79
  velocity of 31, 74-6, 79, 133
linguistic mind 96, 250-1
logic vii, xii, 23, 31, 35, 43, 53, 61, 113-4, 121, 137, 142-3, 145-7, 149-50, 217, 222-3
  synthetic 115, 136-7, 147
Lord 2-4, 6, 8
Luke 3

Index | 350

M

machine 104, 153, 297-8
magnetic
  density 71, 77, 79, 80, 133
  field 65-7, 69, 70, 73, 75-80, 83-5, 88-90, 106, 188, 196-7, 207, 218
    changes 71, 74, 77
    density 72-4, 84
  monopoles 76-7, 79, 82
  space vi, 77-81
magnitude 185-7
Manifest Constitution vii, 303-4, 306, 308, 310, 312-4, 316, 318, 320, 322, 324, 326, 328, 330, 332, 334
masculine 35, 178, 180-2, 184-7, 192, 195, 199, 200, 205, 207
mass 11, 14, 22, 30-1, 63-5, 68-70, 76, 78, 81, 83, 115-7, 124-6, 147, 188, 193-7, 283-5
  conversion of 30-1, 67
  motion of 188
  objective 133, 188
  political 297
Mass Control Field Magnetic 187, 192
mathematics 55, 60, 65, 67, 117-8, 120-1, 124-6, 133, 137, 147, 160, 174, 182, 185, 187, 191
matter 22, 36, 47-8, 53, 61-4, 66-8, 71, 74-5, 77, 79, 80, 84-5, 112, 124-5, 130-1, 195-6, 218-20
Matthew 4
measurement 40, 77, 90, 125, 168, 187, 190-3, 197, 203
Meletus 235, 241-2
memory 54, 92, 102-4, 108-10, 222-3, 247, 249
mercy 43, 187, 189, 191-4, 197, 203, 209, 213, 215, 229, 243
metaphysical theory 218-20
miles 120
modifier 118-21, 124-5, 160, 165, 168
  subjective 123, 128
molecule 72
momentum 69, 81, 125, 188, 297

money 189, 216, 232, 234, 238, 243, 260-1, 268-9, 272-5, 278, 285, 297-8, 325-6, 331, 333-4, 339
moneychangers 300
monism vii, 218-9, 221
Moses xv, 6, 8, 17, 105, 291
motive 16, 20, 23, 25, 34, 56, 115-6, 148, 161, 163-4, 166-8, 214-6, 222, 226-7, 245, 259-60
  hidden 213, 215
  subjective 148, 167
  unconscious 25, 205, 212, 214-5
Muhammad xv, 5-9, 11-2, 14
  words of 5, 7
mysteries 6, 83, 176, 196, 199, 216
myths 24, 175-6

N

nanoseconds 73
national government 253, 262, 298, 312-3, 333
Navajo 98
net reality state 116
new concepts 52, 162-3, 215
nickels 123
numbers 10, 50, 79, 123, 125, 154, 173, 179, 181-5, 187, 191, 194, 198-9, 201, 210, 261
numerator 121, 124, 126, 133

O

Objective vi, 179, 184, 187, 192-3, 197, 203
objective reality vi, 52, 61-2, 64-6, 68, 70, 72, 74, 76, 78-80, 122-3, 157-8, 193-4, 196, 207, 228-9
objective reason 50-1, 114-5
objective state 65, 118, 122, 131, 229, 303, 306-8
objectivism ix, xvii, 50, 53, 55, 219
objectivity ix, xvi, 49, 50, 53, 60, 64, 115, 124, 126, 155, 157, 159, 196-7
objects
  external 137, 158
  real 55, 141
oil 334-5, 340
Old Testament 2, 3, 291

oral knowledge 172, 174, 178, 206
oral traditions 1, 174, 179, 232-4, 303

P
particles 22, 31, 66-7, 70-1, 74, 77, 81-2, 103, 126, 188, 195, 220
partisan politics 280-1, 285-6
party 149-50, 280-5, 287-90, 301, 315, 317-22, 324, 335
  control 285, 289
  polarized 281-2
  politics 281, 283, 285-7, 289, 311, 319, 322, 335
  powers 289, 320
  system 281, 283, 285, 288-9, 321
Paul xv, 4, 5, 9, 127-8, 130, 307
perfection 198, 201, 203, 279
perspective 101-2, 191, 200, 205-6
Pharisees 10
Phillips, Christopher 35, 48, 343
philosopher 22-3, 41, 45, 49, 50, 52, 58, 61-2, 138, 141, 147, 161, 168, 174, 249, 256-7, 266
  king 198, 258
philosophers use words, modern 50
Philosophic Understanding 343-4
Philosophical Motive vi, 17-8, 20, 22, 24-6, 28, 30, 32, 34, 87
philosophize 37, 40, 247
philosophy i, ix, x, xii-xvii, 15-7, 39-41, 47-53, 55-8, 141-3, 158-61, 167-9, 176-7, 204-10, 217, 219-20, 224-5, 228-9
  branch of 213
  changes labels 227
  classical xiii, 49
  epistemological xii, xiii
  foundation of xiii, 36, 191
  history of ix, 42, 51, 59, 253
  indeterminate 53
  teacher of xiv, 149
photon 65, 68-70
  numbers 68
physics 11, 28, 53, 60-2, 64, 76-7, 82, 85, 116, 120-1, 128, 139, 147, 182, 185, 191-5

modern xv, 11, 30-1, 53, 62, 64, 72, 76, 115, 120-1, 130, 133-4, 137, 162, 168, 188-9
piety 235-8, 242-3, 245, 306
  the essence of 238
Plato xiv, xv, 14, 39, 40, 52-60, 122, 138, 159-60, 170-3, 206, 209-12, 231, 234-5, 244-5, 247-51, 254-68, 345-6
Platonic 122, 172, 197, 249, 259, 271, 297, 304, 341
Platonic Idiom ii-x, xii-xiv, xvi, xviii, 1, 3, 5, 7, 9, 11, 13, 15, 17, 169-71, 195-7, 263
Platonic idioms 255, 262, 266, 333
platonic method 263, 340
Platonic Position vi, 49, 50, 52, 54, 56, 58, 60, 343
Platonic State vii, 247-8, 250, 252, 254, 256, 258-60, 262-4, 266, 268, 270, 289, 345
Platonic State Cont 346
Platonic states 341
Platonists 138-9, 298
Plato's
  conclusions 234, 248
  dialogues 39, 235
  inability 306
  reality 159
  terms xvi
  time 53
Plato's Republic xvi, 12, 58, 248, 250, 344
Plato's Republic Book 343, 345-6
pluralism vii, 220
poetry 240, 256
poets 39, 236, 240
political parties 59, 142, 275, 277-8, 280, 282-4, 316, 319, 321, 324, 336
politicians 43, 49, 50, 99, 132, 149, 212, 215, 239-40, 249-50, 319, 329
popular vote 131, 282-6, 289, 317-8, 324
Popular votes 317

Index | 352

position ix, x, xiii, xiv, xvi-xviii, 14, 27, 44, 48-53, 138, 150-1, 159, 177, 181, 187, 196, 274-5, 277-8
  objective xiii, 51
  philosophical xix, 23
possession tax 329-31
possessions 231, 292, 294-5, 329-31, 333-5, 337, 339-41
power xvi, 19, 20, 24, 38, 45-6, 81, 170-1, 193, 271, 274-8, 280-3, 285-6, 288-90, 313-24, 336, 340-1
  financial 318-9, 321
  icons 304, 323
  political 291, 301, 316, 321, 323, 334, 337
  representative 317-8, 320
pragmatists 141, 183-4
preach 2-4
predicate vi, xiv, xviii, 42-3, 50-1, 57, 60, 126, 133-4, 141-2, 156-62, 166-8, 192-3, 206-7, 222-4, 305-6
  act x, 131, 148, 157, 219
  concept 135-6
  connotations 43
  dynamics 304, 306, 308, 313
  process vi, 60, 154, 157-8, 163, 168
  proportion 127
  reality xiv, 27, 42, 51, 78, 119-20, 122, 128, 130, 136, 142, 149, 157, 159-61, 180, 192-3
    demands adherence 201
    long overdue xiii
  state 118, 131
  terms 42, 124, 136, 160, 187, 213-4
  time 119, 162
predicative vi, 77-8, 117, 119-20, 122, 125, 129, 132, 154, 157-8, 165-8, 178-80, 184, 187-8, 192-3, 222
  process 126, 158, 207
predicativism vii, ix, xvi, xvii, 57, 116, 132, 134-6, 138, 201, 219, 228-9, 267

preexisting intelligence 87, 90, 98-9, 104
preposition 128, 160, 199
president 52, 272, 280-1, 285-6, 289, 297, 314-5, 317-8, 324
  vice 280-1
presidential electors 282
pressure 66, 68, 124-5
  reality of 124, 126
Priesthood 192-3, 197, 201, 203
priests 8, 172, 175, 178, 245, 292
principles xiii, 19, 20, 25, 54, 56-7, 104, 132, 166-7, 170-1, 225, 252-4, 259-60, 263, 266-7, 275, 303-4
  third 185, 218, 220, 224
proof 23, 87, 103, 165, 167
property 291-5, 315, 320, 331, 337, 340
  taxes 291, 293-4, 296, 332, 337-8
  low 293-4, 339
  tithe 291-2
prophets 1, 3-9, 11, 14, 249
  of antiquity xii, 232-4
  dead 11
proportion ix, 53, 60, 81, 88, 119, 126, 133, 145-6, 151-4, 156-7, 185-7, 189-90, 192-4, 197-8, 295-6
  direct 120, 124, 126, 128, 154, 182
  inverse 119, 126
proposition 31, 135-7
  analytic 135
  synthetic 135-6
protestant 9, 96, 98, 127, 293
psychological motive 17, 19, 34, 56, 59, 105, 199, 214-5, 238-9, 241, 250
psychological problem 20-1, 30, 60, 85, 218
psychology ii, x, 24-5, 27, 52, 60, 81, 86, 91, 105, 109, 215-6, 229, 247-8, 254-5, 259-60
Pushing Reality vii, 205-6, 208, 210, 212, 214, 216, 218, 220, 222, 224, 226, 228-30, 345
Pythagoras 172-4, 176, 185, 199, 201, 267

R
rational statements   119, 133, 137-8
Rationalism   vii, 142, 221-2
rationalists   221, 223
real estate   340
realist   59, 141, 296
reality   xiii, xiv, xvii, 26-7, 41-4, 62-5, 85-90, 108-11, 116-22, 124-34, 136-9, 156-63, 166-9, 175-7, 180-2, 206-7, 217-21
  changing   136
  conservative   271
  conserving   117, 137
  correct   116, 121-2
  electric   65, 83, 208
  the essence of   128
  fundamental   219-20
  holistic   60, 228
  intuitive   128
  objective exchangeable   63
  physical   xiii, 64, 218-20, 227
  positioned   xvii, 166
  proper   50, 78, 134, 163, 165, 200, 202
  pushed   217, 229
  scarecrows of   i, 40
  single objective   64, 88
  state   116, 118-9
  three-part   180
reason philosophy   27, 193
reasoning   20, 30-1, 66, 111, 114-5, 164, 205, 217
refraction   69, 71-2
rejection   10, 17, 21-5, 27, 33, 36, 40, 110, 166, 169-70, 215, 261
relationship   58, 66-7, 71, 75, 83-4, 90, 93, 102, 107, 119, 146, 148, 152, 178-9, 184-7, 208-10
relativism   vii, 224-5, 227
relativity   11, 13, 22, 53, 71, 73, 76-7, 80, 85, 130, 133, 159, 162, 196-7, 238-9, 241-2
religion   ii, xvi, 6, 10, 12, 16, 18-21, 23, 26, 28, 35, 42-3, 45-7, 53, 150-1, 214-5
representation   vii, xviii, 97, 132, 171, 199, 202, 206, 256, 269, 283, 296, 299, 308, 310, 312-6

equal   258, 308, 310, 312-3
equitable   301, 310, 313, 315, 317, 319, 324
representatives   258, 272, 280, 312, 314, 316-9, 321-4
republic   vii, xv, xvi, 56, 59, 138, 171, 210, 231, 235, 245, 247-8, 257-8, 269-70, 277-9, 289, 314
true   258, 319, 341
responsibility   viii-xii, xv-xviii, 12-4, 21-3, 28, 35-6, 51-2, 58-9, 169-72, 197-8, 201-3, 225-9, 271-2, 295-7, 300-2, 305-7
  denial of   105, 161, 218
  element of   177, 326
  human   190, 271
  individual   57, 170, 172, 211, 250-1, 307
  local   294, 341
  pass   296, 298
  personal   12, 28, 58-9, 170, 251, 264, 302
  predicate reality of   xvii, 14, 161, 246
  social   12-3, 59, 60, 298
Responsibility Equity   192-3, 197
resurrection   9, 25, 84
rhetoric   131, 139, 169, 245, 248, 250, 278, 311
  platonic   xviii, 58
righteousness   305
rights   iv, 60, 138, 263, 279, 307-11, 313
  equal   303-4, 307, 309, 311
  inherent   307, 311, 313, 342
ripples   79, 218
rod   239
Rome   291-3
ruler   233-4, 264

S
sacrifice   17-21, 25, 40, 130, 151, 193, 195, 220, 227, 234, 248, 255, 276-7, 291, 297
sales tax   290, 329-30
salvation   xviii, 110, 127, 129-30, 255, 307
Sartre   226

science 36-7, 40, 42-3, 53, 55, 60, 80, 88, 103-4, 159, 167-8, 176, 199, 200, 207-10, 218, 220
scientist 22, 78, 87, 115, 158, 161, 167, 212, 217-8
scores 94, 96-7, 100
scriptures 3, 4, 7, 14, 127, 175, 182-3
security, social 252, 263, 297, 334
self-evidence 135-7
selfishness 144, 146-7, 228, 232, 244-5, 274-5
Sephiroth 199
Shakespeare 1
sleep 89, 106-10
  state of 89, 106, 109
society 36, 38, 42, 47, 84, 100, 106, 111, 225, 266, 307-8, 323
Socrates vii-ix, xii, xiv-xvi, 1, 14, 34-5, 37-40, 54-7, 138-40, 172, 176, 206, 231-48, 255-6, 303-6, 345-6
  philosophy of xv, 231
  point 236-7
  wisdom of 27, 233
Socrates Café 48, 343
Socratic 43, 46, 250, 253, 266, 272-3, 284, 286
  anti 283-4
  constitution 304
  dialogue 272, 285
  discussion 39, 215, 273, 283-4
  open 251, 253
  method xii, 38-9, 171, 212, 275, 279
  responsibility 249
  statement 303
  thinking 35, 172
Socratic Method vi, 34-6, 38, 40-2, 44-8, 56-7, 178, 209, 216, 276, 283, 286, 343
socratizing 35, 37-8, 45-6
sound principles 131, 283, 303
space 11, 42, 72, 75, 77-80, 83, 116-7, 120-1, 124, 133-4, 137, 162, 186-7, 193-4, 196, 241-2
  empty 162

state ix, x, xviii, 129-30, 211, 233-4, 237, 247-50, 257-8, 261-3, 265-6, 281-2, 285-7, 304-8, 311-2, 323-5, 333
  control 56, 138
  objective 229
  governments 263, 298, 312, 333
  legislatures 280, 282, 286, 319
  subjective 201, 305-7
statement
  normative 327
  objective 327
status quo 37, 39, 41, 152, 252, 257, 276, 278
studied science 172-3
subject xiv, 20, 31, 35, 57, 60, 76, 83, 87, 101, 103, 135-6, 157-60, 199, 200, 233-4, 306-7
  concept 135
Subjective vi, xvii, 160, 179, 184, 187, 192-3, 197, 203, 306
subjective intent 148-9
Subjective Reality 87, 110, 122, 196, 229
  and Intelligence vi, 87-8, 90, 92, 94, 96, 98, 100, 102, 104, 106, 108, 110, 112, 344
  and Reason vi, 113-4, 116, 118, 120, 122, 124, 126, 128, 130, 132, 134, 136, 138, 140, 344
subjectivism ix, xvii, 50, 53, 55, 219, 245
subjectivists 50, 53, 59, 130, 219, 229
subjectivity xvii, 51, 106, 114-5, 126-7, 131, 159, 161, 191
substance 2, 61-4, 79, 81, 127, 130, 173
sun 52, 73, 77, 107, 173
Symmetry 187, 192-3, 197, 203
synonyms 126, 190
synthesis 135-6
synthetic statements 136, 146, 223
system
  belief 18-9, 88, 112
  large 295-6
  small 295-6

T
tax 59, 171, 262, 289-90, 292-6, 298, 309, 311-2, 327-34, 340-1
taxation vii, xvi, xviii, 58, 60, 171, 290-1, 295, 299, 308-9, 311-3, 316, 325-9, 332, 334
  equitable 301, 309, 311, 313, 316
taxing 171, 310, 327, 329
technology 89, 107, 202, 206, 338
terms
  classical 107, 144
  common 114, 238
  new 11, 117, 153, 161-3
  objective 43, 160, 194, 306
  philosophic 267
  proportional 117, 120, 124
  reality of 126, 133-4, 139
  religious 130, 161
  single 121
  subjective 122, 162, 214
  subordinate 122
  twisting of 15, 29, 31
test 54, 90, 92, 94-8, 200, 217, 249, 303, 340
Thales 172
theory 72, 75, 83, 90, 100, 170, 180, 217, 219, 224, 248, 254, 327
third reality ix, xvi, xvii, 50, 53, 85, 219
Thrasymachus 231-4
time
  predicative 78, 116
  Socrates 235
tithes 291-3
tree 149, 177, 180, 191-2, 199, 201
Tree of Life 199, 201-2, 221
truth xiii, 7, 8, 10-3, 23, 32, 38, 44-5, 50-1, 54-5, 121, 132, 158-9, 165, 168-70, 200-1, 223-4
  objective 111, 114-5, 168, 209
  upside 169-70
types xiii, 13, 18, 52, 55, 62-3, 89-96, 98-101, 103-5, 109, 126, 188, 218-20, 249-51, 259-60, 340
  intelligent 96, 99, 104-5

U
ultimate truth xviii, 11, 13, 205

unconsciousness 106, 109
United States 286, 289-90, 296-7, 318, 324, 326, 336
United States Constitution 271, 291
units, atomic 154-5
universe 28, 75-6, 81-5, 87-8, 110, 113, 133-4, 187-8, 196, 226-7, 238, 257
  electric 82, 84, 87

V
values
  adding 105, 189, 294, 336-7, 339
  highest xvi, 243-4
  intrinsic 269
  undefined 275
Vanishing Republic vii, xvi, 271-2, 274, 276, 278, 280, 282, 284, 286, 288, 290, 292, 294, 296, 298
velocity 43, 70-1, 74, 79, 81-2, 117, 120-1
verb xvii, 57, 60, 62-3, 111, 113, 122, 125, 128, 135-6, 149, 157-60, 167, 180, 184-5, 306-8
  equality 125-6, 155
Victory 187, 192-3, 195, 197, 203
vote 131-2, 171, 245, 262, 272-4, 276, 279-83, 285-7, 290, 309, 311-2, 314-21, 323-4
  electoral 280-1

W
war 15, 116, 230, 261, 263, 339
warp 79, 132, 162
Washington 73, 289, 314, 325-6
  George 287-9
wealth 58-9, 261, 268-9, 274-80, 282, 290, 293-4, 313, 326, 331
wealthy 290, 292-3, 331
welfare 94, 292, 297-8, 300, 325
Williams, Walter 326-7, 339, 346
wisdom 1, 2, 144-5, 151-2, 174-6, 181, 183, 186-7, 205-7, 211, 224, 234, 238-42, 244-5, 254, 281-4, 286-7
Wisdom Space 192-3, 197

women 97, 146, 152, 254, 258, 264, 279
words
  contrasting 191
  democratic 258
  fundamental xiii, 247
  philosophy xvi
  predicate 160, 212
  spoken 1, 3
world
  academic viii, xiii, xiv
  objective 59, 87, 194
  real 45, 229, 268
worldviews 17-8, 21, 25, 29, 30, 34, 41, 43, 56, 65, 141, 200, 204, 230, 275
  common 17
worship 6, 8, 10, 17, 20, 255
writers ix, 1, 51-3, 58, 73, 149, 160, 213, 251-2, 288

Y
youth 25, 37, 44, 46-7, 216-7, 250-1, 261

www.ingramcontent.com/pod-product-compliance
Lightning Source LLC
Chambersburg PA
CBHW031307150426
43191CB00005B/114